I-Language

An Introduction to Linguistics as Cognitive Science

D0874940

OXFORD CORE LINGUISTICS
GENERAL EDITOR

David Adger, University of London

PUBLISHED

Core Syntax: A Minimalist Approach

David Adger

I-Language: An Introduction to Linguistics as Cognitive Science

Daniela Isac and Charles Reiss

IN PREPARATION

Core Semantics

Gillian Ramchand

Introduction to Theoretical Linguistics

Peter Svenonius

I-Language

An Introduction to Linguistics as Cognitive Science

Daniela Isac
and Charles Reiss

OXFORD
UNIVERSITY PRESS

OXFORD

UNIVERSITY PRESS

Great Clarendon Street, Oxford OX2 6DP

Oxford University Press is a department of the University of Oxford.
It furthers the University's objective of excellence in research, scholarship,
and education by publishing worldwide in

Oxford New York

Auckland Cape Town Dar es Salaam Hong Kong Karachi
Kuala Lumpur Madrid Melbourne Mexico City Nairobi
New Delhi Shanghai Taipei Toronto

With offices in

Argentina Austria Brazil Chile Czech Republic France Greece
Guatemala Hungary Italy Japan Poland Portugal Singapore
South Korea Switzerland Thailand Turkey Ukraine Vietnam

Oxford is a registered trademark of Oxford University Press
in the UK and in certain other countries

Published in the United States
by Oxford University Press Inc., New York

British Library Cataloguing in Publication Data
Data available
Library of Congress Cataloging in Publication Data
Data available

Typeset by SPI Publisher Services, Pondicherry, India
Printed in Spain by Cayfosa Quebecor

ISBN 978–0–19–953419–7 (Hbk.)
ISBN 978–0–19–953420–3 (Pbk.)

1 3 5 7 9 10 8 6 4 2

Contents

Preface

Our original goal was to write a popular book that would lead the reader through some fairly technical analyses of linguistic data. Instead of just reporting on the claims and results of modern linguistics, we wanted to show the reader how to think like a linguist. In the end, we realized that a textbook format was more suitable, given the depth and breadth we are aiming at. We foresee the book serving as an introduction to linguistics for students planning to continue in the field, as well as for those with interests in other branches of cognitive science. Throughout the book, linguistic issues are related to topics in vision, philosophy, ethology, and so on. We hope that we can inspire our readers to continue the search for unifying themes among these fields.

All the material in this book has been presented to undergraduate students in large classes (often over one hundred students). Much of it has also been presented to middle school students, prison inmates, and non-academic audiences. In developing and teaching the materials, we have had the advantage of being a team of a syntactician and a phonologist, but we hope that any enthusiastic teacher will be able to understand the material and help motivated students work through it. We think that the ideas are important, but, in fact, not very difficult when broken down. Additional exercises and links to material related to the text can be found on the book's companion website: http://linguistics.concordia.ca/i_language/

As an introduction to linguistics the book is very narrow. There are no chapters on sociolinguistics or historical linguistics, for example. And yet, we strongly believe that the best results in these fields can be attained by incorporating the approach to the study of language we develop, basically the framework of generative grammar developed by Noam Chomsky and collaborators since the 1950s. In some sense the book is an exegesis of the Chomskyan program or, rather, our understanding of the program.

In the course of writing we often found each other to be frustratingly thick-headed about various topics. The resulting heated arguments have helped us to achieve deeper understanding and greater intellectual humility and, we hope, to produce a better book. We expect that even sympathetic readers will find much to object to in our presentation, but we think that we have succeeded in laying out a coherent position, sometimes by openly attacking other positions, that can at least serve as the basis for fruitful debate. If any of our claims or arguments manage to get students' "blood pressure up to an appropriately high level" (to quote Morris Halle) where they seek to challenge our point of view, we will consider this to be a successful textbook.

Acknowledgements

There is probably nothing original in this book, and thus we are beholden to the community of linguists and other scholars from whom we have liberally borrowed. In some cases we have acknowledged specific debts, but in general we have not. Most obviously, the book is inspired by and draws heavily from the work of Noam Chomsky. We excuse our general failure at careful attribution by adopting Chomsky's own attitude that full attribution is not only impossible but also fairly unimportant. Our common goal as a community is to understand the object of study—the language faculty and the human mind, in general.

That being said, we will point out that several authors have been most inspiring in helping us to achieve our understanding of the place of linguistics in cognitive science. We mention these to encourage you to consult them on your own. We include their work in the readings for the course that this book grew out of, *Language and Mind: The Chomskyan Program* at Concordia University. Specific works by these cognitive scientists are listed in the reading suggestions at the end of each chapter: Albert Bregman, Morris Halle, Donald Hoffman, Ray Jackendoff, Zenon Pylyshyn. The course that this book grew out of was originally built around Jackendoff's *Patterns in the Mind*, and that book was so useful in developing our own understanding of the place of linguistics in cognitive science that it was actually a challenge to us as authors to move away from its excellent structure around three fundamental arguments.

Many of the articles in the four-volume *Invitation to Cognitive Science*, edited by Daniel Osherson, have also been instrumental as teaching resources, and we recommend them to students interested in making connections among the various branches of cognitive science.

We are also most grateful to our reviewers, Sam Epstein, Virginia Hill, and Ur Schlonsky, and the Core Linguistics Series Editor, David Adger, for useful feedback and for pushing us to not take the easy way out when dealing with technical linguistic topics. Their input has vastly improved the manuscript. It has been a pleasure to work with John Davey, our

Consultant Editor at Oxford, whose encouragement and flexibility are greatly appreciated.

Two non-linguists read early drafts of the book. Harold Golubock provided encouraging feedback—we originally wanted to write a popular book for the intelligent lay reader and Harold was the perfect guinea pig. Lesly Reiss managed to proofread the entire first draft, and she was fascinated... fascinated that anyone would find this material interesting, a sentiment she repeatedly shared with us. We are grateful to Chris Eldridge for particularly helpful insight into the mind–body problem.

The hundreds of Concordia undergraduate students who took our course and helped us develop the materials that have become this book must be acknowledged. Of all our students, Hisako Noguchi deserves special mention. She not only took the class but she has served as a teaching assistant too many times to count. Her input has been crucial to the success of the course and the development of teaching materials. Michael Gagnon and Alexis Wellwood provided excellent comments and Sabina Matyiku was very helpful with the graphics. Francis Murchison and Kevin Brousseau contributed exercises on Kuna and Iyinu (Cree) based on their own research. Michael Barkey's work to develop the Concordia Linguistics Outreach Project (CLOUT) was instrumental in getting us to think about how to introduce difficult material to diverse audiences. These audiences are also to be thanked for their patience and feedback, especially the inmates and teaching staff at Clinton County Correctional Facility in Dannemora, New York, where CLOUT presented several workshops.

Our friend and colleague Alan Bale has taught the Language and Mind course twice, and the book owes a lot to the influence of the materials he developed and his own spin on topics we discuss.

It is impossible to say which examples, arguments or discussions contained herein were taken directly from Mark Hale—we have discussed every issue in this book with him at some point over a very long period of time. His influence on our thinking as reflected in these pages cannot be overestimated.

Finally, we are grateful to our respective spouses who, despite the sometimes cantankerous nature of much of our interaction, managed to deepen their relationship with each other while we were engaged in this writing process.

We would like to dedicate the book to our parents and our children.

List of Figures

PART I

The Object of Inquiry

1

What is I-language?

In the summer of 1991 Charles lay in an Istanbul hotel room burning with fever, 15 percent lighter than his normal weight. In the other bed lay his friend Paul, who had just golfed his way to an MBA, also hot with fever, the inside of his mouth covered with blisters.[1] Paul had paid for the room on his credit card, so it was several steps above the dives they had been staying in. He had gotten the name of a doctor in Istanbul from his mother back in Kansas and was now on the phone with the hotel receptionist, who, given the price of the establishment, spoke excellent English. In vain, Paul was asking her to find the number of Dr. Ozel—"That's right, it's o-z-e-l, Ozel." It wasn't happening.

From the depths of his delirium and intestinal distress, Charles finally found the strength to call out in a hoarse voice, "Tell her to try o with two dots," referring to the Turkish letter ö, so *Özel*. Much to Paul's surprise, she found the number immediately. "Reiss, that's amazing—how did you know that?" Paul asked, fully aware that Charles did not speak Turkish, and also

---

[1] Charles had recommended that he rinse his mouth in the alkaline waters of Lake Van, but that hadn't helped at all.

annoyed with himself for having spoken to him civilly, since they were at one of the points in the trip when they wanted to strangle each other. "If you had listened to me on the bus ride from Bucharest to Istanbul, instead of obsessing about what pork products we would sample on the passage through Bulgaria, you would know," Charles replied brightly, suddenly energized by his ability to gloat.

So, what had Charles tried to explain on that bus ride, in the thirty seconds before Paul's eyes glazed over? How *did* he know? The answer lies in Charles's understanding of vowel patterns in Turkish, an example of a most wonderful linguistic phenomenon called vowel harmony. Understanding of Turkish vowel harmony happened to have a practical value in this situation, something neither of us has ever again experienced, but its real beauty lies in the fact that it reflects some of the deepest workings of the human mind.

Our goal in this book is to get you to accept this rather grandiose claim about the vowel patterns in Turkish words. We will introduce many new ideas, some of which will initially strike you as ridiculous. However, we will try to convince you with logical arguments, data-based arguments from both familiar and less familiar languages, and also appeal to general scientific methodology.

Building on linguistic phenomena, our discussion will touch on some of the most longstanding and difficult issues in philosophy including the following:

 Big philosophical issues we will address
- The Nature–Nurture debate: How much of what we are is innate and how much depends on our experience?
- What is knowledge? How is it acquired?
- What is reality?
- Whatever reality is, how can we get access to it?
- Is there a principled distinction between mind and body?
- How can our study of these issues bear on social questions and educational practice?

Given both the incomplete nature of all scientific inquiry and the limited space we have, we will not propose complete and final solutions to all these problems, but we do hope to offer a real intellectual challenge in a fascinating domain. This should lead you to experience frustration... confusion...annoyance...and ultimately (we hope)...understanding and insight and pleasure.

1.1 Jumping in

Not only the average person but also experts in fields like psychology, engineering, neuroscience, philosophy, and anthropology are willing to make proclamations, sometimes in the pages of respected scholarly publications, about language—its evolution, its acquisition by children and adults, its relationship to thought, and so on. But there is a question that is prior to all of these issues, namely *What is language?* We aim in this book to provide you with a deeper appreciation of the nature of language than that of the average academic in the fields listed above.

This book is not a catalogue of cool facts about language, nor is it a report on the exciting findings of modern linguistics over the past fifty years—there are several excellent books on the market for those purposes. Instead, our strategy is to get you to think about language the way linguists do. With this in mind, we'll jump right in with some data (not Turkish—we'll come back to that later), before we even explain the somewhat obscure title of the book. We won't even tell you what "I-language" means yet. By the end of the chapter, we hope you will have an appreciation of the term that is much deeper than you would have if we just handed you a definition.

Let's begin with a simple example, the relationship between singular and plural nouns in Warlpiri, an Australian Aboriginal language.

 Warlpiri plurals

SINGULAR	PLURAL	
kurdu	kurdukurdu	child/children
kamina	kaminakamina	girl/girls

In English, we form the plural of most nouns (but not all—look at *children*) by adding a suffix to the singular, as in *girl-s*. As you can see, it looks like the plural of a noun in Warlpiri is formed by repeating the singular. This is a real plural—*kurdukurdu* does not just mean "two children," it means "children" and is used to denote two or a hundred children—any number greater than one. You can probably guess the plural form of the word *mardukuja* "woman"—it is *mardukujamardukuja*.

Processes of word formation that involve repeating material from a basic form (all or just part of the basic form) to create a derived form are called processes of reduplication. Reduplication processes are very common in the languages of the world with a variety of meanings, but are not productive in English.

Even with this simple example, we can learn a lot about the nature of language:

 Some lessons about language based on Warlpiri plurals

    a. Some aspects of language are simply memorized—it is necessary to remember certain arbitrary links between sound and meaning, for example, that *kurdu* means "child" in Warlpiri but *child* means "child" in English.

    b. Some aspects of language involve rules or patterns. Your ability to correctly guess the Warlpiri form for "women" shows that the form can be generated by a rule.

    c. If there are rules, they have to apply to some kind of input and produce some kind of output. The Warlpiri plural formation rule highlights an important aspect concerning the nature of rules of language—the units of language, the elements that rules affect, can be quite abstract. We cannot give a definite answer to the question "What sound corresponds to the plural in Warlpiri?" because the answer varies depending on context. We will illustrate this point by discussing the rule in more detail below.

    d. The rules apply to elements that are only definable in linguistic terms—for example, the Warlpiri plural rule applies to nouns, not verbs, and the noun-verb distinction is a purely linguistic one.

The first item is fairly obvious, although the arbitrary nature of the sound-meaning links of human language was only really fully appreciated about one hundred years ago by the Swiss linguist Ferdinand de Saussure, the inventor of structuralism. The point is just that one of the requirements for language is memory. A system, device, organism without memory cannot generate Warlpiri or English plural forms from singulars, since it has no way to store the singulars.

The second item will be dealt with again and again in this book. A Warlpiri speaker has to memorize that *kurdu* means "child", but not how to say "children," since *kurdukurdu* is generated by a rule that repeats any noun in the singular form to make a plural. Of course the rule or pattern itself must be memorized, but this is an even more abstract kind of information than that required for memorizing words.

This discussion of reduplication illustrates a property of language central to our approach: languages are *computational* systems. This term scares some people, but all we mean by it is that language can be analyzed in terms of explicit rules that apply to symbols. Given an input symbol and a rule that applies to that symbol, we can say what the output form will be. The symbols and rules are different ones than those that are familiar in math, but the goal of a computational approach is to make them as explicit as the formulas of math or the mathematical formulas used in sciences like physics or chemistry.

To illustrate the third item, let's compare Warlpiri to English, although we will simplify greatly. In English, we can say that the rule for pluralization is something like "If a noun is of the form x, then the plural of that noun is of the form x-s" as in *girl-s*. In Warlpiri, the rule must be something like "If a noun has the form x, then the plural of the noun is of the form xx." Both the English and the Warlpiri rules show that the rules of language must refer to VARIABLES. A variable is a kind of symbolic placeholder that can change in value each time a rule is applied. This is particularly clear for Warlpiri— the plural marker is not a constant "piece" of sound, as it apparently is in English regular forms, but rather a copy of the noun. Sometimes the variable has the value *kurdu*, sometimes *kamina*, *etc*.

Variables in this sense are just like the variables of math—in a function like $y = 2x + 3$, we can plug in different values for the variable x and derive values for the dependent variable y. If x is set equal to 4 then $y = 2 \times 4 + 3$, which is 11; if the variable x is set equal to 5, then $y = 2 \times 5 + 3$, which is 13; and so on.

In contrast to the Warlpiri rule that tells us to repeat the singular in order to generate the plural, the English rule for regular plurals takes the variable corresponding to a noun and adds a constant -s ending.[2]

If we really want to make the parallel to math explicit, we can think of pluralization as a function mapping members of the set of singulars (the domain of the function) to a set of plurals (the range of the function). In Warlpiri, the pluralization function is something like

1.4 $f(x) = x^\frown x$

where the variable x is drawn from the set of singular nouns and the symbol $\frown$ denotes CONCATENATION— $a^\frown b$ means "a followed by b."

In English, the function would require a variable drawn from the set of singulars and a constant corresponding to the suffix:

1.5 $f(x) = x^\frown s$

---

[2] As we said above, we are oversimplifying, but probably only those readers who have taken a linguistics course know what details we are glossing over. If you do not, you are better off, since you can concentrate on our point about variables and constants.

Concatenation is not the same as mathematical addition or multiplication, but it may still be useful to draw a parallel in math. A function like $f(x) = x + 3$, where the output of the function, typically shown on the y-axis of a graph, depends on the value assigned to the variable x added to a constant, 3.

It is probably apparent that the notions of rules and variables are intimately related. By virtue of the fact that they refer to variables, rules apply to classes of entities. That is what makes the rules productive. The Warlpiri rule that says "Repeat the singular x to make the plural xx" applies not just to *kurdu*, but to *kamina*, *mardukuja*, and in fact to all nouns.

With respect to item (1.3d.), note that nouns are just one of the categories that linguistic rules operate on, but all linguistic categories are just that—linguistic. They cannot be reduced to categories of physics, biology, psychology, or any other domain. The category noun cannot be defined as "a person, place, or thing", despite what your English teacher told you. We'll come back to this later.

1.2 Equivalence classes

Let's elaborate on the notion of "variable" used above. The various nouns of Warlpiri have different pronunciations, and yet we are able to treat them all as members of a set or class of elements that are all subject to the same rule. In other words, any noun can stand in for the variable x in the Warlpiri rule to give the output $x^{\frown}x$. One way of understanding this is that the rule ignores the differences among various nouns and treats them all as members of the abstract category or class "noun."

However, there is another kind of abstraction that is necessary before we even can refer to the nouns in this class. If five Warlpiri speakers utter *kurdu*, the actual sound will be different coming from each speaker—there are differences in the shapes and masses of their vocal apparatus, so that an old man and a young child will produce tokens of *kurdu* with very different physical characteristics. And yet someone hearing all five speakers can perceive *kurdu* in each case.

Even more fundamentally, each pronunciation of *kurdu* by even a single speaker will be physically distinct with respect to the sound wave that reaches a listener, due to differences in ambient noise, the moisture in the speaker's vocal tract, variability in muscle control of the speech organs, etc.

We will come back to these issues in several subsequent chapters, but what they illustrate is a point made about eighty years ago by the great linguist and anthropologist Edward Sapir: "No entity in human experience can be adequately defined as the mechanical sum or product of its physical properties." In modern parlance, human perception and cognition depends upon equivalence classes—symbolic representations that may be derived from experience (tokens of a word heard) or somehow manifested in behavior (tokens of words uttered), but whose relationship with actual experience is quite complex. As Sapir noted "it is notorious how many of these physical properties are, or may be, overlooked as irrelevant" in a particular instance. In Chapter 2, we will illustrate these ideas with both linguistic examples and examples from other cognitive domains.

Scientists, when they conduct experiments and build theories, also make idealizations and consciously exclude certain observations from consideration. In describing equivalence classes, however, we are saying something different. We are claiming that the human mind and cognitive systems act as a filter on experience—they are built to collapse certain detectable differences when categorizing input.

Returning to Warlpiri, then, we see that we need to recognize that words, themselves, are just equivalence classes. The word *kurdu* is one such class, as is the word *kamina*. But then the category noun is also an equivalence class, an abstraction over the set of abstractions that correspond to words.

In Fig. 1.1 we see that individual nouns represent an abstraction from various tokens of words that are spoken and perceived. The category noun is itself an abstraction over the set of individual nouns. The use of symbols that represent equivalence classes is one of the most important notions for understanding language.

There is much more philosophizing to be drawn out of the Warlpiri example, but just for fun we will broaden our empirical base with another example of reduplication before returning to big picture issues.

1.3 Partial reduplication in Samoan

In the case of Warlpiri, the input symbol corresponded to the singular form of a noun, call it x, and the output form could be denoted $x \frown x$. This pattern is called "total reduplication" because the whole base form is repeated. In

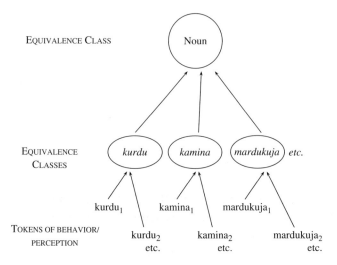

EQUIVALENCE CLASS

Noun

EQUIVALENCE
CLASSES

kurdu   *kamina*   *mardukuja* etc.

kurdu₁   kamina₁   mardukuja₁

TOKENS OF BEHAVIOR/
PERCEPTION

kurdu₂   kamina₂   mardukuja₂
etc.   etc.   etc.

Fig 1.1 The equivalence class of nouns is itself an abstraction from equivalence classes abstracted from sets of tokens of individual nouns.

the following discussion of Samoan, we will discover a pattern of partial reduplication, where only part of the base is repeated.

In Samoan, the singular of the verb "sit" is *nofo* "she sits" and the plural is *nonofo* "they sit" as shown in (1.6).

1.6	Samoan verbs: sg-pl		
	nofo	nonofo	"sit"
	moe	momoe	"sleep"
	alofa	alolofa	"love"
	savali	savavali	"walk"
	maliu	maliliu	"die"

If you compare the singular with the plural, are you tempted to posit a rule that adds a prefix *no-* to the singular to get the plural? We can reject this by considering some more data: the singular and plural for the verb "sleep" is *moe/momoe*—clearly there is no prefix *no-* here. So, maybe the rule in Samoan involves reduplication, just as in Warlpiri, but in this case reduplication just repeats part of the base word, say the first syllable.[3] Well, this idea fails when we get to another pair, the forms for the verb meaning "love": *alofa/alolofa*—the first syllable of the singular *alofa* is *a-*, and this is not repeated in the plural. Instead, the syllable *lo* is repeated in

---

[3] We will assume that you have an intuitive notion of what a syllable is—it is a technical term in linguistics.

alolofa. Perhaps these forms show us that the correct rule involves starting at the beginning of the word, looking for the first consonant and the vowel following that consonant, and then repeating the two of them. This would work for the three verbs considered so far, but there is more data to consider: the last two verbs in example (1.6) show the forms *savavali* and *maliliu*, which shows that the correct rule involves copying the second to last syllable of the singular to make the plural.

We thus see that the Samoan rule requires a variable that constitutes a part of a root word. We won't worry too much about how to represent this—it is an advanced topic, beyond the scope of this book, but here is one approach: suppose that we represent each verb as a sequence of numbered syllables starting from the end of the word. So a two-syllable verb would correspond to (1.7a.) and a three-syllable word to (1.7b.), where the symbol σ stands for a syllable.

1.7	Representing syllable sequences
	a. $\quad\quad\sigma_2\text{-}\sigma_1$
	b. $\quad\quad\sigma_3\text{-}\sigma_2\text{-}\sigma_1$
	c. $\sigma_n\text{-}\ldots\text{-}\sigma_2\text{-}\sigma_1$

The representation in (1.7c.) corresponds to a word with an arbitrary number of syllables, n. The rules for plural formation can now be stated by referring to the variable σ_2:

1.8	If $\sigma_n\text{-}\ldots\text{-}\sigma_2\text{-}\sigma_1$ is a singular verb, then the plural is $\sigma_n\text{-}\ldots\text{-}\sigma_2\text{-}\sigma_2\text{-}\sigma_1$

We will revise our view of Samoan later, but for now we have an idea of what is needed. The Samoan and Warlpiri both are instances of the same process of reduplication. What differs is the nature of the variable that gets repeated in each case: a full word in Warlpiri, a syllable in Samoan. It is exactly because we are able to abstract away from the different nature of the two variables that we can see that the two languages are in fact using the same computational process, reduplication.

Our discussion of Samoan has also illustrated a crucial aspect of linguistic analysis—we examined pieces of data and made hypotheses that we have then tested against more data, revising the hypotheses as necessary to match the full data set. This is a good example of how language data can be subjected to the scientific method. The same methodology is used in all sciences. However, as we will discuss later, there is a deeper level of analysis than just coming up with a rule that is consistent with the data.

1.4 Mentalism

We have posited some rules to account for patterns of nouns in Warlpiri and verbs in Samoan. Let's now ask what those rules are. Well, in some sense, they are our creation, hypotheses we made to account for data sets on the page. However, unless we have some kind of mystical view of our own creative powers, and assuming the data on the page is somehow related to what Warlpiri speakers and Samoans say, it seems reasonable to think that these rules reflect something that existed prior to our analysis—in other words, we have discovered them, not invented them.

Even if the data we analyzed had never been written down, it seems that the rules describe a property of Warlpiri and Samoan speakers. In fact, the memorized singular forms needed to generate the plurals also describe a property of the speakers. Actually spoken words have a sound associated with them, but the rules and the variables they refer to do not—and, as we have seen, even the constant parts do not, since each token is different physically. The rules, the variables, and also the memorized forms of the singulars constitute properties of Warlpiri and Samoan speakers. Similarly, the information that *cat* is pronounced as it is, that it is subject to the regular plural formation rule, and that this rule adds -*s* to the end of the singular is a property of you. We will assume that these properties are a kind of information somehow encoded in the brains of the speakers, and we will refer to that kind of information as a kind of knowledge in the mind of the speakers. Linguistic analysis aims to discover what speakers know—we have discovered, for example, that Samoan speakers *know* (that is, have as one of their properties) a rule that generates plural verbs by reduplicating the second to last syllable of the singular.

The preceding discussion falls under the *mentalist* approach to linguistics. It considers the information and rules and patterns that can be used to analyze linguistic behavior to reflect mental properties, properties of the minds of individuals—the mind consists of information and rules and patterns, some of which constitute knowledge of language. We will later argue that what is mental is part of the biological world, and thus our approach is also known as *biolinguistics*.

Neuroscientists who are trying to understand how cognition arises from the physical matter of the brain need linguists to tell them what kinds of powers inhere in the brains they are studying. If they cannot come up with a model of the brain that accounts for the ability to memorize words (like

Warlpiri singulars) and also store and apply rules that contain variables (the pluralization via reduplication rule of Warlpiri and Samoan, for instance) then their work is not done.

1.5 I-language

You now have all the pieces that are necessary to understand what I-language is. An I-language is a computational system that is encoded in, or a property of, an individual brain. It is a system of rules (a grammar) that computes over symbols that correspond to equivalence classes derived either from experience or other symbols. The mind contains (or perhaps is composed of) many such systems, for vision, language, etc., and an I-language is the name given to that one of these systems that generates the structures associated with speaking and understanding speech.

The I-language approach to linguistics thus studies *individual* mental grammars, entities that are *internal* to each person. In addition to these two words beginning with the letter *I*, there is a third relevant term implicit in the notion of a grammar as a system of rules or patterns. In mathematics a set can be defined *extensionally*, by listing its members, or *intensionally*, by providing a formula or description that characterizes all and only the members of the set. For example, {2, 4, 6, 8} extensionally defines the same set as the intensional description "even numbers less than 10." Notice that an intensional definition is more practical for large sets, and required for infinitely large ones like the set of *all* even numbers. A Warlpiri speaker need not store the set of plurals as an extensionally defined list, since the reduplication rule defines this set intensionally as a function from the set of singulars.

> **1.9**   Two characterizations of the set of Warlpiri plurals
>
> **Extensional:** {kurdukurdu, kaminakamina, mardukujamar-dukuja, ... }
>
> **Intensional:** $\{x^\frown x$ such that x is a singular noun$\}$

The intensional characterization reflects the rule-governed nature of the relationship between singulars and plurals. I-language is meant to suggest all three of these notions—internal, individual, and intensional.

The study of the shared properties of all I-languages is thus the study of what is sometimes called the human language faculty. This study is sometimes called Universal Grammar, the goal of which is to discover the core of properties common to all I-languages.[4] We will address implications of the I-language approach and also contrast it with other approaches throughout the book.

1.6 Some implications of mentalism

This mentalistic, I-language approach to language has several implications. First of all, we need to recognize the difference between our conscious knowledge of Warlpiri and Samoan reduplication that we developed as a scientific analysis, and the unconscious knowledge that the speakers have. Samoans, for example, may have no idea what a syllable is, and thus could not tell us how the singular and plural verb forms they produce are related. They acquired these rules as pre-literate children without any direct instruction from their parents—they were not given organized data sets as you were.

Furthermore, if all speakers of Warlpiri were to die tomorrow, then nobody in the world would have the kind of knowledge that they have, and the language would cease to exist. We might have some writings that describe our analysis of aspects of their language, but that is all. A language, for linguists, is a system of representations and rules in the mind of a person. If the person ceases to exist, that particular person's language ceases to exist. In other words, we have been talking about the Samoan language and the Warlpiri language, but we have been doing so informally. From a linguistic perspective, each Warlpiri speaker and each Samoan speaker has his or her own set of symbols and rules, what we call his or her own *mental grammar*, his or her own I-language.

If this is so, that each Warlpiri speaker actually has his or her own individual mental grammar, then how can Warlpiri speakers communicate with each other? Why do they seem to have the same grammar? The answer is simple—they have mental grammars that are quite similar because they are all humans and they were exposed to similar linguistic experiences when they were acquiring their language as children.

---

[4] Just as the terms *physics* and *history* refer both to objects of study (the physical world or the events of history) and the study itself (as in "He failed physics"), the term Universal Grammar is also used sometimes to refer to the common core of the human language faculty.

Everything we have just said about Warlpiri and Samoan holds as well for English. If we take the mentalistic approach seriously, then we have to admit that there is no entity in the world that we can characterize as "English." There is just a (large) bunch of people with fairly similar mental grammars that they can use to communicate in a way that is typically more efficient than between what we call Japanese and English speakers, because the so-called English mental grammars are more similar to each other. We will continue to use terms like "the English language," "Warlpiri plurals," and "Samoan verbs," but bear in mind that each name is a just practical label for a set of individual mental grammars that are identical with respect to a given phenomenon under analysis.

1.7 Summing up

So, at this point, we hope you have an idea of the I-language approach. The ultimate goal is an understanding of the human language faculty, which is instantiated in individual minds/brains, in the same way that we talk of a human visual faculty. Each individual person, based on their particular experience of language acquisition, ends up with a language faculty that is in a particular state.

We told you earlier that we would not review the major findings of modern linguistics, but we have changed our mind—here they are:

 The fruits of linguistic research
- Every language is different AND
- Every language is the same.

Believe it or not, both of these claims have elicited virulent criticism. Obviously, we have stated the claims like this for rhetorical effect, but we have suggested that they can both, in fact, be true in some non-trivial way. The two claims are complementary rather than contradictory.

We have illustrated the sense in which linguists say that each language is different: each language corresponds to information in a particular mind. Since each person has at least slightly different experiences of language acquisition, it is not surprising that each ends up with different grammars, different bodies of information. When we say that two people speak the same language, it is rather like saying that they are "near" each other. This is a useful expression whose definition depends on numerous factors—Montreal is near Kingston, only three hours away; we work near Mary, only three blocks away; we are sitting near Mary, only three feet away; Paul's liver is near where his gall bladder used to be, only three inches away (N.B. We know nothing about anatomy). What does *near* mean? There is no formal definition of the everyday word *near*, and there is no formal definition for the everyday term "English." Linguistically, there are no dependable criteria for defining a speaker of English—some dialects share properties with Hungarian that others dialects do not share, for example.

The situation becomes even clearer if we look at other languages (using the term in the everyday sense). Spanish and Italian are called different languages, but speakers of the standards feel like they can communicate with each other quite well. On the other hand, the various Italian dialects are often mutually incomprehensible—they are called dialects of the same language because they are spoken within the political boundaries of Italy, not for any linguistic reasons.

The second claim is just the hypothesis of Universal Grammar, an idea we have already hinted at. We will try to show in later chapters that Universal Grammar is more of a logical necessity than a hypothesis. However, in order to understand the claims, and to decide whether to accept or reject them, we propose to continue developing an understanding of what language is.

As promised, we have already argued for one apparently ridiculous notion, the non-existence of English! As with any scientific endeavor, it is to be expected that our results will surprise us from time to time, and that they will be at odds with our everyday intuitions and common sense. In the same way that modern science departs from our common sense, which tells us that light should behave as either a particle or a wave, not both, or that our bodies and our cars must be made of fundamentally different substances, we expect the scientific study of language to overturn some of our most dearly held intuitions. This commitment to science and its ability to surprise us is expressed well in the following quotation from Zenon Pylyshyn, a psychologist and computer scientist whose work inspired much of what you will find in the following pages:

[I]f you believe *P*, and you believe that *P* entails *Q*, then even if *Q* seems more than a little odd, you have some intellectual obligation to take seriously the possibility that *Q* may be true, nonetheless. [Zenon Pylyshyn (1984), *Computation and Cognition*: xxii]

Throughout the book, we intend to mind our *P*s and *Q*s in accordance with Pylyshyn's dictum.

1.8 Exercises

Exercise 1.8.1. **Ethnologue:** Throughout the book we refer to languages in the everyday sense of English, Warlpiri, Spanish, and so on. Find information about where languages are spoken, how many speakers they have and what family they belong to by consulting the *Ethnologue* at http://www.ethnologue.com. Go to the website and write up a description of the language that immediately follows your family name alphabetically and the language that immediately follows your given name. (If your name is James Jameson, or something else that gives the same language twice, use the language that *precedes* your family name alphabetically.)

Exercise 1.8.2. How do you express the meaning *very* in Pocomchí? Fill in the blanks.

adjective		*very* + adjective	
saq	white	saqsaq	very white
raš	green	rašraš	very green
q'eq	black	q'eqq'eq	very black
q'an	ripe		very ripe, rotten
nim	big		very big
kaq	red		very red

Exercise 1.8.3. Can you see how to generate the set of definite nouns (like *the bird*) from the set of bare nouns (like *bird*) in Lyele? Note that vowels in Lyele can bear one of three tones: a = mid tone; á = high tone; à = low tone. These tonal differences are distinctive—they can differentiate meaning.

kúmí	bird	kúmíí	the bird
yálá	millet	yáláá	the millet
kùlí	dog		the dog

Things may be a bit more complex than you thought:

nà	foot	nàá	the foot
yijì	church	yijíì	the church
ya	market	yaá	the market
cèlé	parrot	cèléé	the parrot

To make the definite form (*the* + N) repeat _____ but always use a _____ tone.

What equivalence classes are relevant to a discussion of these Lyele noun forms?

Exercise 1.8.4.   Is it English? Here are some sentences rendered in Standard orthography that we have heard spoken in various places that are referred to as English-speaking places. Identify differences from your own variety of English, if you can figure out the intended translation into your own dialect. Are these sentences all English? How does the I-language approach bear on the issue?

1. We are allowed running here. (Montreal)
2. We are allowed to run here. (Brooklyn)
3. I did nothing today. (Brooklyn)
4. I didn't do nothing today. (Brooklyn)
5. The government has decided to raise taxes. (Montreal)
6. The government have decided to raise taxes. (London)
7. I'm going to the dep to get some cigarettes and beer. (Montreal)
8. That's all the faster I can run. (Michigan)
9. That's as fast as I can run. (Brooklyn)
10. I might could go. (Alabama)
11. I might be able to go. (Brooklyn)
12. He been try make me mad. (Cajun English, Louisiana)
13. I ate a egg. (Ypsilanti)
14. I ate an egg. (Brooklyn)

Further Readings

- Chapters 1 and 2 of *Patterns in the Mind* by Ray Jackendoff (1994). This is an excellent book that inspired much of this book—we actually recommend reading it all.

- Recapturing the Mohawk Language by Marianne Mithun and Wallace Chafc, in Timothy Shopen (1979) (ed.) *Languages and their Status*, (3–33). We have our students read this partly because Mohawk is spoken in the vicinity of Montreal where we teach, and partly because it gives interesting illustrations of productive grammar in a language that is very different from English. There are aspects of the article we disagree with, but this can lead to useful discussion.

2

I-everything: Triangles, streams, words

In the last chapter we introduced two important notions related to I-language: computation and equivalence classes. As we suggested, these ideas have quite broad relevance for an understanding of the human mind, and in this chapter we will provide demonstrations from various domains in addition to linguistic ones. Abstracting away from physical properties and providing analyses in terms of equivalence classes is something that all scientists do, including linguists and other cognitive scientists. In the case of cognitive science, this process of forming equivalence classes actually constitutes the object of study. The human mind/brain automatically filters incoming stimuli in such a way as to collapse even grossly distinct signals and treat them identically. This kind of information processing is what cognitive science studies.

2.1 A triangle built by the mind

Look at Fig. 2.1. If you are a normal human being you will see a white triangle with its vertices at the center of the three Pac-Man figures. You can see the edges of the triangle and trace them with your finger, but if you cover up the Pac-Men the edges seem to disappear. The area of the triangle is exactly the same shade of white as the background of the page, so it is not

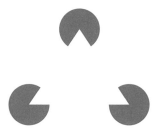

Fig 2.1 Triangle constructed by visual system.

surprising that no edges remain visible. But why do you see a triangle in the first place—are you hallucinating? If so, why does every other human who looks at such a page also see the triangle?

From the point of view of physics, which can measure things like the light reflecting off the page, there is no distinction between the area inside the triangle, its edges and the background. So is the triangle not *real*? We could decide to say that the triangle is not part of the real world and thus adopt a pure physicalist definition that accepts as real only that which can be defined using the categories of physics, like mass, wavelength, velocity, etc. But that is not very satisfying—it leaves us with a big mystery: Why does everyone who looks at the page see the triangle? Isn't *that* a real fact about real humans?

So, is there really a triangle on the page? The solution offered by cognitive science to the triangle mystery is this. The human visual system interprets certain stimuli in such a way as to construct a representation of a triangle. In other words, the triangle is not a physical property of the page but a result of how you process physical stimuli like this page under certain circumstances—for example, when your head is oriented correctly, your eyes are open, and it is not pitch dark in the room. In other words, your mind imposes the triangle interpretation on the page. Now, one could just declare that there is no triangle since its edges cannot be physically detected. One could decide that the only things that are real are those that can be described in physical terms, and the edge of the triangle has no mass, or charge, or luminance, and so it is not a physical entity and thus not real. If the edges aren't real, the triangle itself cannot be real.

As we said, one can arbitrarily decide to use the term *real* in this way, but this puts us in an uncomfortable situation. On the one hand, we have to accept that every single person who looks at the triangle figure sees the same thing, a triangle, and so do certain animals, as can be shown by experiment, despite the fact that the thing they see is not real. Are we all deluded? How come we are all deluded in exactly the same way, then? On the other hand, if we want to study the human visual system scientifically, we have to accept the idea that science can study what is not real. Rather than arbitrarily defining the *real* to include only that which has mass, charge, luminance, location, and so on, we can recognize that physics contains certain categories and vision science others, but it is not the case that the categories of one are necessarily more real than those of the other. In fact, the categories of modern physics are so remote from our everyday experience of what we call the physical world, that they too must be considered abstractions. We'll elaborate on this later on.

People sometimes think that the fact that we see a triangle on the page has to do with the fact that we have the word *triangle* that we can apply to certain experiences. There are at least two problems with this view. The first problem is that if we couldn't recognize triangles in the first place, we would not know what to apply the word to—it just doesn't make sense to say that the word allows us to perceive the object.

The second problem is that our visual system constructs percepts of edges and corners that compose objects even when we have no name for them. Fig. 2.2 contains an illusory regular polygon with thirteen sides. You experience the illusion even if you do not know that such a figure is called a *triskaidecagon* by mathematicians.

We even see illusory shapes that nobody has a name for, as in the blob of Fig. 2.3.

We see the contours of a blob because of the way our visual system processes the information received by our eyes. The triangle or blob we perceive is not part of the physical input to our eyes but is rather an information structure, or representation, constructed by the visual system based on the input it receives and its own rules.

Note that we make no effort to see the triangle or the blob, and in fact we can't help but see the edges of these figures, even when it is pointed out that there is no difference in luminance between the figure and the background. Our visual system works the way it does despite contradictory conscious knowledge.

We mentioned that certain animals will also see shapes when presented with a display with illusory contours like Fig. 2.1. Nieder (2002) reviews the evidence for animal perception of such shapes: for example, bees have been trained in a Y-shaped tunnel to choose the correct branch to a sugar

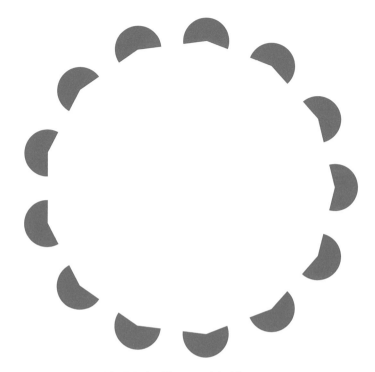

Fig 2.2 An illusory triskaidecagon.

solution when that route is marked with stripes oriented in a particular direction, say rising towards the right. The bees are then tested with the rightward rising pattern replaced by various displays. If the display contains a solid rectangle or one with illusory edges as in Fig. 2.4, the bees treat it like stripes with the same orientation.

However, if the display contains a solid triangle with the wrong orientation, or crucially with the Pac-Men oriented in a way that does not produce illusory contours (even for us humans), the bees treat the display as different from the rightward rising stripes. The two sides of Fig. 2.4 are

Fig 2.3 Unnamed form constructed by visual system.

Fig 2.4 Rectangles constructed by visual system—of humans and bees, who can be trained to treat the two figures as members of an equivalence class in terms of orientation.

processed as members of an equivalence class that excludes the two sides of Fig. 2.5. Clearly, from a purely physical perspective, one could argue that each side of Fig. 2.4 is more like one of the members of Fig. 2.5 than like the other member of Fig. 2.4. However, the well-defined contours of the solid rectangle and the illusory contours of the other figure can be treated as equivalent by a bee (and a human).

However, we can't just say that the rectangle or triangle is "out in the world." If they were out in the world, then a computer vision system with a robotic eye that is way more sensitive than a human eye should be able to detect these shapes at least as easily as a person can. However, it is, in fact, very difficult to get an artificial system to recognize these displays as a rectangle or triangle. It is only a rectangle or triangle to a system that processes information about incoming patterns of light in such a way as to construct the representation of such shapes. Nature has given us such a system, but we haven't yet figured out how to endow computers with such a system. The rectangle or triangle is a symbolic representation, a member of an equivalence class, that is internal to the entity (bee, cat, human,

Fig 2.5 The bees do not treat the illusory rectangle above as the same as either of these two figures.

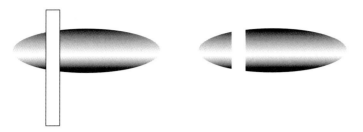

Fig 2.6 How many objects on the left? How many on the right?

whatever) that is constructing it. Since we assume that bees do not have words for various shapes, we now have a third argument against relating our perception of the triangle to our linguistic experience.

We now have a nice parallel to the discussion of the non-existence of languages from the previous chapter. There is no such thing as Warlpiri or *the* Warlpiri word for "child" or *the* Warlpiri reduplication rule; there are just a bunch of humans whose minds contain similar kinds of rules and symbols that we informally group together as Warlpiri. Similarly, there is no triangle or rectangle on these pages, but humans (as well as members of some other species), who all share the same kind of visual system, all construct the same percept upon exposure to this page. Our nervous systems just process information in this way. (As an aside, note that there are, in fact, *no* triangles in the physical world—triangles are geometric figures with sides consisting of perfectly straight line segments meeting at vertices whose angles add up to exactly 180°. Perfectly straight line segments, for example, do not exist in the physical world.)

2.2 More visual construction

Our discussion of vision has already led us to some surprises, and further consideration will, as you suspect, only show us greater complexity. Let's assume a computational approach to vision that parallels in many ways the approach we introduced for language in Chapter 1. On the topic of representation in perception Bregman (1990:3) makes the following point:

In using the word 'representations', we are implying the existence of a two-part system: one part forms the representations and another uses them to do such things as calculate . . .

Let's now apply Bregman's observation to Fig. 2.6.

On the one hand, our visual system must clearly detect and represent shading, textures, and edges. On the other hand, it must perform the calculations or inferences that lead us to see the left side of the figure as representing an ellipse partly occluded by a rectangle, to group the two gray regions together. Note that our visual inference system cannot help but see things this way, and it does not matter that there is no right way to experience the image—it may be a picture of a rectangle occluding an ellipse, or it may be a picture of three distinct objects, as suggested by the right-hand side of the figure. In fact, it is just a pattern of ink on the page: we can specify its physical properties; and we can tell you what numbers we entered in the graphics program that we used to design it. But none of this matters—we, as humans, cannot help but perform the computations that lead to the perception of one object occluding another on the left-hand side. Note that the only difference between the two sides is the black perimeter of the rectangle on the left. The fill of the rectangle and the empty space perceived on the right-hand side are both just regions of the page without any ink.

The output of the visual system, representation of objects with colors, textures, shapes, and sizes feeds into other systems that also appear to involve computations and constructions.

Consider Figure 2.7. On the one hand, we see a nose, a snout, some ears, eyes, and lips, but, on the other hand, we see a picture of Oonagh and Baby Z. Is there any reason to even make such a part/whole distinction, or are we just being pedantic? Well, consider the following description of the condition *prosopagnosia* from the Preface of Hoffman's (1998) *Visual Intelligence*:

After his stroke, Mr. P still had outstanding memory and intelligence. He could read and talk, and mixed well with the other patients on his ward. His vision was in most respects normal—with one notable exception: he couldn't recognize the faces of people or animals. As he put it himself, "I can see the eyes, nose and mouth quite clearly, but they just don't add up. They all seem chalked in, like on a blackboard...I have to tell by the clothes or by the voice whether it is a man or a woman...The hair may help a lot, or if there is a moustache..." Even his own face, seen in a mirror, looked to him strange and unfamiliar. Mr. P had lost a critical aspect of his visual intelligence.

So, Mr. P appears to see normally in the sense of seeing objects like ears and noses and lips, but further computation by the face recognition system, involving the output of the visual system, is somehow impaired. We

Fig 2.7 Mouths, snouts, lips, eyes, and ears or Oonagh and Baby Z?

typically think of faces as objects in the world, but this case suggests that face perception requires construction of a complex symbolic representation from the objects that themselves are constructed by the visual system. These processes of construction occur inside individual minds/brains according to rules and principles (we might say grammars) of vision and face recognition.

2.3 Auditory scene analysis

Just as our mind actively constructs the objects of visual perception and face recognition, it also constructs the objects of auditory perception, what we hear. Imagine you are listening to the hum of an air conditioner and then hear the footsteps of someone walking down the hall to your office. The hum is continuous, but the footsteps are a sequence of short sounds. From a physical point of view, each step is a separate event, yet you perceive the sound of footsteps as a single auditory "object." Your mind integrates the sequence of steps into what is called a single auditory stream. Notice that the continuous hum of the air conditioner constitutes another stream. Although this may seem obvious, in fact there is a tremendously

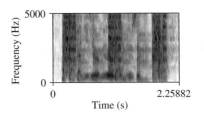

Fig 2.8 Spectrogram of a complex wave consisting of music and speech.

complicated issue to explain. Every time a footstep occurs, the sound originating from the step combines with the sound of the hum, and the vibrations that reach your ears are a composite of these two sources and any others that may be present, such as a person talking on the phone at the next desk. Yet your mind is somehow able to segregate the complex sound wave into two or more separate streams.

Auditory scene analysis is a framework for studying auditory perception developed by Albert Bregman and his collaborators. Auditory scene analysis can be broken down into two main components. One problem, given the fact that sound waves from various sources are combined into a single wave that reaches the eardrum, is that of simultaneous spectral integration and segregation. The auditory system integrates into a single representation parts of the sound spectrum reaching the ear within a temporal window that "go together." Of course, the decision that spectral regions "go together" is determined by properties of the auditory system, and in the case of an illusion, the decision may lead to a non-veridical percept. An example of spectral integration is the perception of a played musical note and the overtones that give the instrument its unique timbre as emanating from the same source. The process of assigning parts of the spectrum to different perceptual sources is called spectral segregation: attending to speech while a fan provides a high-frequency hum in the background requires spectral segregation.

The other main component of auditory scene analysis is sequential integration—acoustic events occurring separated in time may be integrated into a single auditory stream. Examples of streams include a sequence of footsteps or the continuous sound of falling rain. Individual sounds of a foot striking the ground are separated by silence or other sounds, yet the steps are integrated into a single perceptual object, a stream.

The complexity of the task of auditory scene analysis can be appreciated by considering the spectrogram in Fig. 2.8. This is the spectrogram of a

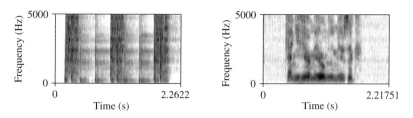

Fig 2.9 The music (left) and the speech (right).

wave created by mixing a sample of recorded speech and some music. The spectrograms of the music and speech separately are shown in Fig. 2.9. In this example, we were able to display the music and speech separately because we had the separate recordings. The mind has to extract such information from a complex stimulus, like the mixed signal, to construct distinct streams from a single physical signal.

The following quotation expresses the extent to which we construct our auditory experience—just as the edges of the triangle above are constructed by our minds, so are the edges of auditory events:

The perceptual world is one of events with defined beginnings and endings...An event becomes defined by its temporal boundary. But this impression is not due to the structure of the acoustic wave; the beginning and ending often are not physically marked by actual silent intervals. [Handel 1989]

This quotation suggests that our minds impose the structure of our auditory perception, just as with our visual perception, and it is pretty easy to find parallels between the two domains. Suppose we remove the border of the rectangle on the left side of Fig. 2.6, giving the right side. It is less likely that you perceive the two curved regions as belonging to a single elliptical object, since they appear separated by "empty space." The presence of the border on the white region on the left lets us perceive it as belonging to a white object which can mask the non-visible part of a (continuous) ellipse. An exact parallel can be designed for audition.

If we take a tone and replace a portion of it with silence, we'll hear the resulting sound as having a gap in the tone. However, if we replace the silence with broad-frequency white noise of a loudness that would be sufficient to mask the tone, then we actually perceive the tone as continuing behind the noise. Interestingly, we will be able to fill in a gap in a sound behind a mask even if the surrounding portions are not constant. For

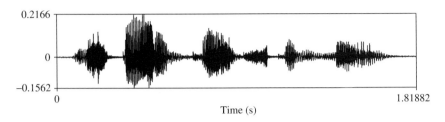

Fig 2.10 Waveform of a sentence.

example, a gap in a tone that rises in frequency can be restored by our perceptual system if it is masked by noise.[5]

In vision and in audition the mind plays an active role in constructing our experience. In the next section we will discover that the perception of boundaries applies even to sound corresponding to speech—even word boundaries are constructed by our minds.

2.4 Words are built by the mind

So, what is this discussion of vision and audition doing in a book on linguistics? The point is that just as our visual and auditory percepts are due to active mental processes, our linguistic cognition is also a function of processing by our mental grammar. This is most easily demonstrated by our perception of speech sounds and their organization into words.

Before we proceed, note that speech perception depends upon prior general auditory processing, since the words we hear are sounds. This relationship between audition and speech perception is somewhat like that between object perception and face recognition discussed above: the output of one system is fed into another.

The display in Fig. 2.10 shows a waveform of a recorded utterance, *The spotted cat skidded by*. The horizontal axis shows time and the vertical axis is basically a record of the loudness of the signal at each point. When the display reaches up and down from the horizontal axis, the speaker's voice was most loud, and where the waveform is basically just a horizontal line, the speaker was silent. (Because of background noise there is never perfect

---

[5] A demonstration and further discussion of this phenomenon can be found http://ego.psych.mcgill.ca/labs/auditory/Demo29.html, which is accessible from the webpage of Al Bregman whose work inspired much of this discussion.

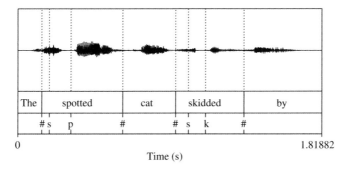

Fig 2.11 Waveform of *The spotted cat skidded by*.

silence indicated.) Based on this information, try to figure out where each word of this sentence begins and ends.

You were probably tempted to place your word boundaries wherever the display indicates a silence. However, you will be surprised to see the transcription we have provided of some of the sounds and the word boundaries in Fig. 2.11. There are two particular aspects of the display to note. First, approximate word boundaries are indicated by the symbol #, but note that there is not necessarily silence between words. Second, note that there is sometimes silence (apart from the slight noise in the signal) inside of words—this is normal when the utterance contains sounds like those corresponding to the letters *p, t, k*. In the words *spotted* and *skidded* there is an *s* before a consonant in the same word, yet the waveform shows that there is silence between the two sounds.[6]

On the other hand, there is no silence between the words *the* and *spotted*. This situation is typical, and if we presented you with recorded speech from an unfamiliar language, you would not be able to find the word boundaries by either looking at the waveform or listening to the recordings. You need a mental grammar of the language to impose word boundaries on the signal.

We learn from this example that, like the triangle we saw, the words we perceive in speech are the result of information processing. The sound wave that reaches our ears does not inherently contain words. Our minds impose words on signals we hear; the words are not part of the signal.

In the case of the perceived triangle, it turns out that any normal human (or bee) who can see will see the triangle, because we all have a visual system that processes information in the same way. In the case of language, there

---

[6] This silence is there because of the way these consonants are articulated—a detail you would learn more about in a phonetics course.

is some learning involved—we perceive word boundaries in speech in ways that depend on the languages we have learned. So linguistic information processing appears to be more plastic, more influenced by experience, than visual information processing.

We will not go into further detail analyzing waveforms here, but we will just mention that our perception of speech as consisting of discrete segments is also due to processing by our speech perception cognition— the actual signal does not consist of a well-defined sequence of segments, as you can perhaps tell by examining the waveform above. The portions of the waveform corresponding to each speech sound blend together, showing us that, like words, our perception of segments is due to the constructive information processing carried out by our minds.

The point we have just made about triangles, auditory streams, faces, and words turns out to be true of all categories of human experience—they are not definable by their actual physical properties. For example, to again cite Edward Sapir, there is no way to define in physical terms, the difference between a club and a pole. An object is called a club if we use it as a club or believe that it was intended to be used as a club by the person who fashioned it—there are no necessary and sufficient physical criteria to make something a club as opposed to a pole.

Similarly, there are no necessary and sufficient physical criteria to determine where word boundaries fall in a waveform. The perception of word boundaries depends on which mental grammar is being used to process the signal. The signal itself has no information about word boundaries, since words are not physically definable entities. We could even imagine a situation in which a given signal would be parsed into different words by speakers of different languages.

Even closer to home, we have all had the experience of misparsing, of assigning word boundaries in a fashion not intended by the speaker. Misassignment of word boundaries is one of the sources of "mishearing" that leads to *mondegreens*[7] like hearing Jimi Hendrix say *'Scuse me while I kiss this guy* instead of the intended *'Scuse me while I kiss the sky.* The [s] of *sky* is misparsed as belonging to the previous word. As we will see in Exercise 2.6.2, [k] after [s], is usually indistinguishable from [g].

---

[7] According to the Wikipedia, the term was coined by Sylvia Wright in *Harper's Magazine*, November 1954, in a discussion of her understanding as a child of the poetic phrase *And laid him on the green* as *And Lady Mondegreen.*

2.5 Summing up

So, to reiterate, the triangles and the words we perceive are related in a very complex and indirect fashion to the physical stimuli we receive. The fact that we can imagine words and triangles in our mind's ear and eye, without any outside stimulus at all, further demonstrates that perception of these entities is due to construction by the mind.

So why is this chapter called "I-Everything"? The "I" of *I-language* is chosen to suggest *individual*, *internal*, and *intensional*. It should be obvious that the triangle you see, the auditory streams you hear, and the words you identify in an utterance are all the output of "I"-systems. For example, each of us has our own individual visual system, and this system is clearly internal to us, part of our make-up as organisms. Moreover, it is not the case that we can only perceive a limited number of objects whose images are stored in some kind of mental list. Like the productivity of our linguistic grammars, our visual computational systems are productive. They construct edges given an infinite range of stimuli. You do not see a triangle only when looking at Fig. 2.1 from a single angle under one set of lighting conditions from a particular distance—try moving the page around or visit http://www.cut-the-knot.org/Curriculum/Geometry/EdgeIllusion.shtml to explore the visual grammar that lets you construct the edges of a triangle.

2.6 Exercises

Exercise 2.6.1. **Word boundaries:** The purpose of this exercise is to give you firsthand experience with the abstractness of linguistic representation. You will see that the word and segment boundaries we perceive are typically not present in the acoustic signal, but instead are imposed by our minds. This is a linguistic example of the construction of experience that we have discussed in relation to vision and hearing.

You will work with a recorded sentence and try to find word boundaries. Using a sound editing program such as Praat (www.praat.org) examine the waveform of the sound file ilang.wav available from the companion website. If you have trouble saving the file from your browser, then download the .zip file containing all the materials you need and unzip it. You'll end up with a folder containing the sound file.

There is also an image of the waveform on the website, but you need a sound editing program to zoom in and play selections. You may find it useful to print this waveform, or one from within Praat, to mark your word boundaries on. In order to complete the exercise you need to be able to see the waveform (a graph of intensity vs. time) and select and play portions of the sound file. You also need to be able to find points in time in the waveform window. This is pretty easy in Praat and most other phonetics programs.

You can also get a manual from the Praat homepage or get a manual written by our former student Tom Erik Stower from the companion page. (This manual contains more detail than you will need.) Write your answers down on scrap paper as you proceed, so that you do not lose your work if the computer crashes or if your session is interrupted.

a. Provide an orthographic transcription of the sentence—that is, just write it in normal English writing.

b. For each word of the ten or so words in the sentence, write the ending time of the word in milliseconds. (Count contractions like *can't* as two words, if there are any.) For example:
   End word 1 "the": 136 msec
   End word 2 "cat": 202 msec
   and so on.

c. Are there any cases of silence within a word? Give at least one example and say where the silence occurs—between which sounds? Example: The word "Casper" has silence between the *s* and the *p*. This can be heard and also seen because the waveform has almost no amplitude between those two sounds.

d. Is there generally silence or a pause between words? Give an example of two adjacent words where you had difficulty deciding on where to place the boundary. Example: It was hard to decide on the boundary between "the" and "apple."

e. Comment on any difficulties or interesting issues you encountered in any part of this exercise. (Say something coherent and relevant—if you found nothing interesting, fake it.)

Exercise 2.6.2. Take either a pre-recorded sentence or record your own and mark the segment boundaries on the waveform. In other words, find the division between adjacent sounds, like the *s* and the *k* of a word like *sky*. Comment on any problems you run into. See how your results compare to those of your classmates. Tom Erik's manual will tell you how to mark the boundaries on a waveform in Praat and print out the results.

Exercise 2.6.3.   More construction: Visit a website with optical illusions and find examples of illusions that demonstrate your mind's role in the construction of color, motion, and shape. Here is one excellent site: http://www.michaelbach.de/ot/index.html

Further Readings

These readings are all fantastic, and we have borrowed freely from them in this book. *Visual Intelligence* is the most accessible.

- Chapters 1, 2, 7 of *Visual Intelligence* by Donald Hoffman (1998).
- Chapter 1 of *Auditory Scene Analysis* by Albert Bregman (1990).
- "The problem of reality" by Ray Jackendoff. *Noûs*, Vol. 25, No. 4. Special Issue on Cognitive Science and Artificial Intelligence (Sep., 1991), pp. 411–33. Reprinted in Jackendoff's *Languages of the Mind: Essays on Mental Representation* (1992).
- "Seeing more than meets the eye: Processing of illusory contours in animals" by A. Nieder (2002). *Journal of Comparative Physiology* **188**: 249–60.

3

Approaches to the study of language

People have a lot of strong feelings about what language is. The term *language* may bring to mind communication, literature, poetry, persuasion, and propaganda, among other things. On the other hand, for the linguist, or at least for the kind we are interested in telling you about, an inquiry into human language involves examining patterns that reveal the existence of rules, the rules of I-languages. The question we want to address in this chapter is why is it that linguists choose to focus on this notion of language as opposed to others, say, language as a means of communication.

Before we answer this question, it is useful to notice that notions of language as a system of communication, or as a conveyor of culture, are commonsense notions of language, part of the intuitive and "untutored ideas people have about the world and how it works" (Nuti 2005:7). In contrast, I-language seems to be a rather narrow term, with a technical definition, one that does not seem to correspond in any direct way to our commonsense intuitions about language. This is not surprising, since the words and concepts of everyday life appear to be insufficient for the task of understanding in every other domain of scientific inquiry. The disconnect between normal experience and the scientific worldview appears to require the invention of a technical vocabulary in all fields of study.

3.1 Commonsense views of "language"

This point about terminology can be easily illustrated with the term *language*. Let us take a look at some of the most common concepts of language.

3.1.1 Language is a form of expression

People may talk about the *language* of the body, the *language* of the hands, or even, like an artist we know, about the *language* of string balls thrown on the floor. It is probably apparent that a concept of language that included all these, as well as the kind of phenomena we have discussed, is way too vague to constitute the object of scientific inquiry—pretty much any expressive thing can be called a language in everyday discussion.

3.1.2 Language as an instrument/result of thought

Another commonly held belief is that language should be defined in its relation to thought and reasoning. Whether it is language that allows us to have (new) thoughts or whether it is thought that controls language is a matter of debate. Under one view, language shapes our perception of reality and predetermines what we see in the world around us. Thus, according to the so-called Sapir–Whorf hypothesis, we conceptualize nature along lines laid down by our native languages. In contrast, under the other view, thoughts exist independently of language and language just matches (some of) the thoughts or concepts that exist independently in our mind. Whatever stand we take on this debate, we find out nothing about the nature of language, and about why it has the properties it has. The "language shapes thought" position would amount to saying that language has the properties it has because it shapes thought. However, no real constraints on the properties of language can be derived from this, since it is not very clear what the boundaries of our thoughts are and how to derive these boundaries. Similarly, the "thought controls language" position is just as unrevealing as to the properties of language. Under this view, one would have to say that language has the properties it has because it is predetermined by thought. This again leaves us with the task of identifying the limits of our thoughts, which are at least hard to define.

3.1.3 Language as a repository of culture

Another commonsense belief about language is that the language used by a culture primarily reflects that culture's interests and concerns, and thus that language can be defined as a medium of culture.

As an illustration, consider the following quote from *Mother Tongue* by Bill Bryson (1990):

Originally, **thou** was to **you** as in French **tu** is to **vous**. **Thou** signified either close familiarity or social inferiority, while **you** was the more impersonal and general term. In European languages to this day choosing between the two forms can present a very real social agony. As Jespersen, a Dane who appreciated these things, put it: "English has thus attained the only manner of address worthy of a nation that respects the elementary rights of each individual."

We won't comment on the assumptions inherent in such a statement, but anyone who maintains illusions that there are interesting connections among linguistic form and race and culture can look forward to enlightenment by reading Franz Boas's 1911 *Introduction to the Handbook of American Indian Languages*, reprinted in Boas et al. (1966). Boas shows that basically every positive or negative correlation among race, language, and culture can be illustrated with cases from the American Northwest Coast Native peoples. Geoffrey Pullum's 1990 essay "The Great Eskimo Vocabulary Hoax", about the notion that Eskimos have a lot of words for snow, is also useful in this regard.

3.1.4 Language as a system of communication

Maybe the most widespread conception of language is that it is a communication system. While there is little doubt that language is used for communication purposes, keeping this in mind does not help at all to identify the properties of this particular system of communication. Language is not the only way people communicate; we also use gestures and facial expressions, for example. At the same time, other species are also able to communicate and they do so by using a communication system as well. Saying that language is a system of communication leaves questions like the following unanswered: Are all these systems alike? Or are they different? And if language is different, how is it different?

Morris Halle, the founder of generative phonology, argues that there are good reasons not to think of language as a communication system:

Since language is not, in its essence, a means for transmitting [cognitive] information—though no one denies that we constantly use language for this very purpose—then it is hardly surprising to find in languages much ambiguity and redundancy, as well as other properties that are obviously undesirable in a good communication code. [Morris Halle 1975]

Halle, who spent ten years trying to apply engineering concepts from the study of information and communication to human language, came to believe that it is actually more productive to treat languages as arbitrary rule systems, like codes or games, in order to get insight into their structure.

3.2 I-language

The views sketched above try to elucidate our everyday thinking about language and they are inappropriate for scientific accounts of language itself. In a way, they presuppose that the concept *language* is already clearly defined, and they address questions related to the relation between language and other phenomena like socialization, or culture.

To give a concrete example, let's consider briefly a view that language acquisition and use is "just a matter of socialization." This is a view that is sometimes presented to students in branches of psychology like child development. Now, even if we had some idea what was meant by socialization, we would still need a mentalist, computational theory, one based on I-language. It must be mentalist, since whatever it means to be "socialized" must at least include encoding in memory. If a child is socialized to cover certain body parts in public, then he or she must somehow remember to do so. Explicit rules against showing those body parts and implicit rules of plural formation must all be encoded in memory if they are to have any influence on behavior. No social interactionist theory can deny that what the Warlpiri child is "socialized" to do is reduplicate to make plurals, whereas the English-speaking child is "socialized" to suffix. Each child ends up with a rule or pattern that can generate—be used to produce and understand—new forms. Thus, the "socialization" process must have led to a specific computational system. So, invoking the vague notion of socialization does nothing to characterize or explain the human capacity for language.

At this point you might be thinking that all there is to it is a matter of taste: linguists are interested in I-language, and people who focus on the relation between language and culture, language and thought, etc, just aren't! That is, of course, true. But the point is that the choice is not arbitrary. It's not just a matter of taste. The choice is dictated by the aim of the pursuit. A scientific pursuit aims at discovering laws and principles that govern the way things are, and it does so by using logical reasoning and by making predictions that can be tested. In order to achieve such goals, scientists have to use terms in a narrow way. Just as physicists use *energy* and *field* in a special way, we will use *language* and *grammar* in a way that appears to define a topic that is amenable to scientific study. We choose a scientific terminology that makes distinctions that we believe correspond to real distinctions in the structure of the world.

Other uses of these terms are fine for ordinary discourse. In fact, the non-scientific terms have priority—scientists borrow words from everyday language and use them in a special way. People use the term *water* to refer to a vast range of solutions containing not only H_2O, but also many other substances, whereas chemists use *water* to refer only to H_2O. The everyday word (or its linguistic ancestor) was in use before the development of chemistry, and it is an arbitrary fact that chemists borrowed this term to refer to a pure molecular substance. Chemistry did not do the same with the other basic elements of ancient times: earth, air, and fire. It would not have been inconceivable for chemistry to have applied the name *air* to what it called instead *oxygen*. Chemistry did not discover the true meaning of the word *water*; rather chemistry borrowed the word for its own uses. It is crucial to distinguish everyday and scientific language when talking not only about chemistry but equally when talking about language itself.

The issue here is not whether the commonsense concepts of language can be used in deriving some kind of knowledge. Someone may believe for example that a certain degree of insight and reflective knowledge is achieved by the following passage from Jespersen's *Growth and Structure of the English Language* (1911).

To bring out clearly one of these points I select at random, by way of contrast, a passage from the language of Hawaii: "I kona hiki ana aku ilaila ua hookipa ia mai la oia me ke aloha pumehana loa." Thus it goes on, no single word ends in a consonant, and a group of two or more consonants is never found. Can anyone be in doubt that even if such a language sound pleasantly and be full of music and harmony the total impression is childlike and effeminate? You do not expect much vigour or energy in a people speaking such a language; it seems adapted only to inhabitants of sunny regions where the soil requires scarcely any labour on the part of man to yield him everything he wants, and where life therefore does not bear the stamp of a hard struggle against nature and against fellow-creatures.

How much insight can be gained from this is debatable, but none of the statements in these passages can be either proved or disproved objectively on the basis of logical reasoning. There is no indication as to why the language of Hawaii should be considered childish and effeminate, except as a totally subjective opinion. Given this, no predictions can be formulated as to what kind of "total impression" some random language would give. This is what makes such statements different from scientific statements.

3.2.1 Narrowness

Some people object to the narrow sense in which Chomsky and those influenced by him use the term *language*. Critics see this as a kind of linguistic imperialism. However, Zenon Pylyshyn (2003), in discussing his narrow use of the term *vision*, basically in recognition of the many ways that the terms vision and seeing are used, as we discussed above, points out that "To use the term 'vision' to include all the organism's intellectual activity that originates with information at the eye and culminates in beliefs about the world, or even actions is not very useful, since it runs together a lot of different processes." The same arguments apply to our terminology for language.

If we ask you to raise your right arm over your head, and you do so, we can ask a physiologist for an account of your behavior that will be highly detailed. He or she will be able to tell us about electrochemical events in your brain and the neurons leading to your arms; contraction and relaxation of various muscles; adjustments in systems responsible for balance and equilibrium; and the actions of proprioceptive systems that let you know, even with your eyes closed, that your arm is raised.

However, there are many, many, many things about which the physiologist (or neurologist or anatomist) will have to remain silent. He or she will not know how it is that you understood the words addressed to you; or how you decided to interpret them as a request; or how you decided to honor the request; or how your intention actually set off the chain of events that can be described in electrochemical and biomechanical detail alluded to above; or how you knew when your intention had been fulfilled. He or she may also not be aware of or care about the fact that you often raise your arm in a similar fashion to pick apples or to paint ceilings.

In other words, there are many mysteries connected with our arm-raising event. Yet, we do not decide that arm-raising as whole is a complete mystery and that physiology should be abandoned as hopeless. We don't give up scientific methodology for the areas where it seems to work, for example in characterizing the chemical reactions in the synapses between neurons. Instead we try to identify areas in which some understanding is possible, and dissect our study of arm-raising accordingly—some things have to be put aside, other questions can be fruitfully explored. One could accuse physiologists of being narrow or unfair for excluding from their textbooks vast questions associated with arm-raising, but nobody does so.

We can also consider what vision scientists study. Their results may have relevance to a wide range of issues, and perhaps give insight into a vast range of phenomena, but we do not expect vision scientists to explain and discuss trends in interior design, art history and the relative salaries of various fashion models, despite the fact that all of these topics are somehow related to what people see.

Chomsky (2000:68) makes the same point with respect to linguists' "failure" to account for communication in general:

The proper conclusion is not that we must abandon concepts of language that can be productively studied, but that the topic of successful communication in the actual world of experience is far too complex and obscure to merit attention in empirical inquiry, except as a guide to intuitions as we pursue research designed to lead to some understanding of the real world, communication included.

If Vişinel tells Wang *I love you*, a linguist cannot figure out why he chose to communicate this particular idea; or whether he is lying; or whether he is not lying, but is trying to get a favor from Wang; or why he didn't use some other way of conveying his message, like *I am quite attached to you and find you attractive and would do anything for you*. But a linguist can tell you that in the sentence that Vişinel did say, *I* is the subject, *love you* is the predicate, *you* is the object, and so on. Structures, rules, patterns—that's the kind of stuff linguists talk about—not what we use language for; not what having language allows us to achieve; and not why we say particular things on particular occasions.

A major premise of this book is that human language can be and should be an object of scientific study, like other aspects of the natural world, including, say, chemical bonds and mammalian reproductive systems. The idea that language can be studied scientifically is rejected by many people as ridiculous. They claim that as an artifact of human invention language is too flexible, too amorphous. It is not difficult to discern that people who hold this opinion are just not willing to accept the kind of narrow delimitation that is necessary in any scientific undertaking. Notice however, that this kind of narrowness does not imply a claim that I-language is the only thing that is worth investigating. In fact, Chomsky (2000:77) himself recognizes that his approach is narrow:

Plainly, a naturalistic approach does not exclude other ways of trying to comprehend the world. Someone committed to it can consistently believe (I do) that we learn much more of human interest about how people think and feel and act by reading novels or studying history or the activities of ordinary life than from all naturalistic psychology, and perhaps always will; similarly, the arts may offer appreciation of the heavens to which astrophysics does not aspire.

He sees the narrowness of focus as a necessity for naturalistic inquiry, the approach of the natural sciences, but this narrowness has no bearing on the richness of all human experience or on the validity of other ways of thinking about the world.

Rather than arguing about the issue of whether language can or should be studied scientifically, our attitude will be that the proof is in the pudding—if the explicit mathematical analysis of Warlpiri and Samoan reduplication yield interesting results, then this suggests our approach is worthwhile. Of course, we can't demand that you find the results interesting—if reduplication turns you on, then scientific linguistics is for you. If you wonder how reduplication reflects the Warlpiri and Samoan worldview and are not satisfied with the answer "Not at all!," then formal linguistics is not for you.

3.3 The kind of stuff we look at

We have delimited the range of what we call language in a very narrow fashion. In order to give you a sense of what such narrowness can do for us, we now present some puzzles involving very simple patterns in English. Your interest may or may not be piqued by these examples—if it is not, read no further. If you are intrigued, then, as suggested by the following quotation, you are ready to begin scientific inquiry into the nature of human language:

The beginning of science is the recognition that the simplest phenomena of ordinary life raise quite serious problems: Why are they as they are, instead of some different way? [*Language and Problems of Knowledge* Chomsky 1988:43]

The puzzles we present in the following section will resurface later in the book. Here we present them just to illustrate the kind of things modern theoretical linguistics takes as amenable to scientific inquiry, the kind of patterns that can give insight into our object of study, the human language faculty. As you will see, we do not need to go to the Australian outback to find intriguing puzzles, the following are all drawn from English.

3.3.1 A puzzle concerning questions

Consider a sentence like the following:

3.1   The boy is singing.

To make a YES/NO question out of such a sentence you would probably say the following:

3.2   Is the boy singing?

Now make a YES/NO question with this next sentence:

3.3   The boy who is dancing is very tall.

And with this one:

3.4   The boy is kissing the dog that is whining.

We are sure that you had no problem coming up with the following questions:

3.5   Is the boy who is dancing very tall?

3.6   Is the boy kissing the dog that is whining?

But coming up with a general rule for how to form YES/NO questions from declarative sentences is actually pretty hard to do. If you think it is not so hard, consider additional sentences like the following:

3.7   The boy whose mother can sing well may chase the puppy that is recovering from an injury that it received from a man who can be quite nasty.

We may have slowed you down a bit, but you can probably recognize that the corresponding question is this:

3.8   May the boy whose mother can sing well chase the puppy that is recovering from an injury that it received from a man who can be quite nasty?

In other words, it is kind of hard to state the rule relating declaratives and the corresponding YES/NO question, but it is pretty easy to make the relevant sentences, at least until the sentences get quite long.

Compare this situation with the following. Here is a rule that is easy to state:

3.9   Rule 1. Reverse order of words in a sentence A to form sequence B.

Thus the following sequences of words are related by Rule 1:

3.10   The dog saw a cat.

3.11   Cat a saw dog the.

We are sure you will agree that Rule 1 is very easy to understand—you just start at the right edge of A and read off words from right to left to get B.

Now consider the following sentence:

3.12   The tall man who is crying can drop the frog that is croaking.

Say the sentence to yourself a few times, then turn it into a question. We assume this is easy to do. Now, look away from this page and apply Rule 1—reverse the order of the words.

⋮

Now that you are looking back, we are willing to bet that you failed miserably at applying Rule 1 to the last example. Try with a shorter sentence like this:

3.13   Three blind mice ran across the track.

We bet that you failed with this simple sentence too—or maybe you succeeded, but you had to go really slowly.

Our first puzzle is the following: Why is the question formation rule, which is so hard to state, so easy to apply; and why is Rule 1, which seems easy to state, so hard to apply.[8] Obviously, we have not defined any explicit way to measure "hard" or "easy," so we rely on intuition at this point.

---

[8] One might suggest that the YES/NO rule involves displacing a single word, whereas Rule 1 involves manipulating all the words in the sentence—to counter this replace Rule 1 with a rule that just moves the fourth word of a sentence A to the front in order to form B—is this easy to apply?

3.3.2 Puzzles concerning relations among words

Consider the following:

a. Bill is perplexed. John kissed himself. (*himself* = *John*, *himself* cannot be *Bill*)

b. Bill is perplexed. *Mary kissed himself. (*himself* cannot be *Mary*, *himself* cannot be *Bill*)

c. Bill is perplexed. John kissed him. (*him* cannot be *John*, *him* can be *Bill*)

d. Bill is perplexed. *Himself kissed John. (*himself* cannot be John, and *himself* cannot be *Bill*)

e. Bill is perplexed. He kissed John. (*he* cannot be *John*, but *he* can be *Bill*)

In (3.14a.) *himself* must refer to the same person as *John*, and cannot refer to a person mentioned outside the sentence that contains *himself*, such as *Bill*. In (3.14b.) *himself* cannot refer to the same person as *Mary*, even if *Mary* is in the same sentence, and it cannot refer to *Bill* either. In fact, there is no grammatical interpretation of this string, a status denoted by the '*'. In (3.14c.), *him* cannot refer to the same person as *John*, which is in the same sentence as *him*, and it has to refer to a person that is not mentioned in the sentence, someone from outside of the sentence, say *Bill*, or some other male. In (3.14d.) *himself* cannot refer to *John*, which is in the same sentence as *himself*, and it cannot refer to *Bill*, which is in a different sentence, either. Like (3.14b.) there is no grammatical interpretation of this string. In the last example, (3.14e.) *he* cannot refer to *John*, which is in the same sentence, but it may refer to *Bill*, which is outside of the sentence where *he* occurs.

The form *himself* appears to be dependent for its interpretation on another noun phrase.[9] It appears that the relevant noun phrase must be in the same sentence as *himself*. But notice that this is not all. In example (3.14d.) there is a nominal expression in the same sentence as *himself* that the latter could potentially enter a dependency relation with, yet the sequence is ungrammatical, perhaps because *himself* precedes the other expression. In contrast, the form *him* appears not to be subject to these conditions.

It turns out to be very difficult to explain the distribution of words like *him* and *himself* with respect to other nominal expressions, despite the fact

---

[9] We'll clarify this notion later—examples of noun phrases are *that tall man, the boy with the yellow hat*, and *Mary*.

that they are very common words used even by small children. Thus, the distribution of these words constitutes a puzzle on its own, and we will offer a solution to this problem in a later chapter.

We now want to draw your attention to a deeper puzzle, one that relates the patterns we have just seen to other patterns. Consider the following examples:

3.15
    a. Bill is perplexed. John didn't kiss anybody.
    b. Bill is perplexed. John never kisses anybody.
    c. Bill is perplexed. *John kissed anybody.
    d. Bill is perplexed. *John always kissed anybody.
    e. Bill isn't perplexed. *John kissed anybody.
    f. Bill isn't perplexed. *John always kissed anybody.
    g. Bill is perplexed. *Anybody didn't kiss John.

Examples (3.15a.–d.) suggest that *anybody* is somehow dependent on a negative word like the contracted *n't* or *never*. Examples (3.15e.–f.) show that having a negative word in the immediate context of a preceding sentence is not sufficient—such a negative cannot license the appearance of *anybody* in these examples. Like *himself*, the interpretation of *anybody* appears to involve a relation or dependency among words within the sentence containing *anybody*. The parallel between (3.15g.) and (3.14d.) is also striking—like *himself*, *anybody* seems to need to follow the word it is dependent upon.

The examples we looked at are short, simple strings with familiar English words, and the judgments of what is and what is not grammatical are easy to make. For us, these phenomena present puzzles that are crying out for an explanation in the same way as the proverbial apple that hit Newton on the head. A sense of wonder about the complexity of everyday events is a necessary starting point. We will not tell you here what the detailed analysis of these examples is. At this point, all we want to do is illustrate the surprising parallelism between the distribution of *himself* and *anybody*. We will show later on that the accounts of these elements can be brought together: each of them can be explained with the same basic notion—what we will call c-command.

Needless to say, questions like the ones we discussed above can easily arise under an I-language approach, but not under the other views of language we mentioned earlier. If language is viewed as a repository of culture or as a vehicle for our thoughts, for example, questions like these couldn't even be

Fig 3.1 Which two of these look most alike? Baboon image (left) used by permission © Art Parts.

formulated, and even if they could, no insight could be gained regarding the observed restrictions, since there is no cultural restriction against assuming, for example, that *him* in (3.14c.) can refer to the same person as *John*, and since it is certainly possible to think about *him* as referring to the same person as *John*.

3.4 Methodological dualism

We have advocated an I-language approach on the basis of the fact that the narrowness of this concept allows for a scientific study of language. However, there is a lot of resistance to the idea that language can at all be the object of scientific inquiry.

Suppose you see around campus a poster with a picture of a baboon, advertising a talk on the communication system of this primate species. Who do you expect to show up at the lecture? Probably a bunch of calculator- and backpack-toting science nerds. Same if the poster shows a photograph of the Crab Nebula, an astronomical entity 7,000 light years away from earth. However, if the poster advertises a lecture on language or on the English language with a picture of a small human, you might get people from the education department, the English department, the communications department, and very few science students. Why is this? Don't the baby and the baboon look much more alike than the baboon and the nebula in Fig. 3.1?

When discussion falls within the domain of the physical sciences, pretty much everyone agrees that everyday, commonsense conceptions or categories do not map directly onto scientific ones. And a scientist has no qualms about postulating unobservable entities and new theoretical concepts with limited application in everyday experience if these provide the best solution to whatever problem is at stake—the physicist doesn't worry if the layperson finds genes, valence or quarks unintuitive. In introducing these concepts the scientist is not concerned if the solution he proposes bears little resemblance to pre-theoretic discourse or understanding. Humans do not have an immediate understanding or any intuitions about electrons, protons, or neutrons, or the position of planets, and yet we are ready to accept that scientific pursuits that rely on the postulation of these entities are valid. Any scientific pursuit leads to this kind of gap between the commonsense concepts and understanding and scientific concepts and understanding.

Since Newton posited gravitational fields to explain action at a distance, the effect of the moon on the tides of earth's oceans, for example, our everyday conception of how the world works and our scientific models have drifted further and further apart:

At one time there was no very profound difference between the two versions. The scientist accepted the familiar story [of the perceiving mind] in its main outline; only he corrected a few facts here and there, and elaborated a few details. But latterly the familiar story and the scientific story have diverged more and more widely—until it has become hard to recognise that they have anything in common. Not content with upsetting fundamentally our ideas of material substance, physics has played strange pranks with our conceptions of space and time. Even causality has undergone transformations. Physical science now deliberately aims at presenting a new version of the story of our experience from the very beginning, rejecting the familiar story as too erratic a foundation. [Sir Arthur Eddington, "Science and Experience." 1934]

As the familiar story and the scientific story diverge it becomes impossible to understand in any direct sense what the world is like according to the scientific view.

However, when it comes to language, or to any scientific theory of the mind, there appears to be a double standard. Although many scholars in various fields do not explicitly acknowledge their views, they are typically not willing to accept a gap between everyday and scientific notions in the domain of mental phenomena. In the case of language, it seems that philosophers are the main supporters of this double standard. As Jerry Fodor notes:

To a remarkable extent, and really out of thin air, philosophers have taken it upon themselves to legislate conditions under which empirical inquiry into the mental must proceed. [Fodor 2000, "It's all in the mind," *Times Literary Supplement* review of Chomsky 2000b]

The resistance is not necessarily due to assuming a dualist position, i.e. that mental phenomena are to be kept apart from physical phenomena. Even supporters of a monist position, who assume that the mind is somehow amenable to physical explanation, are usually skeptical about the possibility of applying naturalistic scientific methodology accepted for the study of the physical world to the study of the mind. This kind of double standard is called methodological dualism.

What methodological dualists propose instead as tools for the study of mental phenomena is the use of intuitions about the mind provided by common sense, contrary to the practice used in other areas of naturalistic inquiry. Accounts are expected to be cast in terms of recognizable, familiar concepts. For example, when it comes to language, philosophers tend to assume that the notion of language investigated should be one that corresponds to commonsense notions such as communication, and that the concepts that will be instrumental in figuring out the properties of language are concepts like truth, reference, belief, meaning, in their everyday intuitive sense.

The explanations that are cast in terms of such familiar concepts are preferred to accounts that use specialized concepts that depart from commonsense notions. Such latter attempts are dubbed as "dubious" and "outrageous" on the grounds that they are counterintuitive, but nobody objects to the theory of relativity or biological theories of cell reproduction on such grounds.

Explanatory theories of mind have been proposed, notably in the study of language. They have been seriously challenged, not for violating the canons of methodological naturalism (which they seem to observe, reasonably well), but on other grounds: "philosophical grounds," which are alleged to show that they are dubious, perhaps outrageous, irrespective of success by the normal criteria of science; or perhaps that they are successful, but do not deal with "the mind" or "the mental"...[S]uch critiques are commonly a form of methodological dualism, and...advocacy (or tacit acceptance) of that stance has been a leading theme of much of the most interesting work in recent philosophy of language. [Chomsky 2000:77]

The stand we take in this book is a monist one, both from the point of view of the object of study—mental phenomena are natural phenomena in the world, just as physical phenomena are; and from a methodological point of view—we expect our explanations of the mental to depart from commonsense intuitions in the same way that scientific explanations of gravity, optics, thermodynamics, and genetics do.

3.5 Biolinguistics

The view we are adopting has more to it than just being a monist view in the sense explained above. One could potentially believe that I-language is a legitimate object of scientific study, and that the methodology used to perform this study should be the usual scientific methodology employed by all sciences, but assume no necessary connection between I-language and biological cognitive structures. Much work in cognitive science actually adopts this stance. The idea is that cognition should be studied as abstract computational-representational systems that, in principle, could be implemented in a wide variety of physical devices.

Under this view, the *desire* for a hamburger, the *intention* to pay for it on Tuesday, or the *pain* of a toothache each have computational-representational essence that is independent of their existence in the mind of a human desirer/intender/sufferer. Even more strongly, some researchers think it is important to characterize cognition in such a way that it necessarily abstracts away from the physical system in which it happens to be instantiated, so that we can accept the possibility that Martians, who may have very different physical structures from us, can be correctly said to have *the same* desires/intentions/pains that we do. The arguments for Martians apply equally to digital computers.

Under this view, the implementation of an I-language could be in a human brain, but also in a computer, for example, and whatever theory one would come up with for accounting for the linguistic computational properties of the human mind will also apply to machines.

The view advocated in this book is that I-language is directly related to an organ of the human body, i.e. to some part or structure of the brain, and that I-language is the physiological function of such a structure in the brain. Such an approach is only partly supported by the findings reported by brain scientists—*we* know language is in there, but *they* have not made much progress in identifying its neural correlates. In our view, the "pure computation" approach to the study of language actually has a potentially deleterious effect on the search for understanding, an issue we will elaborate on in the next chapter.

We thus adopt the term *biolinguistics* in this book to emphasize the fact that we are studying a property of organisms, their language faculty. We are doing this in the same vein as studies of dolphin communication systems, or the navigational abilities of wasps—they all require complex computational systems that are constrained by the genetic endowment of the organisms that engage in the relevant behaviors. In this sense, linguistics is just a branch of cognitive ethology, the study of the computational systems that underlie animal behavior.

3.6 And so?

Each one of us has a digestive system that releases enzymes, breaks down complex molecules and provides nourishment to the whole body. There are "digestologists" who try to understand the workings of this system, the details of which are inaccessible to the conscious knowledge of most of us. And this is in spite of the fact that we each have a more or less functional human digestive system. Similarly, each of us who speaks "English" has a mental grammar that is comprised of rules and patterns that relate to the puzzles illustrated in Section 3.3. Our goal, as the digestologists of the language faculty, is not to teach you how to speak or listen but rather to unveil these rules and patterns.

Again and again, we will return to the themes of computation and equivalence class within the framework of I-language. We do not aim for fairness or completeness in our presentation of what language is and what linguistics is—the book represents our own biases and judgments about what is crucial, as well as the shortcomings in our knowledge and understanding. However, we will present some phenomena of reasonable complexity, in a way that we hope will render them accessible.

People tend to think of science as belonging to an elite few in our society. However, we suggest that the spirit and practice of science is accessible to anyone who can appreciate the following proclamation by Democritus, the father of atomic theory:

I would rather find a single causal law than be the king of Persia. [Democritus 5th century BC]

Part of the beauty of linguistics is that it is a fairly young field, and interesting data is easily accessible for investigation. It is relatively easy for a newcomer to enter the field and start making real discoveries and contributions. We do not need complex measuring devices to start making hypotheses and collecting further data that can bear on our two puzzles, for example. The devices and the source of data are readily available in our mind. In fact, several linguists have argued that when funding for science education is scarce and when the general public is fairly ignorant about the nature of science, the accessibility of linguistics makes it an ideal vehicle for teaching skills of hypothesis formation and testing. In this spirit the authors and their students have begun lecturing about linguistics outside of the university setting—in high schools, public libraries, and even prisons.

If you decide to pursue the following discussion, if these puzzles intrigue you, we promise an overview of linguistics, as grounded in cognitive science, that will stretch your mind and give you an appreciation derived from experience that will be more broad and also more profound than that of many academics and professionals in fields that are concerned with some aspect of human language. With this experience-based knowledge, you will not be able to avoid the conclusion that many widely accepted views concerning the nature of language are as misguided and empty as we now know the claims of alchemy and astrology to be.

3.7 Exercises

Exercise 3.7.1.   Ask three friends the following questions:

- What is language?
- Can you characterize language without mentioning what we use it for?
- Can language be studied scientifically, like biology or physics?

Discuss their responses in terms of the approaches introduced in this chapter.

Further Readings

Like most of Chomsky's writings, these are difficult, but we hope the discussion we have provided makes them more accessible.

- Chapter 1 of *Knowledge of Language* by Noam Chomsky (1986).
- "Linguistics and brain science" by Noam Chomsky in A. Marantz, Y. Miyashita, and W. O'Neil (eds), *Image, Language, Brain*, pp. 13–28.
- "Language as a natural object" by Noam Chomsky (2000a). Chapter 5.

4

I-/E-/P-Language

By now, we hope that the internalist approach to linguistics, the approach that takes the object of study to be the human language faculty and the states it can attain, is clear. The computations and representations that we have been discussing are always assumed to be computations and representations of specific human "computers" and "representers," individual humans whose linguistic experience has caused their language faculty to end up in a certain state.

In the first chapter we looked at the formation of complex words via reduplication in Warlpiri and Samoan. This kind of phenomenon falls in the realm of morphology, the study of word formation from the *morphemes*, the minimal units of meaning that a speaker must have in memory. In this chapter we will look at an aspect of *phonology*, the sound patterns of language. In particular, we will focus on word *stress*. We will use this discussion of word stress to gain further insight into the implications of adopting the I-language perspective.

4.1 Computation in phonology

You probably have an idea of what stress is, and you probably know that the location of stress in English is unpredictable. For example, the character in the non-*Rocky* film series starring Sylvester Stallone is **Ram**bo, with stress (basically, extra loudness and duration, and higher pitch) on the first syllable. In contrast, the name of the poet played by Leonardo di Caprio in *Total Eclipse* is *Rim***baud** with stress on the second syllable. Aside from this difference in stress, which is not predictable from other aspects of the names, such as what sounds they contain, the two names are identical in our dialects of English.

Some languages contrast with English in that the placement of stress is predictable, and thus stress cannot be used to distinguish two names or two different word meanings. Since our interest here is in computational aspects of language, those that can be expressed by rules, we will focus now on languages with non-distinctive, rule-governed, predictable stress patterns. The discussion relies heavily on discussion by Bill Idsardi in his 1992 thesis from MIT, *The Computation of Prosody*.

In general, stress is realized on the vowels of a word, but it is traditional to attribute stress to syllables. For our purposes, we will assume that each vowel corresponds to a syllable. The symbols *i,u,e,o,a* represent vowels in the following discussion, and so each one of these symbols will correspond to a single syllable. Finally, we note that words can have more than one stress, a primary stressed syllable, marked with an acute accent on the vowel, like *á*, and secondarily stressed syllables marked with a grave accent on the vowel, like *à*. We'll assume that the stress system of I-languages is rule-based and that the input to the stress system is a string of syllables with no stress assigned, while the output is the same string with the correct stress pattern.

4.1.1 Two simple languages

Let's look first at Weri, a language of Papua New Guinea. The following data is representative of words with an odd number of syllables (the (a.) cases) and those with an even number (like (b.)). We won't even tell you what these words mean, so you can concentrate on the patterns of interest.

    a. àkunèpetál
        b. ulùamít

Each of these forms represents the output of some phonological rule that assigns stress in Weri. The input to this rule is the form without stress.

What we want to discover is the rule that takes these non-stressed forms and outputs the stressed forms.

4.2   a. akunepetal → àkunèpetál
           b. uluamit → ulùamít

Suppose the way stress is assigned to words in Weri is the following:

4.3   An algorithm for Weri stress

- Syllables are grouped into pairs (each grouped pair is called a "foot"), starting from the end of the word as follows:
  a. a(kune)(petal)
  b. (ulu)(amit)
- Leftover syllables are grouped by themselves:
  a. (a)(kune)(petal)
  b. (ulu)(amit)
- Stress is assigned to the syllable at the right edge of each foot:
  a. (à)(kunè)(petàl)
  b. (ulù)(amìt)
- The rightmost stress in the word is made the primary stress:
  a. (à)(kunè)(petál)
  b. (ulù)(amít)

We have thus generated the stress on the listed words, and it turns out that the algorithm will generate stress correctly on all Weri words.

Now consider data from another language called Maranungku, spoken in Northern Australia:

4.4
- tíralk
- mérepèt
- jángarmàta
- lángkaràtefì
- wélepèlemànta

Suppose we proposed the following algorithm to generate Maranungku stress.

4.5   An algorithm for Maranungku stress

- Label the vowels of each syllables with an index from 1 to n, where n is the number of syllables in the word, e.g.:
- ti$_1$ra$_2$lk
- me$_1$re$_2$pe$_3$t
- …
- Assign stress to each syllable whose vowel bears an odd-numbered index.
- Assign primary stress to the syllable whose vowel bears the lowest index.

Just as we successfully generated Weri stress patterns above, we have now developed an algorithm to generate Maranungku stress patterns. These examples illustrate once again the idea that languages are computational systems. However, you should be bothered at this point.

You may have noticed that the stress patterns of the two languages Weri and Maranungku are mirror images of each other. The former has primary stress on the last syllable and secondary stress on every other syllable counting from the last. The latter has primary stress on the first syllable and secondary stress on every other syllable counting from the first. Despite this relationship between the patterns, we have analyzed the two in completely different terms. For Weri we needed to group syllables into feet of two and target the righthand syllable in each foot. For Maranungku we need to label syllables up to an arbitrarily high number, determine if a syllable is labeled with an odd number, and, if it is, stress it.

You probably have figured out that we could have adopted the Weri analysis to Maranungku by just changing the starting point for grouping syllables to the beginning of the word; stressing the leftmost member of each foot, and placing primary stress on the lefthand stressed syllable in the word.

Alternatively, we could have adapted the Maranungku analysis to Weri by assigning our indices from 1 to n starting at the end of the word and again stressing the odd-numbered syllables.

There are three important issues to discuss at this point, and it is crucial to distinguish them:

a. Does it make sense to ask what the correct analysis is for each language?
b. Is it important to provide a unified analysis of the two languages?
c. What is the correct unified analysis of the two languages?

We have developed two equivalent analyses for each language—a grouping analysis and a counting analysis—and if we conceive of a language as just a list of recorded utterances, there is no question of correctness in choosing among equivalent analyses, analyses that will always map the same input to the same output. But if we think of a particular grammar as actually characterizing a property of a particular human mind, then there is a correct grammar corresponding to the linguistic knowledge of each person. More than one grammar can simulate the output of a Weri or Maranungku speaker, but the goal of linguistics is to model the system of knowledge that is actually in a person's mind. So, the answer to our first question is that it does make sense to ask what the correct analysis is.

If we believe that there is such a thing as the human language faculty or, indeed, such a thing as human language, then we are committed to the existence of a unified analysis of stress systems of the two languages. If we analyze them in completely different terms, then we are, in effect, saying that they are two different kinds of thing. Thus, it is important to provide a unified analysis if we think we are faced with two instantiations of the human linguistic stress system.

The final question, the one that asks for the correct analysis, is a hot topic of research. We will postpone giving you an answer, but just to give you an indication of where we are heading, consider the following quotation from Chomsky's *Knowledge of Language* (1986:38), where S_0 refers to the initial state of the language faculty, prior to any experience, and I-language refers to the mental grammar a speaker has.

Because evidence from Japanese can evidently bear on the correctness of a theory of S_0, it can have indirect—but very powerful—bearing on the choice of the grammar that attempts to characterize the I-language attained by a speaker of English.

In other words, evidence from one language's stress system, say that of Weri, should bear on the best analysis of the stress system in other languages, such as Maranungku, since each represents a development of the initial state of the stress module of the human language faculty. Let us look at more data that shows other ways in which languages may differ minimally in their stress systems, while conforming to the same general pattern.

4.1.2 Some more data

The two languages we have just considered are sufficient to make the point we are interested in, but it will be useful to look at two more simple stress patterns.

Here are two words from Warao, a language spoken in Venezuela:

     a. yiwàranáe
        b. yàpurùkitàneháse

The general pattern in Warao is that stress falls on even-numbered vowels counting from the end of the word, and main stress is on the second to last vowel. So in the (a.) form, there is no stress on the first vowel, because the word has an odd number of vowels, but in the (b.) form the initial vowel is stressed because the word has an even number of vowels. Here are the forms repeated with the vowels numbered and with syllables grouped in twos—we don't want to bias our search for the right model just yet:

4.7   a. yi₅wà₄ra₃ná₂e₁
           yi(wàra)(náe)
       b. yà₈pu₇rù₆ki₅tà₄ne₃há₂se₁
           (yàpu)(rùki)(tàne)(háse)

Like Weri, this language builds feet from the end of the word but it differs in that it stresses the *lefthand* member of each foot and does not allow feet of one syllable. Alternatively stated, Warao stresses even-numbered syllables counting from the end of the word.

Finally consider Pintupi, an Australian language in which stress is again predictable. See if you can extract the pattern based on the following forms:

4.8   Rules in phonology: Pintupi (Australian) stress

páṇa	"earth"
tʲúṭaya	"many"
máḷawàna	"through from behind"
púḷiŋkàlatʲu	"we (sat) on the hill"
tʲámulùmpatʲùŋku	"our relation"
ṭíḷirìŋulàmpatʲu	"the fire for our benefit flared up"

Now see if you can predict where the stress would fall on these Pintupi forms:

4.9   Where are the stressed syllables in the following words?

kuranʲuluimpatʲuɻa	"the first one who is our relation"
yumaɻiŋkamaratʲuɻaka	"because of mother-in-law"

You may have figured out that stress in Pintupi is exactly like in Maranungku, except that a final syllable is never stressed, even if it is odd-numbered. If we think about the grouping of syllables into pairs, we can think of this condition as a failure to stress a syllable that is not part of a pair. So this condition applies in Pintupi and Warao, but not in other languages, like Maranungku or Weri. So this is one dimension along which languages may differ minimally, while conforming to the same general type of algorithm for assigning stress.

There are many, many languages like the four we have considered. They provide us with good examples of computation within one small domain, as well as with the kind of (micro)variation that we can find within such a domain.

However, the simplicity of these patterns has allowed us to discuss three questions that have been the subject of very important debates among philosophers and linguists over the past fifty years or so. In general, the philosophical position (e.g. Quine's) has been to deny the validity of trying to choose a correct analysis for some linguistic data. All analyses that made the right predictions were considered equally valid. We will see that this view comes from failing to adopt the I-language perspective that languages (including stress systems) are components of actual individuals.

This is such an important point that we need to expound on it a bit. Recall the discussion of Samoan in Chapter 1. We forced you to make and revise hypotheses as you received new data. Positing a prefix *no-* in the form *nonofo* became less attractive when we expanded the set of data to include *momoe*, and the hypothesis that the first syllable is reduplicated became untenable when we again expanded the empirical base to include *alolofa*. There is nothing surprising about this—a smaller set of data allowed for a wider range of hypotheses concerning reduplication. As soon as we expanded the corpus, however, some of the hypotheses had to be dropped or revised. Chomsky's statement about Japanese and English, cited above, makes basically the same point: there is no good reason to consider only "English" data or "Weri" data—even when trying to figure out the nature of a Weri grammar, data from Maranungku, English, or Japanese could be, or rather should be, considered relevant. The empirical base of potentially relevant data is all linguistic output of all human languages. This position is only available to us once we adopt the I-language, biolinguistic approach. In fact this approach necessitates taking seriously the fact that Weri-type grammars, Maranungku-type grammars, Japanese-type grammars, and English-type grammars are built from the same primitives, primitives that can be part of a computational system realized in a biological organism with the properties of humans.

4.2 Extensional equivalence

Above we developed two competing analyses for the stress systems of each of two languages, Weri and Maranungku. For each language we were able to construct a grouping algorithm and a counting algorithm for generating the correct stress patterns. Two algorithms that produce the same outputs are said to be *extensionally equivalent*, so we can say that the two analyses that we proposed for, say, Weri correspond to extensionally equivalent grammars for Weri stress. Of course we are using the term grammar here not in the sense of "mental grammar" but to refer to the explicit rule systems, the algorithms, that we came up with as linguists. Our goal will be to understand the extent to which these algorithms we posit correspond to the actual mental grammars of Weri speakers.

Since the grammars of human languages are quite complex it may be useful to illustrate this notion of extensional equivalence with a simple mathematical example. Suppose we wanted to devise a rule system to take some input and generate as output a number that is a member of the set $S = \{1, 4, 7, 10, 13, 16, 19\}$. Well, there are actually an infinite number of ways of generating the set S—one way would be to just list the members of the set as inputs and map them to themselves as outputs, but there are other ways. For example, we could define a set of inputs $\mathcal{I}_1 = \{0, 1, 2, 3, 4, 5, 6\}$ and a function $f_1 = 3x + 1$. Then for each element of $\mathcal{I}_1$ we could apply f_1 to it and generate a member of S. This system for generating S, along with two others, is given in (4.10)—you should check that they all work.

> **4.10** Extensional equivalence—three functions for generating a set of numbers:
> $S = \{1, 4, 7, 10, 13, 16, 19\}$.
>
> a. $3x + 1$, $x \in \{0, 1, 2, 3, 4, 5, 6\}$
> b. $3x - 2$, $x \in \{1, 2, 3, 4, 5, 6, 7\}$
> c. $(3x - 4)/2$, $x \in \{2, 4, 6, 8, 10, 12, 14\}$

So all of these functions applied to their respective input sets are extensionally equivalent—they all generate S.

Now, what if we asked what the *correct* function is for generating S. Does this question make any sense? We are just generating a set of numbers, a list of data, so there is no reason to say that any one is more correct than any other. However, if you have a little device that always flashes a number from S after you hit some button corresponding to a number from another set, then it does make sense to ask what is going on inside the device. There is no correct answer to the question "How is *set S* generated?" But there is a correct answer to the question "What is this device doing to generate members of S?" We may not be able to answer the question, or we may be able to only eliminate certain possibilities and claim that the correct answer is one of a certain class of answers. But a correct answer does exist —we can be confident of its existence even if we do not know all of its properties.

Once we adopt the I-language perspective that language is best understood as individual grammars that are properties of individual minds, then we recognize that there *is* a correct answer concerning the true nature of Weri stress.[10] It may be hard to find out what it is, but there is a question of truth of the matter. Our next step will be to see if there is any way to make progress on figuring out what that correct answer is—is it more likely that the correct answer relies on grouping syllables into pairs from right to left and stressing the rightmost member of each group with primary stress in the rightmost group, or on counting up the number of syllables in the word, finding that number n, assigning primary stress to syllable n and secondary stress to syllables $n - 2, n - 4, n - 6$, etc.?

The internalist I-language perspective will help us. Languages are properties of individuals, and they take on their individual properties due to the effects of experience on some initial state of the human language faculty. In other words, humans are born with the capacity to learn any human stress system, but experience, the data a child is exposed to, determines which system is encoded in the learner's mind as the stress grammar. Given this perspective, it is apparent that our goal as linguists should be to discover a single set of primitives of representation and computation that can generate all the stress systems we observe. Since Weri speakers and Maranungku speakers are all humans, we assume that they start out with the same cognitive apparatus for representing equivalence classes of syllables and words and computing stress. So, either both should use the syllable-counting method or both should use the grouping method. If Weri uses the grouping method, then that tells us that the initial state of the language faculty (referred to as S_0 above) allows the learner to represent words by grouping syllables; similarly, if Weri uses the counting method, that has implications for the initial state. So, if we can get both Weri and Maranungku stress with only one kind of primitive (either counting or grouping), then we should do so.

---

[10] Just to be clear, nothing we have said implies that everyone referred to as a speaker of some particular "language" must have the same exact grammar even in cases where the outputs are apparently identical in a restricted domain, like stress. There is a correct answer for each individual Weri speaker. The question of whether all extensionally equivalent stress grammars are identical is an interesting one, but beyond our scope here.

To recapitulate, we have justified the view that there is a correct analysis for the stress system for a language by appealing to the I-language perspective. Since grammars are properties of individuals, there is a correct characterization of what those properties are. Second, since all humans are assumed to be capable of learning all languages from an initial state that has the same basic resources, we have justified the idea that the same fundamental notions should be used to model both Weri stress and Maranungku stress. If we reject internalism, the I-language perspective, then there is no reason to assume that one set of data labeled "Weri" and another set labeled "Maranungku" should be analyzed using the same representational and computational primitive elements. If our goal is to generate data sets or to simulate the behavior of Weri speakers, then we don't need to worry about what the correct analysis is.

So, cognitive biolinguistics is concerned with the correct characterization of Weri stress as a step towards figuring out the nature of the language faculty of humans. People interested in generating sets of data, including many working linguists, are concerned with stating a set of rules that will generate a corpus of observed forms. Artificial intelligence, as opposed to cognitive science, is concerned with simulating human behavior, and someone working in this field may be happy to build a robot that simulates Weri stress patterns but uses a grammar that is completely different in its representations and computations from that internal to a real Weri speaker.

Is there any hope of choosing between the counting and grouping analyses of Weri? We can at least make some suggestive observations. When we turn to syntax in subsequent chapters, we will see that the language faculty never has syntactic rules or structures that depend on counting words. In contrast, the fundamental notion of syntax seems to be that certain words in a sentence are in closer relations than others. Appealing just to intuition, we hope you can agree that in a sentence like *The man ate a fish* there are groups of words that "go together" in some sense: *the man* forms a group; *a fish* forms a group; but *man ate* and *ate a* do not form groups. If you accept this intuition about English syntax, then we propose to attempt to apply this fundamental notion of grouping to analyze as much of language, all languages, as possible. And if we can use grouping, but never appeal to counting, this may indicate that we have discovered a fundamental property of linguistic representations—they are structured.

Young children and many species of animals have been shown to be able to distinguish small numbers of items, such as one versus three or two versus four. It is typically assumed that this is done by a process called *subitizing*, which is an almost immediate perception of number that even appears to utilize only a subset of the brain regions used for counting. Outside of the range of subitizing, animal and child performance on counting tasks degrades immediately, so that even five and ten cannot be distinguished. Although the reports remain controversial, there have been claims that even adults in the Amazonian Pirahã society (which has only about a hundred members) cannot count, but only subitize. In general, counting appears to be a conscious activity that is not actually utilized by other cognitive systems, something that appeared late in human evolution and appears late in development of the individual. It is thus attractive to not posit stress-generating algorithms that depend upon the language faculty counting to arbitrarily high numbers.

So, our conclusion is that English syntax and Weri and Maranungku stress are all best modeled using the notion of grouping—of syllables or words, as relevant. By taking this strong stand we are forced to review our discussion of Samoan reduplication in Chapter 1. We proposed a rule that reduplicated syllable $n - 1$, and this appeared to be able to generate all the data. However, an extensionally equivalent rule that groups syllables from the end of the word into pairs and repeats the leftmost member of the rightmost group is now preferable.

We repeat in (4.11) the Samoan forms with the grouping of the last two syllables, which will make the parallel to stress systems more apparent.

4.11	Samoan verbs: sg-pl		
	(**nof**o)	nonofo	"sit"
	(**mo**e)	momoe	"sleep"
	a(**lof**a)	alolofa	"love"
	sa(**val**i)	savavali	"walk"
	ma(**liu**)	maliliu	"die"

We are proposing that grouping of elements in a string into constituents is a common operation in the construction of linguistic representations—it recurs in syntax, in morphological reduplication, and in the phonology of stress in various languages. The grouping process is part of an algorithm in each case for finding targets of specific processes—targeted syllables may receive stress, as in Weri, or they may be repeated, as in Samoan. We have discovered a commonality, but there obviously must be room for variation as well: in some stress systems, like Weri and Warao, and in Samoan the grouping of syllables must start at the end of the word; whereas in cases like Maranungku and Pintupi the grouping starts at the beginning of the word. Another parameter of variation relates to which member of a group is targeted for special treatment—the leftmost or the rightmost. Next, we have seen that the treatment of syllables that are not part of a binary group must be considered—are they ignored or are they treated like the targeted syllable of binary groups?

Here in (4.12) is the Pintupi data with the grouping of syllables (σ stands for syllable). We can see that grouping starts at the beginning of the word; the leftmost member of each group is targeted; and a syllable that ends up as not part of a binary group gets ignored. This results in the fact that odd-numbered syllables are not stressed when they are final.

4.12	Pintupi stress (again)		
	(pán̪a)	(óσ)	"earth"
	(t^jút̪a)(ya)	(óσ)σ	"many"
	(mál̪a)(wàna)	(óσ)(òσ)	"through from behind"
	(púl̪iŋ)(kàla)(t^ju)	(óσ)(òσ)σ	"we (sat) on the hill"
	(t^jámu)(lùmpa)(t^jùŋku)	(óσ)(òσ)(òσ)	"our relation"
	(t̪íl̪i)(rìŋu)(làmpa)(t^ju)	(óσ)(òσ)(òσ)σ	"the fire for our benefit flared up"

So, yes, Pintupi has a stress system that is different from that of Weri, Warao, and Maranungku, but it can be analyzed in terms of a set of primitive elements, equivalence classes (syllables, for example), and computations (grouping of two elements) that can be used to analyze not only the other stress systems but a wide range of linguistic phenomena including Samoan reduplication.

This discussion of extensional equivalence and the internalist perspective has thus provided us with a framework for understanding how we can pursue a theory of Universal Grammar, a theory of S_0, the intial state of the language faculty. Without the I-language, biolinguistics perspective, it is not even possible to pose the question of what is the correct rule in a given case. The internalist perspective guarantees that there is a correct answer, since grammars are actually instantiated in individual minds/brains. Since each I-language represents a development of the initial state of the language faculty, we can gain insight into the correct characterization by expanding our empirical base from a single language to all attested languages. Finally, the biolinguistic approach encourages us to draw on what we know about other aspects of cognition, neuroscience, and evolution to decide that a stress algorithm that groups syllables into feet is more plausible than one that relies on counting arbitrarily high and referring to the notion of odd or even, a notion not part of any known natural system.

Under the pure computation view that we discussed in Section 3.5, specific evidence from the evolutionary and developmental biology of humans, as well as their general cognitive properties, is denied a part in characterizing the nature of language, since these are just the accidental properties of one kind of language computing-representing system. These biological properties might be absent from Martians who, let's say, can perform the same input-output mappings. In other words, the pure computation approach makes it impossible, and even undesirable, to choose among extensionally equivalent grammars. The pure computation approach is a step backwards to Quine's view that it is incoherent to ask what the best grammar is among ones that all generate the data.

4.3 Non-internalist approaches

While it is probably hard to find working linguists who would deny that humans do store linguistic information in their minds or brains, it is not very hard to find linguists and other scholars who insist that, in addition to the individual, internal "I-languages," as Chomsky calls them, there is another object of study for linguists, that has properties that differ from I-languages.

We will briefly discuss three such examples, but we warn you to be on the lookout for more in your own reading in fields like philosophy, anthropology, psychology, and even linguistics, where both tacit and explicit rejections of the I-language approach are not as rare as one might expect.

Our first example comes from the work of Geoffrey Pullum, a linguist who has actually done a lot of important work on the formal properties of human language in general and on the analysis of particular languages. To give a sense of his range of expertise, we just note that he has co-authored an encyclopedic grammar of English and also done fieldwork and published on several endangered languages of Amazonia.

In an article comparing two approaches to syntactic modeling, Pullum and co-author Scholz (2001) made the following statements:

- millions of different people may be correctly described as speakers of the same language
- *The Times* in the UK, *The New York Times* in the USA, *The Sydney Morning Herald* in Australia, and other papers around the world all publish in the same language

You can probably tell that, coming from a professional linguist, both of these statements reflect a rejection of the I-language approach advocated by Chomsky and adopted in this book.

The second example is mentioned by Chomsky in a paper called "Linguistics and Brain Science" and comes from a very successful popular book by Terence Deacon, a biological anthropologist formerly at Harvard and Boston University, and currently with appointments in both anthropology and linguistics at the University of California at Berkeley. In a discussion of language acquisition in his 1997 book *The Symbolic Species*, Deacon criticizes the view of "Chomsky and his followers" who

assert that the source for prior support for language acquisition must originate from *inside* the brain, on the unstated assumption that there is no other possible source. But there is another alternative: that the extra support for language learning is vested neither in the brain of the child nor in the brains of parents or teachers, but outside brains, in language itself. [105]

The I-language perspective defines languages as mental grammars, encoded in individual brains, but Deacon explicitly refers to language (languages?) as "outside brains." It is hard to imagine a clearer denial of the I-language view.

Finally, we present a quotation from Michel Foucault, a French philosopher who has been most influential in the fields of literary criticism and cultural studies.

Language partakes in the world-wide dissemination of similitudes and signatures. It must therefore be studied itself as a thing in nature. Like animals, plants or stars, its elements have their laws of affinity and convenience, their necessary analogies. [Foucault 1973:35]

At first blush, this passage perhaps appears to support a scientific approach to language that should thus be consistent with the Chomskyan program we have been developing. However, Foucault is not advocating the study of the human language faculty as an object of study of the same status as the human faculty of vision, but rather he is advocating recognition of some abstraction "language" that has an existence of its own, like animals and plants, not part of (human) animals.

Despite the very different approaches of Pullum, Deacon and Foucault, we find them equally incoherent in light of the discussion and discoveries discussed thus far in this book. In the discussion that follows we will clarify why.

4.3.1 E-language

Chomsky makes a distinction in his book *Knowledge of Language* between the I-language approach, that he advocates, and various other approaches to the study of language. It is possible, like Geoffrey Pullum, whom we cited above, to approach the study of language from a formal, computational perspective and build very explicit mathematical models, but to consider the object of study to be linguistic corpora, collections of data. These could be recorded utterances or text collections like a set of articles from a single newspaper or various newspapers, as Pullum suggests in the quotation above. A corpus could also be a collection of utterances from "English" or "Italian," or even the limited corpus of words from "Weri," "Maranungku," "Pintupi," and "Warao" that we looked at earlier in the chapter. This approach is dubbed the E-language approach by Chomsky, where "E-"stands for "external," in contrast to the "I-" of the internal, individual approach we have been developing. It is important to realize that E-language constitutes an attempt to come up with a formal characterization of language, one that differs from everyday notions, and that the goal is to subject E-languages to scientific study.

One problem, however, is that E-language is an incoherent notion—the corpus is very often a collection of utterances produced by several speakers. Newspapers obviously represent the output of many individuals. Thus, there is no guarantee that a particular set of data can be modeled by a single grammar that corresponds to a possible humanly attainable language.

Furthermore, it is obvious that even a single individual can generate output that corresponds to mutiple grammars. Some people are clearly multilingual, with grammars that we may refer to informally as "Japanese" and "English;" in other cases an individual may have grammars that correspond to what are called close dialects of a single language in everyday parlance. Again, even if one focuses on a collection of utterances produced by only one speaker, there is no guarantee that this collection can be generated by a single mental grammar, a grammar that is a possible humanly attainable language.

And, finally, even if one wishes to take into account data produced by only one speaker, in only one language, say Quebec French, one still needs a way to define Quebec French. In fact, this is a more general problem for E-language approaches. How does one decide what constitutes the relevant corpus? If one took all the newspapers published in Montreal, there would be an incredible diversity of grammars represented, including some we would call English or French, and many others. Any study of this corpus as a single system would lead to chaotic results—this would be a really bad way to choose a corpus. On the other hand, someone might get reasonable results by deciding to work on the corpus consisting of the last five years of French newpapers in Montreal. So, depending on the choice of the corpus, one would get results that are more or less satisfactory. In order to eliminate the choice that leads to unsatisfactory results, one has to rely (tacitly) on an everyday notion of language. In a sense, the E-language perspective always tacitly relies upon the everyday notion of languages and speech communities in order to define the corpus that is subject to analysis.

For these reasons, the goal of I-linguistics is not to analyze corpora of data, or to analyze speech behavior, but rather to infer the nature of the human language faculty. E-language approaches are also interested in identifying patterns underlying the corpora, but what differs is whether these patterns are assumed to be rooted in biology or not, whether they are assumed to be dependent or independent of psychological states of individuals. Under an E-language perspective, the rules underlying the corpora are just that, rules that can correctly generate the data. On the other hand, under an internalist perspective grammars are actually instantiated in individual minds/brains. The rules of I-language grammars constitute knowledge, information encoded in the brain of a speaker at a certain point in time. The ultimate task of an I-linguist involves characterizing both the initial state of the language faculty, before exposure to any experience, and the states the language faculty can attain after exposure to experience. As illustrated above, with examples from Weri, Maranungku, Pintupi, and Waori, an internalist view provides a filter for teasing apart rules that can generate a corpus but that are psychologically implausible from rules that both can underlie a corpus[11] and are compatible with what we know about the biology, including psychology, of humans.

4.3.2 P-language

Apart from E-language, there is yet another concept of language that sees language as independent of any psychological states of individuals, as independent of speakers. Actually, such views are not incompatible with the belief in what we have called I-language; the assumption is that in addition to individual I-languages, there exist entities, "languages," independent of the existence of actual human speakers. Under such a view, English, for example, is an idealization, or maybe an idea, like Plato's ideal forms, that is only imperfectly grasped or accessed by actual speakers of English, or represented in actual utterances—much like an ideal triangle cannot exist in the physical world but is somehow manifest indirectly in triangles that we see. This kind of perfect, ideal language is what Chomsky calls P-language ("P" for "Platonic") and such a view is (typically implicitly) at the base of many philosophical discussions of language. It follows from such views that there are words out there in "English" that you might not know, that in fact no speaker might know, but they are part of "English." It also follows that there might be some patterns or rules of "English" that are not encoded in your mind, or in anybody's mind, that are also part of "English." You can probably see what the problem is. It is impossible to define the boundaries of P-English. How many words could there be that are part of "English" but we, as mere mortal speakers, do not know? And how many patterns? And how can we tell whether these unknown words or patterns are really part of P-English and not part of P-Romanian? There is no way to tell because we, as speakers that are only aspiring towards or grasping at the ideal "English," do not have full access to it.

There are other questions that such an approach raises, namely do these P-languages change? Well, if they are ideal, perfect entities, they probably don't change. But then did Shakespeare and Chaucer access the same P-English that we do? How about dialect variation? Do you participate in,

---

[11] The choice of what constitutes the corpus is subject to the kind of idealizations common in all sciences, and also necessary for the E-language approach.

grasp, use, speak, aspire towards the same P-language as Bob Marley and George W. Bush?

It is typically only a certain variety of philosopher that explicitly proposes the existence of entities like P-languages. It is important to point out, however, that in everyday life we all implicitly act as if we believe that such things exist. When we play Scrabble or argue about whether something someone says "is an English word," we implicity assume that there is an entity "English" that a word can be part of. When we ask if *dog*, *snuck*, or *florb* are English words, we do not mean something like "Is there any individual who we would call in everyday terms a 'speaker of English' whose mental grammar contains a lexical item whose phonology is *florb*," etc. We typically treat dictionaries as defining what languages, or at least the words of languages, "really" are. In everyday life we are people, not linguists, and to speak like linguists in everyday life would make us as popular as an astronomer who gave a discourse on the heliocentric solar system and the earth's rotation every time he or she was invited to watch a gorgeous sunset—in everyday terms, the sun does set; in astronomical terms, the earth rotates so that the sun is no longer visible to an observer on its surface. But talking constantly like an astronomer or linguist in everyday life is annoying, perhaps even pathological. This is not a question of right or wrong, but of choosing a way of speaking that is appropriate to the situation—most of us do not find a discourse on the Copernican revolution or Pintupi stress to be appropriate to a romantic picnic with an attractive mate (although we are aware that human perversity ranges quite widely).

4.4 How is communication possible?

If we want to deny the existence in the world of entities like "English" or "Japanese" that correspond to the everyday notions, and we also deny the coherence of the E-language conception implicit in the work of many linguists, as well as the existence of the P-languages implicit in much philosophical work, we perhaps want to say something about why it appears to be the case that two speakers of English or Japanese communicate with each other, whereas speakers of two different languages, one English speaker and one Japanese speaker, say, have great difficulty in communicating.

Communication is a fairly vague notion. We assume that we can walk into a noodle shop in Japan, lay some money down on the counter, point to someone else's bowl and get served the same dish. We may even be able to imitate a pig or a fish to get some pork or a fish with our noodles. Communication can thus take place when people clearly do not have the same grammar.

On the other hand, communication can fail even when the grammars are similar. We can walk into a shop in London and, in New York dialect, ask for some chips, and then become enraged when we are served french fries. What are called *chips* in New York are called *crisps* in London. Why can't we communicate perfectly with other "English" speakers if we are speaking the same language?

Given the I-language perspective, we just assume that some people have I-languages, grammars, that are very similar, based on similar experience and other people have grammars that are not very similar. Suppose we take two football teams trained to play by the rules of the Canadian Football League (CFL). They will play a game in which everyone is playing by the same set of rules. If we replace one team by a team playing with National Football League (NFL) rules, we can imagine that the teams could continue to play with each other, to interact, to compete, to communicate. If, instead of NFL rules, one team has the rules of rugby, things will get more chaotic, but some interaction and play is still imaginable. And so on. Finally, imagine that one team is playing by CFL rules and the other is playing by the rules of Olympic synchronized swimming. Not much competitive interaction is possible—we are in a situation like that in which a Japanese speaker and an English speaker try to interact using their grammars—the rules are just too different.

So, two people can talk to each other and communicate more or less when they have similar mental grammars, similar information and rules in their brains. This is the case because they are both human, so they have most of the same basic physical and cognitive resources, and because they must have had enough experience that was similar in ways necessary to lead to similar grammars. There is no need to posit the existence of languages as entities that exist apart from the existence of speakers, and there is no need to posit conventions or public rules that constitute a language. Chomsky has made this point in many places over the years:

It might be that when he listens to Mary speak, Peter proceeds by assuming that she is identical to him, modulo M, some array of modifications that he must work out. Sometimes the task is easy, sometimes hard, sometimes hopeless. . . . Insofar as Peter succeeds in these tasks, he understands what Mary says as being what he means by his comparable expression. The only (virtually) "shared structure" among humans generally is the initial state of the language faculty. Beyond that we expect to find no more than approximations, as in the case of other natural objects that grow and develop. [*New Horizons* 2000b:31]

Chomsky's point is basically that if you start with two creatures that are identical in relevant respects (they both have a human language faculty), and they have experiences that are similar enough during the process of language acquisition, the ultimate states of their language faculties will be similar to each other. When they interact, such individuals behave as if there is a set of regular correspondences between their languages, and they try to discover and apply such correspondences, with more or less success.

Note that a Spaniard can go to Italy and communicate well, but he does not thus have an Italian grammar. Similarly, we, the authors, can go to Jamaica and speak English and perhaps do worse than a Spaniard in Italy. If you speak to a Portuguese person in Spanish, or a Dutch person in German they might get offended, even if they understand you quite well on the basis of the similarity of their language to the one you use to address them. Speak to them in English and they probably won't get offended, whether or not they understand you. This is a reflection of how one's linguistic self-consciousness is connected to ethnic and national identity, perhaps more strongly than to communication.

A speaker of a Norwegian dialect as opposed to a Swedish dialect is recognized as such if he grew up in Norway and not Sweden. His language may be extremely similar to that of someone who lives two kilometers away but is called a speaker of a Swedish dialect because she lives in Sweden. The language of these two people may be much closer by any measure we want to apply than either is to the national standard of his or her respective country. If the Swede goes to Norway to work or visit, she just speaks Swedish and appears to be understood better than, say, someone with a Glasgow Scottish accent coming to Brooklyn, New York. We tend to label languages and dialects on the basis of historical and political events, or on the basis of labels that others have applied on those bases. Of course it would be an incredible coincidence if the way we referred to speech behaviors—Brooklyn *English* and Glasgow *English* as opposed to *Norwegian* and *Swedish*—determined their properties. To believe this would really be attributing magical powers to our naming practices!

We return to the issue of differences among dialects of "the same language" in Chapter 12. For now, note that the names of languages around the world, and the language-dialect distinction, are notions of everyday language that cannot be the basis of scientific inquiry. If these labels turned out to perfectly define natural divisions in the world, it would be as amazing an outcome as if terms like *household pet* defined a real biological category. Nobody expects genetics or evolution textbooks to have a chapter on *household pets* and, similarly, there is no reason to think that what we refer to as English or Norwegian or Chinese (which includes many mutually unintelligible dialects like Cantonese and Mandarin) should refer to a natural class of grammars.

The difference between Hindi and Urdu is a question of identity. A person who speaks Hindi is typically Hindu and uses an alphabet derived from the Sanskrit one; a person who speaks Urdu is typically Muslim and uses an alphabet derived from the Arabic one. Similarly, a self-described speaker of Croatian is typically Catholic and uses the Latin alphabet, whereas a Serbian speaker is typically Orthodox and uses a version of the Cyrillic alphabet that Russian uses. In the former Yugoslavia, Serbian and Croatian speakers lived in the same town and same houses even, and the schools alternated alphabets by week. There is no linguistic criterion distinguishing Serbs from Croats.

Our friend Bert Vaux has described a group living on the coast of the Black Sea in Turkey who think that they speak a funny kind of Turkish. It turns out that they speak, according to the principles of historical linguistics, a dialect of Armenian. Why do they call themselves Turkish speakers?—because they are Muslim, and they identify with the Turkish Muslim world, and not the Armenian Christian world.

So, there are no necessary or sufficient linguistic conditions for identifying what we call in everyday speech *a speaker of English* or *a speaker of Urdu*. This suggests that a scientific approach to the study of language will not treat these terms as having any status in the theory. This is exactly the practice in the I-language approach.

4.5 Exercises

Exercise 4.5.1. **Stress rules:** Consider the following two made-up words:

4.13

- pakulikamukitakamonisimu
- musinimokatakimukaliku

Imagine that you are (a) a Weri speaker; (b) a Maranungku speaker; (c) a Pintupi speaker; (d) a Waori speaker. What would be the output of your stress assignment rule in each case?

Exercise 4.5.2.   Kuna verbs: Concordia undergraduate student Francis Murchison spent his last semester (Winter 2007) in Panama doing field-work on the Kuna language. Here is a basic morphology problem adapted from his early fieldwork. Each word in Kuna corresponds to a sentence in English. How much can you break up each Kuna word into morphemes, minimal units of meaning?

4.14   Kuna verbs

Kuna	English
anuagunne	I eat fish
beuagunne	You eat fish
weuagunne	She/he eats fish
anmaruagunne	We eat fish
bemaruagunne	You all eat fish
wemaruagunne	They eat fish
anogopgunne	I eat coconut
anuagunnsa	I ate fish

Further Readings

• Chapter 2 of Chomsky's *Knowledge of Language* (1986).

PART II

Linguistic Representation and Computation

5

A syntactic theory that won't work

One of the most important documents of the so-called cognitive revolution of the 1950s and 60s is Chomsky's book *Syntactic Structures*, published in 1957. The work presented in this small volume has had profound effects on linguistics, psychology, computer science, mathematics, and other fields. Surprisingly, the main ideas are relatively simple, and in this chapter our discussion of issues that arise in the scientific study of language is inspired by the first three chapters of Chomsky's book, a mere ten pages of text. Many of the insights still stand, and so the book is of much more than merely historical interest.

5.1 General requirements on grammars

In Part I we presented the biolinguistic approach that focuses on the study of I-language, language as knowledge that is encoded in the human mind, and not on a notion of language as a corpus of texts or as a set of observed behaviors. The study of grammar is a matter of "individual psychology:" our minds contain an abstract system of rules that is one of the factors that play a role in our ability to produce and understand language. The aim of a science of language is to reveal these rules.

Given that I-languages are encoded in people's minds, it follows that they cannot be discovered in the sense in which we discover, say, archeological artifacts buried in the ground. Given the current state of the neurosciences, there is also no hope for the foreseeable future that we can learn about the nature of mental grammars by looking directly at brains—we have no idea how, say, the Pintupi stress rule is encoded in neural tissue, which it must somehow be. Instead, we have to infer the properties of mental grammars on the basis of the kind of modeling and hypothesis formation and testing common to all scientific endeavors.

Our sources of evidence for these inferences come from various domains, including speaker judgments concerning the grammaticality of utterances, as well as work done by psycholinguists and neurolinguists involving measurements of blood flow and electrical activity in the brain, eye movements during reading tasks, reaction times to various stimuli, and others. The biolinguistic approach does not arbitrarily delimit our potential sources of information and insight but rather welcomes findings from any domain that may help in constructing a coherent and biologically plausible model of human language, including its acquisition by children. Our rejection of counting mechanisms in stress systems illustrated an attempt to draw on general considerations of biology and development in selecting among competing grammatical models.

Whatever the details of the system of rules that is relevant for this or that language, there are a number of requirements that all grammars must comply with. These are in part requirements that constrain any scientific undertaking, and partly requirements that spring from the fact that we view languages as a part of the natural, biological world. After sketching some of these requirements, we will examine a particular proposal for the mathematical modeling of grammars and show how it can be demonstrated to be insufficient. Our arguments will rely on your intuitions about your own English-type grammars.

5.1.1 Precise formulation

The following passage from the preface of *Syntactic Structures* (1957) is a straightforward description of Chomsky's proposed methodology. Part of its importance lies in the proposal, not completely novel at the time, yet still controversial to this day, that normal scientific reasoning should be applied to the study of language.

By pushing a precise but inadequate formulation to an unacceptable conclusion we can often expose the exact source of this inadequacy and consequently gain a deeper understanding of the linguistic data. More positively a formalized theory may automatically provide solutions for many problems other than those for which it was explicitly designed. Obscure and intuition-bound notions can neither lead to absurd conclusions nor provide new and correct ones and hence they fail to be useful in two important respects.

As you see, the passage accepts as a normal part of doing science the construction of models that inevitably turn out to be insufficiently powerful for the phenomenon under analysis. Chomsky points out that such models, when formulated precisely, can, by the very nature of their failings, provide insight.

5.1.2 Universality

To some extent we expect that the grammar for each language will have its own specific rules, but the ultimate goal of linguistic analysis "should be a theory in which the descriptive devices utilized in particular grammars are presented and studied abstractly with no specific reference to particular languages" (p. 11). Looking back, we see that this is the idea of Universal Grammar. Chomsky does not justify this statement of the ultimate goal of linguistics, but it seems clear, especially when we are familiar with his later work, that he already saw the aim of his studies to be an understanding of the human language faculty. He refers to the study of *Language*, with a capital L, to distinguish it from the study of particular languages. In more current writings Chomsky and his collaborators have taken the stand, at first blush "more than a little odd," that all languages have the *same* rules, at least in the domain of syntax. We will return to this idea later in the book.

5.1.3 Independence from meaning

In the preceding chapters we looked at rules relating the singular and plural of Samoan verbs, rules relating the singular and plural of nouns in various languages, and rules that provide the stress pattern of words. Clearly, those rules applied to classes of words that were defined independently of meaning. The Warlpiri full reduplication rule, for instance, applies to all nouns, regardless of what the meaning of the noun is. Similarly, the Maranungku stress rule applies to all words, independent of their meaning.

Let us now consider yet other types of linguistic rules—the rules that concern the way in which sentences are constructed in various languages. Linguists call these syntactic rules. Syntactic rules differ from the stress rules that we illustrated earlier, which are examples of phonological rules, rules governing sound patterns. Syntactic rules also differ from the rules of word formation, prefixing, suffixing, and reduplication, for instance, that linguists call morphological rules.

Even though in the case of morphology or phonology, people are ready to accept that the respective rules are divorced from meaning, for some reason, there is a tendency to believe that syntax, the arrangement of words in sentences, cannot be divorced from consideration of what the sentences mean. In other words, structure and meaning are assumed to be inseparable.

However, consider the following now famous example introduced by Chomsky:

5.1   *Colorless green ideas sleep furiously.*

We don't think of abstract nouns like *ideas* as being able to have a color, *green*, and being *green* seems to be incompatible with being *colorless*. We also don't think of *ideas* as being able to *sleep* (although we can clearly say this in some metaphorical sense). Finally, there seems to be something weird in the juxtaposition of the verb *sleep* and the adverb *furiously*.

The point of this example is that despite all these incongruities and the fact that it is hard to imagine a situation in which the sentence would be uttered, it feels intuitively like a well-formed sentence. Compare the sentence above with the following example:

5.2   *Furiously sleep ideas green colorless.*

This just does not feel like a sentence at all. It contains all the same words as the previous example—in fact it just reverses their order—but it is difficult to even read it with normal sentence intonation, and it is even hard to remember in comparison with the well-structured sentence. Without looking back, try to repeat this example, then try to repeat the previous one, the famous sentence.[12]

This discussion suggests the independence of syntactic knowledge from meaning by presenting an example that in some sense is meaningless and yet intuitively well formed, grammatical. It is hard to imagine a situation that would be accurately described by (5.1), and yet we react to it differently than we do to (5.2).

The same point can be made with examples that are easily interpretable but ungrammatical.

5.3   Easily interpretable, yet ill-formed strings
   a. *The child seems sleeping
   b. *John read the book that Mary bought it for him

The asterisk before these examples serves to indicate that they are not well-formed sentences.

However, it is trivially easy to assign an interpretation to both of these sentences. When we hear (5.3a.), we automatically interpret it as meaning basically the same thing as what *The child seems to be sleeping* means. And yet, it intuitively feels like there is something wrong with the structure of the sentence. Similarly, even though (5.3b.) can easily be assigned an interpretation—the same as *John read the book that Mary bought for him*, it is ungrammatical. Once again we see that structure and meaning appear to be independent.

These examples are also helpful for developing a notion of *grammaticality*. A grammatical sentence or word or stress pattern is generated by the grammar under consideration. Anything not generated by the grammar is ungrammatical. In other words, grammaticality is not related to meaning and is not an absolute notion—a grammatical plural in Warlpiri is not a grammatical plural in Telugu.

At the time Chomsky wrote, and even today in certain approaches to computer processing of natural language, the notion of grammaticality is correlated with the probability a sentence has of being uttered: (more) grammatical sentences are those that have a higher probability of being uttered. Chomsky provides the following strings in a discussion of this notion:

---

[12] Many people who read these passages in *Syntactic Structures* do not even realize that the string in (5.2) is the reversal of that in (5.1) until it is pointed out to them—we were among those people.

5.4   Equally improbable utterances
  • *I saw a fragile whale*
  • *I saw a fragile of*

These two strings have basically zero probability of being uttered, and yet the first seems well formed and the second does not. Just as syntactic well-formedness seems to be independent of semantic congruity, it also seems to be independent of questions of probability.

Given the notion of grammaticality that we have developed, it follows that there is no such thing as an ungrammatical *sentence*. Grammars generate sentences, that, by definition, are grammatical; any string of words that cannot be generated by a given grammar is, by definition, not a sentence—it is just a string of words. This distinction is not always made and it is common, even in linguistics, to talk about *ungrammatical sentences*, although we will try to avoid doing so in this book.

To sum up, the patterns of language can be studied independent of the meaning that the patterns happen to be associated with. The patterns are also independent of the notion of probability. This applies to morphological rules, phonological rules, and syntactic rules alike.

5.1.4 Finiteness

Human life is finite in length. It follows from this brute fact both that the longest sentence ever uttered by any person is finite in length, that is, it contains a finite number of words; and it also follows that there can only be a finite number of sentences uttered by any person. These limits on sentence length and the number of sentences a person can pronounce[13] obviously have nothing to do with the nature of grammar.

You probably share our intuition that any two well-formed sentences can be strung together to make a well-formed sentence, like (5.5c.), formed from (5.5a.b.).

 5.5   One way to make new sentences
  a. The unexamined life is not worth living.
  b. I like cheese.
  c. I like cheese AND the unexamined life is not worth living.

---

[13] Yeah, yeah—sentences are mental representations for a linguist, so you never pronounce a *sentence* in this technical sense. Bear with us in our mixing of technical and non-technical language—we'll be more careful later on.

The simple possibility of conjoining sentences with *and* allows us to identify arbitrarily many new sentences with an arbitrarily high number of words.

We have the fact of mortality to explain the limits on observable sentence length and the size of the output corpus of any individual person. We also have as an obvious fact the finite long-term memory and short-term processing and attentional resources of the human brain. This fact further lowers the ceiling on the length of the longest observable sentences. As we explore approaches to syntactic modeling we will see that there is no reason to build into the grammar itself a way to limit the length of sentences, and, in fact, that doing so would complicate our model without providing any benefit or insight.

So, we will not require our models to account for the finite size of observable sentences and observable corpora, sets of recorded utterances. However, we must recognize the fact that grammars are encoded in the finite brains that we have, and this does require that the grammars themselves be finite in size.

We have already introduced these ideas implicitly in the discussion of stress: the stress algorithms we looked at were statable with a small number of rules, and thus they were finite in size. However, despite the fact that our list of data for each language was very limited, the algorithm could be applied to words of any length. Adding a restriction to the length of a possible word into our stress algorithm of, say, Pintupi may reflect a true observation about our corpus, or even about any possible corpus. However, such a restriction would be arbitrary and would complicate the model.

5.1.5 Output representations

The term *grammar* is used in linguistics with a certain ambiguity. In one usage, a grammar is something in the mind of a speaker—the thing that linguists study. In the other usage, a grammar is the linguist's model of what is in the mind of a speaker—the product of a linguist's analysis. This ambiguity is common across disciplines in sciences, social sciences, and humanities—the same term refers to the *object of study* and the *theory* of the object of study. The term *physics*, for example, refers to the properties of the physical world, what physicists study, and to the set of theories and hypotheses developed by physicists about the physical world. When we explain an event by referring to the *physics of the situation* we are referring to hypothesized properties of the world; we are not referring to the study of these properties. *Physics*, in the first sense, has been the same throughout the history of the universe; *physics*, in the second sense, was revolutionized by Newton. (Note that the word *history* has the same ambiguity—which sense is intended in the previous sentence?)

Almost all linguists use the term *grammar* in this ambiguous fashion. More recently, there has been an attempt to avoid this problem by using the term *grammar* to refer only to the linguist's models. The object of study, what is being modeled, is referred to as the *language*. Thus, in more current usage, the phrase *mental grammar* is avoided, and the term *language* is equated with *I-language*. This is a departure from earlier work, including *Syntactic Structures* where Chomsky defines a language as a set of sentences, possibly with an infinite number of members.

These issues rarely cause confusion for the experienced scholar, but some terminological nightmares have become so entrenched that they are impossible to avoid at this point and are worth clarifying for the benefit of the uninitiated. Here is one of them: When we say that a string like *John are leaving* is ungrammatical, we mean that it is not generated by the I-language under consideration, call it L. Our job is to make a model, a grammar of this L. Now if we make a model M, and M generates *John are leaving*, then by definition this sentence is *grammatical* with respect to M. Unfortunately, we will say things like "M is a bad model of L because M generates ungrammatical outputs." But this is oxymoronic—grammatical *means* "generated by a grammar." What we intend is that M (the model of grammar we are currently considering) generates forms that are not grammatical with respect to the object of inquiry (the mental grammar, I-language) L.

So, it should be clear from the preceding discussion that the model we propose should generate all and only the sentences that the (I-)language generates—the model grammar and the mental grammar should be a perfect match. If there are sentences of the language that the model does not generate, then we say that the model *undergenerates*. If there are sentences generated by the model that are not generated by the language, we say that the model *overgenerates*.

It is possible for a model to both under- and overgenerate with respect to a language. Suppose that we want to model Dana's English-type I-language and that the grammar we come up with generates only the following two sentences:

5.6

    a. *I saw a frog dancing down Broadway*
    b. *Three all kiss turtles one more*

From the point of view of the model grammar, both of these strings are grammatical, by hypothesis, since the grammar generates them. However, from the point of view of Dana's mental grammar, of her I-language, only the first string is grammatical and the second one is ungrammatical, as indicated by the asterisk in (5.7b.), below.

5.7

    a. *I saw a frog dancing down Broadway*
    b. **Three all kiss turtles one more*

Now, string (5.7a.) is grammatical both according to the model grammar and from the perspective of Dana's mental grammar. However, Dana's I-language actually generates an infinite number of other sentences in addition to this one, so our model grammar *undergenerates*. String (5.7b.), on the other hand, is grammatical according to the model grammar, but is not generated by Dana's I-language, which means that the model grammar *overgenerates*. You can probably imagine more subtle examples, but the point should be clear: the model grammar must generate ALL AND ONLY the sentences generated by the mental grammar.

5.2 Finite state languages

With this background and set of requirements for our models, we can now explore various classes of model grammars and their suitability for capturing the syntax of human languages. Following Chomsky's discussion we adopt normal scientific methodology to first see if a mathematically very simple grammar would be sufficient. The type of grammar he discusses first is called a *Finite State Grammar* or *fsg*.

In Chapter 3 of *Syntactic Structures*, Chomsky's approach is this: we can view sentences as finitely long strings of words in which certain orderings are allowed and others are not, so let's try to describe a language as some kind of simple string-generating mechanism.

One such device is called a Finite State Machine or Finite State Grammar (*fsg*). In the terminology of *Syntactic Structures*, a *fsg* generates a finite state language.

A *fsg* has the following properties: the system can be in any one of a finite number of states, and moving from one state to another outputs a symbol.

There is at least one initial and one final state. The machine has no memory. Here is a *fsg* that generates a language consisting of just two sentences:

| 5.8 | Simple Finite State Grammar |

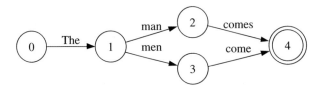

This *fsg* generates the following two sentences:

| 5.9 | • The man comes |
| | • The men come |

In other words, there are exactly two paths through the machine from the start state to the end state.

This *fsg* does indeed generate a set of sentences, and languages can be conceived of as sets of sentences, but this *fsg* lacks one of the most obvious properties of human languages. It is true that each sentence is of finite length, but there is no maximum length to the sentences in a language. Suppose you think that S_1 is the longest sentence of English—well, we can always precede S_1 by *I think that . . .* to give *I think that* S_1, as follows:

5.10	There is no longest sentence
	• S_1 = *Bill claims that Mary says that Tom claims that Alfred saw Claire bite the frog.*
	• S_2 = *I think that Bill claims that Mary says that Tom claims that Alfred saw Claire bite the frog.*

This new sentence S_2 is longer than S_1, and we can easily come up with another sentence S_3 of the form *You suspect that* S_2:

| 5.11 | *You suspect that I think that Bill claims that Mary says that Tom claims that Alfred saw Claire bite the frog.* |

There is no limit to how long a sentence can be.

Similarly, there is no limit to the number of sentences a grammar can generate, since if we have some finite set of sentences, we can always double the number of sentences by preceding each sentence in the original set by *I think that . . . .* So, our simple *fsg* fails to capture the fact that there is no longest sentence and that a language cannot be said to consist of a finite number of sentences.

Before we continue our study of *fsgs*, let's be clear about the fact that there is a limit on the longest sentence a person can utter—for example, it cannot be so long that it would take one hundred and fifty years to utter. Similarly, there is a finite number of sentences one can utter in a finite lifetime. However, in this paragraph we have slipped into using the term *sentence* in a non-technical, everyday, intuitive sense that corresponds only loosely to the sense of a string of symbols generated by a grammar. A sentence in the technical sense of the word has no duration, no length in time, although it does have a length in terms of a number of symbols (words). A given sentence may underlie a particular utterance, but that utterance may involve speaking very fast or very slow, and thus utterance duration is not the same as sentence length.

Similarly, there is no highest integer, but there is a highest integer that a person can count to in a finite amount of time, and a highest number of integers that a person can name in a finite lifetime.

Let's return to *fsgs*. It turns out that the challenge of generating an infinitely large set of sentences can be met by *fsgs* by use of a simple device—looping. A loop in a *fsg* is a path that starts at a given node (state) and returns to that same node (state), either immediately or after passing through other nodes. Consider the following *fsg* with a loop that leaves a node and returns directly to the same node:

5.12   Finite State Grammar with a loop

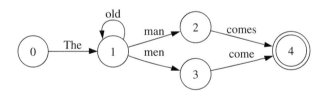

Wow! This *fsg* now generates an infinite set of sentences:

5.13
- The man comes
- The old man comes
- The old, old man comes
- etc.
- The men come
- The old men come
- The old, old men come
- etc.

This *fsg* can generate an infinite number of sentences because there are an infinite number of paths from the start state to the end state. We can choose not to follow the path that writes out *old*, we can choose to follow it once, or twice, etc.

So, while it is clear that *fsg*s are very simple, they does turn out to have the power to capture one of the most salient aspects of language—"language makes infinite use of finite means" in the famous words of Wilhelm von Humboldt (1767–1835). Despite having a finite number of words and rules, human languages have this property of infinity in two different ways: there is no limit on the number of sentences a grammar can generate, and there is no limit on the length of the sentences a grammar can generate. Both of these properties follow from the fact that every language has a way to connect sentences: if "A" is a sentence and "B" is a sentence, then "A and B" is a sentence. And "A and A and B" is also a sentence. All languages also have the means to embed a sentence inside another sentence, as we saw in (5.10), above. Conjoining and embedding are two ways of creating an arbitrary number of sentences, and sentences of arbitrary length.[14]

5.2.1 How do *fsg*s work?

In order to demonstrate how *fsg*s would model, or fail to model, human languages, let's first consider what are called *toy languages*. Toy languages are sets of strings of symbols that are constructed to have the mathematical properties of real human languages, without a lot of distracting detail. Using toy languages, we can focus on the properties of human languages we are interested in.

We can discuss a set of languages built out of just two "words," the symbols *a* and *b*. Each language is a set of strings (sequences) of *a*'s and *b*'s. For practice, here are two languages that Chomsky does not discuss:

5.14   Toy languages not from *Syntactic Structures*
- L_a {ab, aabb, aabbbbbb ...} = $a^n b^m$
- L_β {ab, abab, ababababab ...} = $(ab)^n$

The notation a^n means "the symbol *a* is repeated *n* times." Similarly, b^m means "the symbol *b* is repeated *m* times." The first language thus consists

---

[14] Actually conjoining is a kind of embedding, but it is useful to distinguish the two here for expository purposes.

of strings that contain one or more *a*'s followed by one or more *b*'s. By using different symbols, *n* and *m*, we show that the number of times that *a* and *b* are repeated are independent of each other—they may be different. Of course, they may be the same as well in a particular sentence.

Can you make a *fsg* to generate all and only these sentences—in other words, can you characterize L_a using a *fsg*?

Your solution should be something like this:

5.15   A *fsg* for L_a

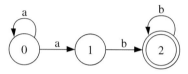

The start state is labeled "0" and we mark the final state (or states) with a double circle. The other numbers have no meaning and are just for reference. From the start state, one can proceed immediately to node 1 spelling out one *a*, or one can follow the loop from state 0 back to 0. Each time this path is followed, we get an *a*. The machine cannot stop until we reach state 2, and the path from 1 to 2 will guarantee that we get at least one *b*. The stop state 2 is a place where we *can* stop, but it is not necessary to stop; we can follow the *b* loop an arbitrary number of times before stopping.

As an exercise, you can make a *fsg* that allows the number of *a*'s and *b*'s to be zero.

Let's move on to the second toy language, L_β. We are going to assume that each transition can spell out at most a single symbol, and also that there are no null transitions, so that each transition spells out exactly one symbol. With these constraints on possible machines, we can offer the following solution for the language L_β that generates arbitrarily long strings of repetitions of *ab*.

5.16   A *fsg* for L_β

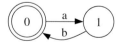

In this *fsg* state 0 is also the termination state. You will notice that this *fsg* can generate completely null strings (strings of zero length) because it is possible to never leave state 0, to terminate without taking any transitions. How would you change the *fsg* to ensure that the shortest string it generates is *ab*?

Now consider the following *fsg*:

| 5.17 | An uninteresting *fsg* |

What strings consisting solely of *a*'s and *b*'s will this *fsg* in (5.17) generate? You can see that it will generate any such string. We can follow the *a* loop thirty-seven times, then the *b* loop twice, then go back to the *a* loop another thirty-seven times and then stop. Any string consisting of only these two symbols can be generated by this *fsg*. This power is what makes this machine completely uninteresting even from the point of view of toy languages. It is true that the *fsg* in (5.17) can generate all the sentences of L_α ($a^n b^m$) or L_β (($ab)^n$), but at the same time it will also generate strings that are members of neither L_α nor L_β.

The point of a grammar is to generate all the strings of a set and nothing else. A proposed grammar should generate all and only the grammatical sentences of the language we are modeling. Otherwise, it does not characterize the set of sentences in the language, since it does not distinguish them from non-sentences.

5.2.2 Why a *fsg* is not sufficient for English

In spite of its simplicity and its ability to generate an infinite number of sentences with finite means, Finite State Grammars have a serious drawback. There are whole classes of languages that *fsg*s cannot model. There are sets of sentences that human grammars generate that can only be generated by a *fsg* that will necessarily generate lots of undesirable strings as well, strings that a human grammar cannot generate. In other words, if we make a *fsg* powerful enough to not undergenerate, then it will overgenerate—a *fsg* cannot, by its very nature, match the power of languages with certain properties, properties that human languages have. Please be patient—this will become clear.

Here are some examples of languages that Chomsky presented in *Syntactic Structures* that cannot be modeled by a *fsg*.

| 5.18 | Toy languages from *Syntactic Structures* |

- L_1 = {ab, aabb, aaabbb, ...} = $a^n b^n$
- L_2 = {aa, bb, abba, baab, aaaa, bbbb, aabaa, abbbba, ...} = mirror image
- L_3 = {aa, bb, abab, baba, aaaa, bbbb, aabaab, abbabb, ...} = XX

So, why can't a Finite State Machine be made to generate these languages? The first consists of sentences containing some number of *a*'s followed by the same number of *b*'s. The second consists of sentences containing any string of *a*'s and *b*'s followed by the same string in reverse order (with perhaps a single "pivot" symbol between the two parts—in other words, each sentence in this language consists of a string and its mirror image). The third language consists of sentences that contain any string X of *a*'s and *b*'s repeated twice in a row. So, every sentence has the form XX. There is a common property shared by all these languages that makes it impossible to devise a *fsg* that will generate them—they all require arbitrary amounts of memory, and, by design, a *fsg* does not have any memory.

They require memory because points in the string depend on previous points that can be arbitrarily far away. In the first language, for example, the number of *b*'s must exactly match the number of *a*'s. In the second language, the last symbol in a sentence must match the first symbol; the second to last must match the second; etc. In the third language, the whole second half of a sentence must match the first half exactly.

The reason Chomsky gives these examples is that there are sentences in actual languages, including English, that have the same structure as that of the sentences in the toy grammars that cannot be generated by a *fsg*. For example, any sentence that involves the construction *if* ... *then* ... requires keeping track of each *if* and matching it with a *then*. Similarly for the construction *either* ... *or* .... So by creating sentences of English using such constructions we produce the logical structures seen in the languages that cannot be generated by a *fsg*. We can show this in various ways, for example by labeling the first half of the relevant constructions with *a* and the second half with *b*.

| 5.19 | Some $a^n b^n$ structures in English |

- *If$_a$ John is singing then$_b$ it is raining*

- *If$_a$ either$_a$ John is singing or$_b$ Bill hates Tony then$_b$ it is raining*
- *If$_a$ either$_a$ John either$_a$ loves Mary or$_b$ hates Tony or$_b$ Tom dances well then$_b$ it is raining*

There has to be the same number of elements labeled *a* and *b*. We could also label the relevant word pairs with their own indices to illustrate a mirror-image structure:

 5.20   Labeling to show mirror-image structures in English

- *If$_a$ John is singing then$_a$ it is raining*
- *If$_a$ either$_b$ John is singing or$_b$ Bill hates Tony then$_a$ it is raining*
- *If$_a$ either$_b$ John either$_c$ loves Mary or$_c$ hates Tony or$_b$ Tom dances well then$_a$ it is raining*

We have first an *if... then* structure; then we embed an *either... or* structure inside of it; then we embed another *either... or* structure inside the first one. These sentences become hard to understand as the embedding gets more complex, but they conform to the rules of English-type grammars. Although Chomsky does not dwell on this point in *Syntactic Structures*, he later stresses this important distinction between grammaticality, conformity with the patterns or rules or principles of the grammar, and processability. A very long sentence or one with lots of embedding may be hard to understand because of limits on memory and attention, yet it may conform to the rules of a grammar.

5.3 Discussion

The previous demonstration of the insufficiency of *fsg*s may have gone by a bit quickly, so we will now revisit some of the basic points using examples based on real English sentences. The two simple sentences of (5.21) show agreement in the form of the subject and the verb—the first has a singular subject and a singular verb form, whereas the second has a plural subject and a plural verb form. The fact that the subject of the first sentence is singular is encoded by the form *man*, as opposed to the plural subject encoded by *men* in the second sentence.

5.21   A language with two sentences

- The **man** here **is** leaving
- The *men* here *are* leaving

If we want to generate these sentences using a *fsg* we run into a problem that you may not have considered. We can surely generate the two sentences using a *fsg* like (5.22), but such a grammar will also generate sentences that are ungrammatical in English.

 Bad *fsg*

The grammar in (5.22) will generate only the two grammatical English sentences as long as we follow the two dotted transitions or the two dashed transitions as we proceed from start to end state. However, by its very nature, a *fsg* does not have the capacity to guarantee this. When the grammar is in state 3, there is no memory of how it got there, whether via the dotted transition or the dashed transition between states 1 and 2. Such a grammar is said to overgenerate, since it generates sentences that are not grammatical in the actual human grammar that we are trying to model. This *fsg* grammar, in addition to generating the two sentences we are interested in, will also generate strings that are not grammatical in English such as the following:

5.23   The grammar in (5.22) overgenerates

- *The man here are leaving
- *The men here is leaving

If we want a *fsg* to generate all and only the sentences of the fragment of English we are considering, we need something like the following grammar, where the dashed and dotted pairs of lines need have no special status, since they lie on separate paths.

5.24   Good *fsg*

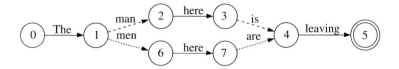

This grammar in (5.24) will generate the two sentences we want and not generate the two undesirable strings, but at a price—the grammar must encode
the word *here* twice, even though the two sentences intuitively appear to
contain the same word. It does not seem right to encode the word *here* twice,
but the words *the* and *leaving* only once.

It may be apparent at this point that a *fsg* can be written that will generate
all and only the sentences of any finite corpus—say all the strings that
appeared in *The New York Times* last year, or all of Shakespeare. The
simplest way to achieve this is to have a distinct path from the start state
to an end state corresponding to each sentence in the corpus.

However, such grammars will need to contain massive amounts of
redundancy—words, and even identical strings of words, will have to be
repeated numerous times. This point will be clearer if you try Exercise 5.5.7
at the end of this chapter.

The examples raised by Chomsky involving mirror-image structures or
repeated sequences, as well as the examples we have given of subject verb
agreement, all demonstrate the incapacity of *fsgs* to capture the fact that
part of sentences involve so-called *long distance dependencies*. Parts of a
sentence that are dependent upon each other may be arbitrarily far from
each other in terms of the number of words that intervene between them.
Again, doing Exercise 5.5.7 will reinforce this idea better than any further
discussion can.

5.3.1 Why did we go through it, then?

Why did we bother going through this long discussion of an approach to
syntax that clearly is not sufficiently powerful to capture the syntax of natural language? Chomsky's *Syntactic Structures* is of historical significance
as an early attempt to formalize the study of natural language—remember
that most people still think of language as something to be studied in
the humanities, an amorphous, fluid, human construction. So one reason
is just to give you an idea of what it means to explore the question of
how much computational power a mathematical model of language needs.
It was revolutionary at the time even to ask such questions; the answer
is still being vigorously pursued. Chomsky went on in his book to propose a more complex theory, aspects of which we adopt in the following
chapters, but the book is a founding document of the cognitive revolution

of the mid-twentieth century, and we hope to have shown that it is very accessible.

Second, our concern here is not to provide a final answer concerning the nature of human language but rather to demonstrate a methodology, to show how one can explore the computational properties of human language. We are trying to model the computational properties of human language, so we start out with the simplest device that seems reasonable, something that can generate an infinite number of strings of unbounded length. However, we then find that *fsgs* are not sufficiently powerful and we need to try something with more computational power. Third, even failed attempts at modeling can be useful as we discussed in Section 5.1.1.

In our particular case, identifying the failings of *fsgs* gives us immediate understanding of the fact that a syntactic model should conform not only to the list of general requirements mentioned above for possible grammars but also to the need to account for long-distance dependencies, such as subject-verb agreement and *if... then* constructions, and so on.

5.4 Power of grammars

We mentioned that *Syntactic Structures* presents work that was influential even in formal language theory, a branch of theoretical computer science. As Chomsky attempted to understand human language, he presented more and more powerful models. The set of grammar-types he defined fall along a hierarchy of complexity now known as the Chomsky Hierarchy. To just give you a taste of what it means to order languages in such a hierarchy, consider how one would solve the problem of generating structures of the form $a^n b^n$.

One possibility is to provide the grammar with a counter: keep track of the a's and match them with b's. In other words, we can reject the constraint that the language has no memory. However, if we want to maintain the idea that there is no grammatical limit on the number or length of sentences, then we cannot choose the counter option. No actual counter in a real physical device or organism can count arbitrarily high.

If we do not want to endow our grammars with a counter, then we can achieve the desired effect by allowing the grammar to introduce an a and a matching b together. Let's illustrate. Suppose that a grammar consisted of rewrite rules that generated sentences by replacing symbols like S with "words" like a or b. Let's explore one such grammar, G_1 with the following properties:

| 5.25 | The grammar G_1 |

- Symbols:
  - Non-terminal symbol: S
  - Terminal symbols: a, b
- Rewrite rules:
  - i. $S \rightarrow ab$
  - ii. $S \rightarrow a\,Sb$

Let's assume that a sentence is generated by starting with S and applying the rules until only terminal symbols remain. Here, then, are some possible sentences generated by G_1.

| 5.26 | Sentences of G_1 |

- $S \rightarrow ab$ (by application of rule i.)
- $S \rightarrow a\,Sb \rightarrow aabb$ (by application of rule ii. followed by application of rule i.)
- $S \rightarrow a\,Sb \rightarrow aa\,Sbb \rightarrow aaabbb$ (two applications of rule ii. followed by application of rule i.)
- $S \rightarrow a\,Sb \rightarrow aa\,Sbb \rightarrow aaa\,Sbbb \rightarrow \ldots aaaaaaa\,Sbbbbbbb \rightarrow \ldots aaaaaaaaaaabbbbbbbbbbb$ (nine applications of rule ii. followed by one application of rule i.)

Since the rewrite rules introduce matching a's and b's, it is unnecessary to have a counter. By introducing an a and a b together, we get the same effect as a counter, but we can do so without setting an arbitrary limit on sentence length.

Now, how does this kind of grammar, that uses rewrite rules, compare with Finite State Grammars? Rewrite grammars can certainly do something that Finite State Grammars cannot do, namely they can produce structures of the form $a^n b^n$. But can rewrite grammars deal with everything that Finite State Grammars can? In other words, is it the case that rewrite grammars are more powerful than Finite State Grammars? Chomsky shows that Finite State Grammars have the same power as rewrite grammars, but only if a number of restrictions are set on the rewrite grammars. We will not provide the details of the formal proof that Chomsky goes through, but here is the general pattern of reasoning behind his proof. Since rewrite grammars with restrictions are less powerful than rewrite grammars without restrictions, and given that rewrite grammars with restrictions have the same power as

Finite State Grammars, it follows that rewrite grammars (without restrictions) are more powerful than Finite State Grammars.

Here are the restrictions that, when added to rewrite grammars, will turn the latter into grammars of equal power to the power of Finite State Grammars.

5.27   Some restrictions on a rewrite rule grammar
- rewrite rules can only spell out a single terminal symbol OR
- a single non-terminal symbol OR
- a single terminal, followed by a non-terminal

It turns out that with such restrictions, we get a grammar that has the same power as Finite State Grammars. In other words, by using this restricted rewrite grammar we can generate languages like our L_α {ab aabb aabbbbbb...} = $a^n b^m$ and L_β {ab abab abababab...} = $(ab)^n$, just as we can generate them with Finite State Grammars, and we cannot generate languages like L_1 = {ab, aabb, aaabbb, ...} = $a^n b^n$, L_2 = {aa, bb, abba, baab, aaaa, bbbb, aabaa, abbbba, ...} = mirror image or L_3 = {aa, bb, abab, baba, aaaa, bbbb, aabaab, abbabb, ...} = XX from *Syntactic Structures* which require that matching elements be introduced together, just as Finite State Grammars cannot generate these. Here is one such restricted grammar, G_2:

5.28   The grammar G_2
- Symbols:
  - Non-terminal symbols: *S, T*
  - Terminal symbols: *a, b*
- Rewrite rules:
  - i. $S \rightarrow aT$
  - ii. $T \rightarrow b$
  - iii. $T \rightarrow bS$

This restricted grammar can generate L_β.

If we let S be the start symbol, then we can generate the following sentences:

5.29   Sentences of G_2

- $S \rightarrow aT \rightarrow ab$ (by application of rule i. and then rule ii.)
- $S \rightarrow aT \rightarrow abS \rightarrow abaT \rightarrow abab$ (by application of rule i. followed by application of rule iii. followed by application of rule i. followed by application of rule ii.)

- $S \rightarrow aT \rightarrow abS \rightarrow abaT \rightarrow \ldots ababababababababS \rightarrow$
  $abababababababababaT \ldots abababababababababab$ (The sequence
  rule i.-rule iii. applies nine times, then rule i. applies followed by
  rule ii.)

This grammar generates all and only sequences of the form $(ab)^n$, which
means that it characterizes or generates L_β {ab, abab, ababababab...} =
$(ab)^n$.

We will not provide a formal proof, but we hope to suggest to you that
a rewrite rule grammar with the kinds of restrictions we have placed on
G_2, the restrictions in (5.27), has exactly the power of a *fsg*, since it cannot
introduce matching elements that are separated by other elements. It can,
however, achieve the effect of loops in the *fsgs* by having a rule that rewrites
S as something that includes T, and a rule that rewrites T as something that
includes S. If you accept (without proof) the claim that the restricted rewrite
grammars are equivalent to *fsgs*, we can conclude that *fsgs* are less powerful
than rewrite grammars in general, including grammars like G_1.

If you are interested in such topics, you should find a book that discusses formal language theory, such as *Mathematical Methods in Linguistics* by Partee et al. (1990). The Chomsky Hierarchy places *fsgs*
lower in the hierarchy of grammar formalisms than rewrite rule grammars that lack restrictions on how many terminals can be spelled out
in one step, because any set of strings that can be generated with the
restricted grammar can be generated with the unrestricted one, but not vice
versa.

Chomsky's demonstration, as presented here, shows that a restricted
rewrite rule grammar, or equivalently a *fsg*, is not sufficiently powerful to
generate the patterns we find in English. Since English (that is, the set of
grammars of the type that we call English in everyday speech) is a human
language, it can be concluded that *fsgs* are insufficient to model the human
language faculty. Thus, we see how Chomsky's approach licenses claims
about Universal Grammar, even though the discussion looks at only a single
(type of) human language.

Some linguists claim that we need more data before making proposals
about Universal Grammar, and they criticize other linguists, like Chomsky,
who have concentrated on a few languages, say Japanese, English, French,
and German, and then proceeded to make universal claims. However,
such criticism is invalid: *Syntactic Structures* demonstrates that Universal

Grammar must be of at least a complexity greater than *fsg*s. No new data can bear on this conclusion.

5.5 Exercises

In the following exercises, assume these conventions for Finite State Machines:

- Start states are numbered 0
- Other numbers are meaningless
- End states use double circles
- Each transition can only write out a single "word" *a*, *b* or *c*

Exercise 5.5.1.   Make a Finite State Machine that will generate all and only strings of the form $(abc)^n$—that is *abc* repeated any number of times greater than or equal to 1: $L = \{abc, abcabc, abcabcabc, \ldots\}$.

Exercise 5.5.2.   Can you make a Finite State Machine that generates a language whose sentences consist of any nonnull string of *a*'s and *b*'s followed by a single *c* followed by any string of *a*'s and *b*'s of the same length as the first such string? For example, *baabacbabb* is a sentence in this language but *baabacbbbb* is not. Explain why there is no such machine or show the machine if you can.

Exercise 5.5.3.   Can you make a Finite State Machine that generates a language whose sentences consist of any nonnull string of *a*'s and *b*'s followed by a single *c* followed by any nonnull string of *a*'s and *b*'s followed by three *c*'s? For example *baabacbabbbccc* is a sentence in this language and so is *baabacbbbbccc* but *cbabccc* is not. Explain why there is no such machine or show the machine if you can.

Exercise 5.5.4.   Can you make a Finite State Machine that generates a language whose sentences consist of any (possibly null) string of *a*'s and *b*'s followed by four *c*'s followed by any nonnull string of *a*'s and *b*'s? Explain why there is no such machine or show the machine if you can.

Exercise 5.5.5.   Can you make a Finite State Machine that generates a language whose sentences consist of any nonnull string of *a*'s and *b*'s followed by between one and four *c*'s followed by any (possibly null) string of *a*'s and *b*'s? Explain why there is no such machine or show the machine if you can.

Exercise 5.5.6.   Make a rewrite rule grammar that obeys the restrictions in (5.27) that can generate L_a. In other words, turn the *fsg* in (5.15) into a rewrite rule grammar. (Hint: You need two non-terminal symbols.)

Exercise 5.5.7.   Try to develop a *fsg* to generate all and only the sentences in the following list. Ideally you should build up your grammar, for example, by making one for the first sentence, then the first two, then the first three, and so on.

    a. The boy is washing
    b. The boy with blue eyes is washing
    c. The boys are washing
    d. The boys with blue eyes are washing
    e. The boy is washing himself
    f. The boys are washing themselves
    g. The boy with blue eyes is washing himself
    h. The boys with blue eyes are washing themselves
    i. Both the boys with blue eyes are washing themselves

Further Readings

- Chapters 1, 2, 3 of *Syntactic Structures* by Noam Chomsky (1957).
- *Syntactic Structures Revisited* by Lasnik et al. (2000).
- *Mathematical Methods in Linguistics* by Partee et al. (1990).
- "Chomsky Hierarchy" on *Wikipedia* is a useful overview for readers with some technical training.

6

Abstract representations

6.1 Abstractness

If linguistics studies grammars as properties of individual minds, then linguistics is part of psychology. Now, no book on psychology can do without some anecdotes concerning experiments done on rats, so here we go.

According to results obtained by Seth Roberts, a psychologist at the University of California at Berkeley, a rat can be trained to press a lever for food after hearing a tone play for forty seconds.[15] We found this to be pretty surprising, but, once one accepts the validity of the result, it is perhaps not so shocking that the rats can also be trained to press a lever for food after being exposed to forty seconds of a visual stimulus, like a lamp being illuminated.

The really exciting result comes when the rats, after being trained to press the lever after forty seconds of sound, and also after forty seconds of light, are exposed to twenty seconds of sound and then the sound goes off and the light goes on. What do they do? Do they wait for the full forty seconds of light? No! They press the lever after twenty seconds of light.

---

[15] Obviously there is some pressing a bit early and some a bit late, but the rats are surprisingly accurate.

This result only makes sense if the rats have not just learned to respond to certain simple stimuli (like forty seconds of light or forty seconds of sound, which is what they have been trained on), but rather have learned something more abstract like "Press the lever after forty seconds of stimulus." In order to learn this generalization, the rats must be able to cognize in terms of an abstract category of duration, not sound duration or light duration, but duration pure and simple. Duration pure and simple cannot be observed, it can only be abstracted from events that have duration. Rats (and humans, for that matter) use duration to construct equivalence classes of stimuli that abstract away from the specific modality in which a stimulus is presented.

Of course, by now, this appeal to abstract categories should not bother you—we have already discussed the fact that triangles we perceive and also words we perceive are constructions of our minds, and not just records of physical stimuli. The fascinating thing is that this abstractness seems to hold in all domains of human (and rodent) experience.

We would like you to keep this notion of abstractness in mind as we embark on a fairly sophisticated exploration of syntax, phonology, and morphology, leaving behind the simple finite state models that we now understand to be insufficient and turning instead to models that have many of the crucial details used by linguists working today. Just as positing a category DURATION appears to be necessary for making an intelligible model of rat behavior, it appears to be necessary to model human linguistic behavior by proposing categories of analysis that are not directly observable, that cannot be defined in terms of what we usually think of as the building blocks of the physical world.

6.2 Abstractness of sentence structure

In this section we illustrate the idea that syntactic computation is structure-dependent. The phenomenon we are going to look at is the distribution of the contracted form of copula verbs in English. We will see that this element is sensitive to a restriction that can only be stated in structural terms.

The examples in (6.1a.–d.) are all question-and-answer pairs.

a. *Do you know if anyone is here yet?*
   I know Mary is here.
b. *Do you know if anyone is here yet?*
   I know Mary's here.
c. *Do you know if anyone is here yet?*
   I know Mary is.

d. *Do you know if anyone is here yet?*
   *I know Mary's.

The question is the same in all the instances, but the answers differ. Some of the question-answer pairs are well formed, as in (6.1a.–c.), whereas (6.1d.) is not. The answer in (6.1a.) contains the copula verb *is* followed by the locational expression *here*. The answer in (6.1b.) is the same, except that it contains the so-called "contracted" form of the copula, *'s*. Sentence (6.1c.) is the same as (6.1a.) with the full copula form, but without *here*. So it seems possible to either contract or not contract the copula, and to have or not have *here* at the end of the sentence. However, for some reason, the answer in (6.1d.), that has both contraction and no *here*, is completely ungrammatical. This is odd. You may discard this by saying that (6.1d.) just doesn't sound right, but the question is *Why not?* As noted in Chapter 3, when we stop to pay attention, even the "simplest phenomena of ordinary life raise quite serious problems."

Before working our way towards the generalization underlying these facts, let us point out that, whatever the generalization will turn out to be, we already know several things.

First of all, we know that the rule will have to be stated in abstract terms. Example (6.2) shows us that it is not the *sound* of (6.1d.) that makes it ungrammatical. If the string *I know Mary's* occurs as an answer to a different question, as in *Mary's mother*, then the string is well formed.

6.2	Do you know anyone's mother?

I know Mary's.

No doubt you will have noticed that the difference between the answer in (6.2) and the answer in (6.1d.) is that *'s* is the possessive ending of *Mary* in (6.2), and in (6.1d.) it is the copula verb. So, the account of the ungrammaticality of (6.1d.) will have to be expressed in terms of abstract morphemes like possessives, nouns, copulas.

Second, we know that the weirdness of (6.1d.) should be based on a rule or pattern, not on a list of exceptions; the rule will have to explain why possessive -*s* behaves differently from the so-called "contraction" of *is*, and why the contraction of *is* is sometimes fine, as in (6.1b.).[16]

---

[16] We say "so-called" since calling the form *'s* a contraction makes it sound like this form is somehow derived from the "full" form *is* by the mental grammar of an English speaker, but it is not at all apparent that this is the case.

Third, notice that most or all of us are unaware of such facts about our grammars. English speakers never produce these weird-sounding contractions like (6.1d.), and they know they are weird without knowing why.

So now let's try to come up with a generalization that underlies these simple facts. One possibility that could come to mind is that the pattern in (6.1a.-d.) is due to some constraint that says: "the contracted copula can't be the last word before a pause." However, sentence (6.3) shows this cannot be the case, since in this sentence the word *and* follows the copula, and the sentence is still ungrammatical.

 6.3   Do you know if anyone is here yet?
    ***I know Mary's and Bill's coming soon.**

So on the one hand, when the contracted copula is followed by a word like *here*, as in (6.1b.), the result is grammatical, but when it is followed by a word like *and*, as in (6.3), the result is ungrammatical. Maybe it is the nature of the word that follows the contracted copula that matters, then. Let's look at more examples.

 6.4   Do you know if anyone is here yet?
    ***I know Mary's but she has to leave soon.**

Example (6.4) shows that there is another word beside *and* that produces ungrammaticality when it follows the contracted copula, namely *but*. This offers a gleam of hope for our attempt to find a generalization, since *and* and *but* are both members of the same category—they are both *connectors*. We could now say that

 6.5   The contracted form of the copula cannot be
    a. followed by a connector, or
    b. followed by a pause

We could stop here, and assume that this is the right generalization. If we did, however, we would be missing a generalization—these two conditions under which *is* cannot be contracted can actually be captured by one single statement. This unification is possible because connectors and what we have informally called pauses have something in common. On the one hand, a pause occurs by definition at the end of particular types of strings, i.e. sentences. On the other hand, connectors link two strings that can be of various types; it could be two nominal strings, or two verbal strings, or two other types of strings, but, crucially, it could also be between two sentences.

 Connectors

    a. Mary **and** Peter are here.

    b. Mary opened the window **and** Peter closed it back again.

So it looks like connectors and pauses do share something, namely that they both can occur after sentences. The generalization in (6.5) could now be restated as in (6.7).

 The contracted form of the copula must be followed by another word in the same sentence (inside the smallest S that contains the copula).

So, the generalization does not refer to connectors and pauses, but we can use the presence of these items to identify the end of a sentence. We will get a more detailed understanding of sentences in the next chapter.

It is interesting to note that English orthography appears to be very misleading with regard to the contracted copula. We write *'s* for the contracted copula and orthographically it attaches to the word to its left, the preceding word. However, it looks like the contracted form is actually dependent on the word to its right, the following word. Since the connectors *but* and *and* in our examples are not inside of the first sentence, they are not able to "support" the contracted copula. A word like *here*, on the other hand, is inside of the first sentence, and thus it can be preceded by the contracted copula.

Notice that the crucial distinction here is that between a string of words and a sentence. A string of words is merely a set of words arranged in some sequence. A sentence differs from a string in two ways. First, we assume that SENTENCE is a category of grammatical computation, an equivalence class. Second, members of this equivalence class are structured—they consist of parts and subparts that ultimately reduce to words. We have not yet told you anything about this structure, we will come back to it and offer more details in Chapter 7. For the time being, let us simply adopt a notational convention: a string of words that shows up at the base of a triangle whose top vertex is notated with an S is a sentence, that is it has a certain structure and is a member of an abstract equivalence class, the class of sentences. With this convention we can represent the structure of an example like *Mary's here but Bill is not* as in (6.8). Notice that the contracted copula is not the last word in its sentence, and hence the example is grammatical.

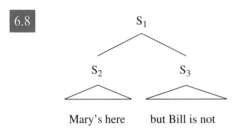

In contrast, if there is nothing following the contracted copula in its own sentence, as in (6.9), the result is ungrammatical.

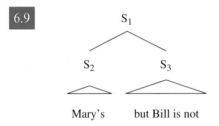

So why are we looking at this? One good reason is to just develop some humility about the complexity of human language. When an educational psychologist or philosopher or anthropologist or neurologist makes a claim about how language is learned or used, ask them to explain the copula reduction facts, to see if they actually have any idea what language is.

Another reason to look at this data is for further illustration of the notions of computation and equivalence class. As we pointed out, there are very precise rules governing where contracted forms can occur. It is not a matter of what "sounds good" in a particular case. And these rules have to make reference to abstract equivalence classes like morphemes and the structures that we represented by means of tree diagrams. These patterns do not inhere in the physical signal; they are pure mental constructs, examples of how the mind processes information. When two words fall under the same S node in one of our trees, that means that they are in a closer relationship than when they do not fall under the same node. These diagrams have predictive power concerning grammaticality in the same way that models of particles have predictive power in physics. Thus, the examples support our argument in favor of treating language from a scientific perspective and our stance against methodological dualism.

The generalization we discovered concerning the distribution of contracted forms is clearly specific to English; it reflects part of what it means to have an English-type grammar, or what we usually refer to as to "know English." However, the examples also have a relevance to Universal Grammar.

Recall that we rejected an account based merely on the linear ordering of words—it is not simply the case that the contraction needs to be followed by some word. Instead, a structural account was necessary—the contracted form and the following word have to be in a certain structural relationship that we can express using our tree diagrams. Well, it turns out that all syntactic phenomena of all languages appear to rely on this notion of structure.

Rules of syntax never rely merely on linear order—they are structure-dependent. This appears to be a fundamental property of the human language faculty, and thus constitutes a fundamental property of the human mind. Note that structure dependence is not a *logical* necessity—we can invent rules that reverse the order of words in a sentence or move the third word to the front of the sentence, but no rules like this exist in human languages, as far as we know.

Recall from Chapter 3 the puzzle concerning the difficulty of reversing the words in a sentence as opposed to the ease of forming a Yes/No question from a declarative. We pointed out that the question-formation rule was difficult to state, but we now can say a bit more—the rule will turn out to be structure-dependent, like the rule for using the contracted form *'s*, and unlike the string-reversing rule that is *not* a possible rule of human language.

6.3 Allophony

In this section we will once again consider some English data, but now in the domain of phonology. In addition to the inherent interest of the phenomena, we can point out that this example illustrates the fact that "English" is not actually an entity in the world. The following discussion assumes a typical North American dialect, that of the second author, and the exercises at the end of the chapter provide a chance to explore other dialects of English.

Consider the following sentence spoken by a speaker of East Coast North American English (a recording is available on the companion website).

6.10   That cat, Atom, didn't want to stare at the two thin rats at ease atop the atomic pot.

How many *t*'s does it contain? Perhaps you paid attention to orthography, the writing system, and counted up the tokens of the *letter t* that appear in the sentence and came up with the number 18 as your answer.

6.11   That cat, **Atom**, didn't want to stare at the two **thin** rats at ease atop the atomic pot.

Now what is the sound corresponding to the letter *t*? Say it aloud a few times—*ta ta ta*. Well, most people will not be surprised to notice that this sound is not pronounced for each written *t*, for example we know that the spelling *th* does not correspond to the same sound in many dialects of English. If you are particularly sensitive to these issues, you may notice that there are actually two sounds corresponding to the writing *th* for most speakers of English that are different from the sound in *ta ta ta*.

The sound of *th* in *that* and (both tokens of) *the* is called a voiced sound, involving vibration of the vocal folds, whereas the one in *thin* is called a voiceless sound, involving no vibration. You can make the difference more salient by plugging your ears with your fingers while pronouncing the two sounds.

If you now consider the remaining 14 tokens of the letter *t*, you may be in for a surprise. If you speak a typical North American dialect you will find a distinct difference between the *t* of *Atom* and that of *atomic*. In fact, you will find that *Atom* and *Adam* are pronounced identical for most North American English speakers. If you pronounce the sentence in a natural fashion—not too carefully or formally—you will probably find that the sound in *Atom* is also found to correspond to the *t* in the phrase *at ease*, but that the sound in *atomic* is that found in *atop*.

Take a break, because things get worse. . . . Now say the word *two* while holding your hand or a sheet of paper in front of your mouth. You will notice that a puff of air makes the paper move, or is felt by your hand. If you now say the word *stare*, no such puff is felt. Is this an idiosyncracy of these two words?—No, as we will see. But why do English speakers think of these words as both containing *t*? Your first reaction might be that we are guided by the orthography, that we think of the various pronunciations of the letter *t* as versions of the same entity, just because we write them the same. We will try to show you that something more interesting is at play.

Consider now the words *cat* and *at*. You should be able to tell that these end in a sound that is very different from the *ta ta ta* sound, at least when the sentence is pronounced naturally. This sound is called a glottal stop. It occurs in the middle of what is written *uh-uh* to mean "no."

Finally consider the part of the sentence written *didn't want to*. In our normal speech, the three written *t*'s have no pronunciation at all—you get something that might be written in a cartoon as *dinnwanna* or *didnwanna*.

So are there any regularities governing the distribution of these different correlates of the letter *t*? Why are speakers so unaware of most of these patterns?

Let's take a word like *cat* and put it in different contexts—compare the *natural* pronunciation (at least for us) of the *t* in each context—again, recordings are on the companion website:

   a. *I saw a cat*—a glottal stop [ʔ], the sound in the middle of *uh-uh* "no."
   b. *The cat is on the mat*—a flap, [ɾ], the sound in the middle of *butter* and *ladder*.
   c. *I saw three cats*—plain old *t*, [t], without a puff of air

And to complete our inventory compare the pronunciation of the letter in the words below:

6.13

   a. *My tie is clean*—an aspirated *t*, [tʰ] followed by a puff of air
   b. *My sty is clean*—another plain old [t], although it actually sounds like a *d* if you cut off the *s*, something you can do with a simple, free computer program like Praat, mentioned in Chapter 2.

The three forms in (6.12) show how alternations in the [t] of a given morpheme, *cat*, can be induced by placing it in various contexts. When nothing follows in the sentence, or when there is a major syntactic break following, as in *I saw a cat, and Sami did too*, we get a glottal stop. When an unstressed vowel follows [t], whether within a word, as in *atom*, or in a syntactically close following word, as in 6.12b, we get a flap, as in *The cat is on the mat*. When an *s* follows within the word we get a plain [t], as in *cats*.

The examples (6.13) do not involve alternations within a morpheme but instead are based on a distributional observation. At the beginning of a word, before a stressed syllable, we find the aspirated [tʰ], whereas we get the unaspirated [t] when there is a preceding *s*. You should confirm that these generalizations hold by coming up with other examples.

Now are these generalizations just a matter of how we have memorized the pronunciation of words like *cat, tie, sty*? Let's test that idea. Imagine we tell you that we just bought two *joots*. You might ask us

6.14   What is a joot?

and we bet you would pronounce the *t* as a glottal stop (if your dialect is like ours). And we might answer "It's like a banana," to which you might reply

6.15   Oh, a joot is a fruit?

And you would totally unconsciously pronounce the *t* of *joot* as a flap and the *t* of *fruit* as a glottal stop.[17] Since, by assumption, you never heard anyone say *joot* before this exchange, and when you heard us say it, it had a *t*, why did you say it with a flap or a glottal stop?

The answer is that your grammar, your I-language, the computational system in your mind that underlies in a very abstract way your pronunciation, treats plain and aspirated [t], flap, and glottal stop as equivalence classes that are themselves realizations of a more abstract equivalence class called a *phoneme*. The traditional notation for this particular phoneme is /t/, which will do for our purposes. Our grammar then has a set of rules that determine the realization of /t/ in various contexts, in terms of the still abstract elements, called *allophones*, plain and aspirated [t], glottal stop, and flap.

Phonemes are traditionally represented between backslash brackets, as in the top of Fig. 6.1. We somewhat arbitrarily have chosen the symbol /t/ to represent the phoneme in this case. The allophones, the conditioned variant forms of the phoneme that show up in the output of the grammar, are represented in square brackets, [t]. Finally, Fig. 6.1 shows a representational format invented by Mark Hale—we have used little body symbols to represent actual tokens of speech. So, each allophone is an abstraction over tokens of speech or speech perception behavior, and each phoneme is an abstraction over allophones. You should compare Fig. 6.1 with Fig. 1.1 from Chapter 1, which represented nouns as equivalence classes.

---

[17] With different intonation, you can produce *joot* with a glottal stop in this sentence as well. This just shows how intonation interacts with other aspects of pronunciation, a complication we don't want to get into here.

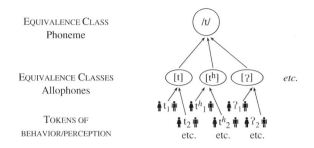

Fig 6.1 The equivalence class of the phoneme /t/ is itself an abstraction from equivalence classes of allophones abstracted from individual utterances.

How did your grammar end up in this state? As you were learning language you were unconsciously learning the patterns of alternation and distribution that we just told you about. Based on these patterns, you constructed equivalence classes, along with a computational system that relates equivalence classes to one another.

These examples are so simple, and if you speak the dialect we are describing they are so hard to view objectively, that we think it is worthwhile to stress that they provide another very strong argument for the construction of experience. Like the constructed edges of the triangle illusion, the identity of the sounds we hear is largely a product of the computations of our minds. Note that our perception of *t* sounds leads to us hearing signals that are physically quite different as the same—we hear, in some sense, the plain and aspirated *t*, the glottal stop, the flap, and even silence (whatever it means to *hear silence*) as tokens of the same type, the phoneme /t/. On the other hand, we can point out that there are other flaps in our English that are not related to /t/ but to /d/—consider the pairs *wed, wedding* and *feed, feeding* that have [d] in the first members and flap in the second.

| 6.16 | Why does perception of *t* show construction of experience? |

- Things that are different physically perceived as the same
  - t/tʰ/ʔ/ɾ/Ø
- Things that are physically the same perceived as different:
  - *wetting* ⤳ [wɛɾɪŋ]
  - *wedding* ⤳ [wɛɾɪŋ]

So, in addition to leading us to experience phonetically distinct sounds (the various forms of /t/) as identical, our grammar also leads us to experience two phonetically identical sounds as different, even when they occur in exactly the same environment, as in *wetting* and *wedding*. Most speakers of dialects in which these words are complete homophones will insist that the words are pronounced differently. They are not, unless one produces a spelling pronunciation, a pronunciation that does not reflect the grammar, as in *I said we*[d]*ing, not we*[t]*ing*, but this does not reflect what the grammar does with /t/ and /d/ inputs in this environment.

We should note that it is perfectly possible to be a native speaker of English and treat flap and plain [t] as allophones of a single phoneme, and also be a native speaker of Japanese, in which [t] and flap represent completely distinct phonemes. Or to be a speaker of both English and Thai, and thus treat plain and aspirated *t* as allophones in English but as separate phonemes that can distinguish word meaning in Thai. In other words, a bilingual person will process information and thus construct experience differently depending on which of the two I-languages is used. The equivalence class is not in the signal but is a result of signal processing.

Before moving on, we reiterate that your own dialect of English may be completely different from ours. For example, you may not have any flaps at all; and you may have glottal stops in places where we do not, as in words like *writer*, as opposed to a [d] in *rider*. We have a flap in the middle of both of these words, and they only differ in terms of the vowels preceding the flap. This is typical of North American English, but it may be hard to convince speakers that it is true. We have provided a recording on the companion website.

6.4 Turkish vowel harmony

We are now ready to return to the analysis of Turkish vowel harmony, the phenomenon mentioned at the very beginning of the book. Consider the data in (6.17) that shows the nominative singular, nominative plural, the genitive singular and the genitive plural of eight Turkish nouns. Nominative is the form used when the noun is subject of a sentence, so *ipler* would be the word for ropes in a sentence meaning "The ropes fell." The genitive is used to show possession, so *ipin* means "the rope's, of the rope." The genitive plural combines the meanings genitive and plural, so *iplerin* means "of the ropes."

6.17   Turkish vowel harmony data[18]

		nom. sg.	nom. pl.	gen. sg.	gen. pl.	
a.	ip	ip-ler	ip-in	ip-ler-in	"rope"
b.	kıl	kıl-lar	kıl-ın	kıl-lar-ın	"body hair"
c.	sap	sap-lar	sap-ın	sap-lar-ın	"stalk"
d.	uç	uç-lar	uç-un	uç-lar-ın	"tip"
e.	son	son-lar	son-un	son-lar-ın	"end"
f.	öç	öç-ler	öç-ün	öç-ler-in	"revenge'"
g.	gül	gül-ler	gül-ün	gül-ler-in	"rose"
h.	ek	ek-ler	ek-in	ek-ler-in	"joint"

As you look over the data you will notice that the plural suffix takes two different forms -ler and -lar. In the genitive singular column, you notice four different forms: -in, -ın, -un, -ün. In the genitive plural column we see the same two forms of the plural, -ler, -lar, but only two forms of the genitive marker.

Here are some questions about these forms:

- What determines the choice of vowel in each suffix?
- How can we represent the suffix?
- Do we have to say that the genitive suffix in the plural is different than the genitive suffix in the singular, since the former has only two forms and the latter has four?

In order to begin to answer these questions, we need to understand a bit about the phonetic correlates of Turkish vowels. We will need to describe them along three dimensions that we will illustrate using English vowels. First, pronounce the word *beat* slowly to yourself and try to pay attention to the position of your tongue and jaw. For our purposes, what is important is just to compare this vowel with that of *bet*. In the latter, you should feel (or see in a mirror) that your tongue and jaw are lower than in the former. We will refer to the vowel of *beat*, whose phonetic symbol is [i], as a HIGH vowel, and to the vowel of *bet*, as a NON-HIGH vowel. For this vowel, we will use the symbol [e], since we will follow the Turkish writing system in this discussion, although the symbol used in the International Phonetic Alphabet is [ε].

Next, compare, by feeling and looking in a mirror, the vowel of *beat* with that of *boot*, which we will write as [u]. You should notice that in *beat* your

---

[18] The symbol ç represents the sound written *ch* in English. The vowel symbols will be explained in the main text.

lips are spread rather wide, whereas in *boot* the lips are rounded. The vowel in *boot* is ROUND, that in *beat* is NON-ROUND.

The last parameter is a bit harder to notice, but it can also be illustrated using *beat* and *boot*. Try to say the words slowly and silently, concentrating not on the lips but on the difference in the position of the tongue. One way to isolate what is happening with the tongue is to try to say a long version of the vowel in *boot* but forcing the lips to stay spread as for the vowel in *beat*. You won't sound natural, and you will look funny, but you should notice that the tongue is pulled further back in the mouth for the *boot* vowel than for the *beat* vowel. The latter is called a NON-BACK vowel and the former a BACK vowel.

The three binary choices NON-BACK vs. BACK, and so on, allow for 2×2×2 combinations, each one corresponding to one of the eight Turkish vowels in the roots of the words in (6.17), as shown in the following table:

	NON-BACK		BACK	
HIGH	i	ü	ı	u
NON-HIGH	e	ö	a	o
	NON-ROUND	ROUND	NON-ROUND	ROUND

You can play with your speech articulators and figure out the approximate pronunciation of the other vowels in the table. For example, [ü] has the tongue forward and high like [i], but it has the lips rounded, like [u]. This sound occurs in German, also written *ü*, and in French, where it is written *u*. If you are familiar with the International Phonetic Alphabet, you will know that the symbol for this vowel is [y].

The photographs in Fig. 6.2 will give you an idea of how these vowels are articulated. You can hear sound files and see more photos on the companion website.

The descriptions in terms of the configurations of the vocal tract that we have provided correspond to equivalence classes of vowels. The label of each class (for example HIGH) is typically called a *distinctive feature* or just *feature* in the linguistics literature. The features correspond to the linguistically relevant distinctions among speech sounds in the languages of the world. Sets of segments that correspond to a feature description are called *natural classes*. For example, the set of HIGH vowels is a natural class (containing i, ü, ı, u), as is the set of HIGH, NON-ROUND vowels (containing i, ı). Note that the more features we list, the smaller the natural class is, because adding features makes the description more specific.

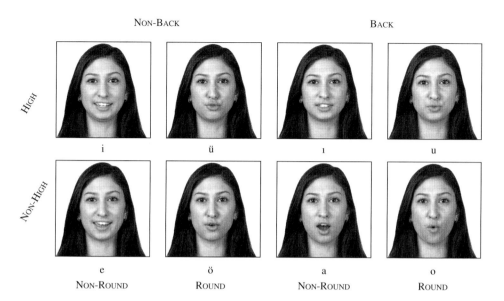

Fig 6.2 A native speaker pronouncing the eight Turkish vowels. See companion website for side views and sound files. The photographer, Sabina Matyiku, and the model, Ezgi Özdemir, are both Concordia undergraduate linguistics students.

For practice, list the members of the natural class of ROUND vowels in the table. Now list the NON-HIGH, ROUND vowels. Now list the BACK vowels.

So we are now ready to analyze the Turkish forms—we have broken down the data to make the presentation clearer. We begin with just some of the nominative singular and plural forms you saw above, as well as some new forms that will make the patterns more apparent. Try to answer the questions before you read the discussion that follows.

6.18   Turkish singular/plural pairs

singular	plural	meaning
dev	devler	"giant"
kek	kekler	"cake"
can	canlar	"soul"
cep	cepler	"pocket"
tarz	tarzlar	"type"
kap	kaplar	"recipient"
çek	çekler	"check"
saç	saçlar	"hair"

şey   şeyler   "thing"

ters   tersler   "contrary"

aşk   aşklar   "love"

a. What are the two forms of the plural suffix? 1.   2.

b. What determines where you find each suffix?

  • Suffix (1.) occurs...

  • Suffix (2.) occurs...

Notice that the plural of *sap* is *saplar* and the plural of *ek* is *ekler*. It turns out that this is a general pattern—if the root has just an *a*, then the plural is *-lar*; if the root has just an *e*, then the plural is *-ler*.

What about the other roots that take *-lar* in the plural? They are *uç*, *kıl*, *son*. What do you notice about the four vowels *a, o, u, ı*?...Right, they are all BACK. And the four vowels that take the suffix *-ler* are all NON-BACK: *e, ö, i, ü*.

| 6.19 | More Turkish singular/plural pairs |

singular	plural	meaning
ip	ipler	"rope"
kıl	kıllar	"body hair"
sap	saplar	"stalk"
uç	uçlar	"edge"
son	sonlar	"end"
öç	öçler	"vengeance"
gül	güller	"rose"
ek	ekler	"junction"

a. What are the two forms of the plural suffix? 1.   2.

b. What determines where you find each suffix?

  • Suffix (1.) occurs...

  • Suffix (2.) occurs...

So to compute which vowel occurs in the plural, we read the NON-BACK/BACK value of the vowel on the bare singular root form and choose the version of the plural whose value agrees with it.

Let's be explicit—what does this show us about equivalence classes? Well, the vowels that are, say, NON-BACK, are not all pronounced with the tongue in exactly the same place—for the purposes of phonology, lots of physical detail is ignored, and these vowels can be treated as identical in some respect.

Why does this illustrate computation? Well, we can formulate an explicit algorithm referring to symbols that corresponds to the patterns we see in the data. Something like this algorithm seems to underlie the behavior of Turkish speakers.

Before we proceed, we should note that Turkish speakers are not physically constrained to obey the patterns of vowel harmony. For instance, they may be bilingual in Turkish and English, so as people their behavior is not always vowel-harmonic. Also, we can ask a Turkish speaker to pronounce, say, *sap-ler*, and he or she will be able to do so—but this does not reflect the computations of the grammar. Grammars do not directly model behavior, and behavior is just one of the sources of evidence for understanding the computations of the grammar.

So what *is* the plural suffix in Turkish? How is it stored in the mind of a speaker? Is its vowel encoded as NON-BACK or BACK? Let's ask some easier questions. What does the plural suffix start with? It seems reasonable to assume that it starts with an *l*, since there is no evidence that it is anything else. We won't worry here about how to express *l* using features (we would need many new ones). It also seems reasonable that it ends with *r*. So the form is something like *-lVr*, where V is the vowel we need to figure out.

The V in the middle of the plural suffix appears never in a rounded form, and it appears never as a HIGH vowel, so it seems reasonable to assume that the stored form is a member of the equivalence classes NON-HIGH and NON-ROUND. What about the value for NON-BACK/BACK? Well, we could assume that it is NON-BACK, basically that the vowel is stored in memory as *e*, and then change it into *a* when it follows a BACK vowel. But we could also assume it is basically BACK and have a rule that changes it to *e* when it follows a NON-BACK vowel.

These two options seem equally valid, and there is no principled way to choose among them. If all we wanted to do was write a computer program to mimic Turkish output, then it would not matter which one we use. However, the cognitive biolinguistic approach assumes that there is some truth to the matter concerning what computations characterize a Turkish grammar.[19] We have a third option, in addition to choosing between *a* and *e*.

---

[19] Obviously, different speakers could have different versions of the rule, even if their grammatical output is the same.

First, let's recognize that a child learning Turkish would find him- or herself in a situation like that of us, the linguists—there is no principled way to decide between basic *e* or *a*. If part of the goal of grammatical theory is to explain how children learn language, then leaving them to make random choices is not much of a solution. A second point to appreciate is that, once we have features, the symbols *e, a,* and so on become unnecessary. These symbols are just abbreviations for highly specific equivalence classes: *e* is just an abbreviation for the intersection of the sets denoted by NON-BACK, NON-HIGH, and NON-ROUND. This realization liberates us to propose that the equivalence class in memory that corresponds to the vowel in the plural suffix is just characterized as NON-HIGH, NON-ROUND—with *no* value for the third contrast NON-BACK/BACK. In other words, the vowel in the suffix has no value along this dimension and the computational system, the phonological grammar, provides it with one. The stored form of the vowel is thus something like this:

$$
\begin{bmatrix} V \\ \text{NON-ROUND} \\ \text{NON-HIGH} \end{bmatrix}
$$

The plural suffix then contains this vowel preceded by an *l* and followed by *r*. As noted above, we will not provide featural representations for *l* and *r*, and thus we represent the suffix thus:

$$
l\begin{bmatrix} V \\ \text{NON-ROUND} \\ \text{NON-HIGH} \end{bmatrix}r
$$

This conclusion not only frees us from being forced to make an arbitrary choice but also leads to an elegant analysis of the rest of the data, as we will now see.

We turn now to an analysis of the genitive singular forms. We need to first identify what forms occur, then determine the environment in which each variant occurs, and finally posit a form that is stored in memory that can be used to compute the output forms.

6.20   Turkish nominative and genitive singular pairs

nom. singular	genitive singular	meaning
ip	ipin	"rope"
kıl	kılın	"body hair"

sap	sapın	"stalk"
uç	uçun	"edge"
son	sonun	"end"
öç	öçün	"vengeance"
gül	gülün	"rose"
ek	ekin	"junction"

a. What are the four forms of the genitive suffix?
   1.   2.   3.   4.
b. What determines where you find each suffix?
   • Suffix (1.) occurs ...
   • Suffix (2.) occurs ...
   • Suffix (3.) occurs ...
   • Suffix (4.) occurs ...

Here are the four vowels that occur in the suffix: *i, ü, ı, u*. What do they have in common? They are all HIGH, so it seems reasonable to suppose that this suffix is stored in memory with a vowel encoded as HIGH.

Now, where does the form *-in* occur? It occurs in the forms *ipin* and *ekin*. These are the forms with root vowels that are NON-BACK, NON-ROUND, which agrees with the vowel *i* of the suffix. Where does the suffix *-ün* occur? It occurs in the forms *öçün* and *gülün*, which have vowels that agree with the suffix vowel in being NON-BACK, ROUND. We get the same pattern with the other two forms of the suffix: *-ın* occurs with *sapın* and *kılın*, which both have BACK, NON-ROUND vowels; and *-un* occurs in *uçun* and *sonun*, where the vowels are BACK, ROUND.

We now see that we don't have to choose a particular vowel to represent the genitive suffix. It is stored in memory as containing a vowel that is specified as just HIGH, and that's it:

$$\begin{bmatrix} V \\ \text{HIGH} \end{bmatrix} n$$

The other features are filled in by the computational system to match those of the vowel that precedes.

The genitive suffix is thus encoded in memory as an abstract entity that starts with a vowel specified as HIGH followed by an *n*. The other features of the vowel get filled in depending on the context by the grammar. Note that the stored forms of the vowels of the plural and the genitive are both lacking specification for some features, but the two vowels are distinct from each other.

We are now ready to tackle the genitive plurals.

| 6.21 | Turkish nominative singular/genitive plural pairs |

nom. singular	genitive plural	meaning
ip	iplerin	"rope"
kıl	kılların	"body hair"
sap	sapların	"stalk"
uç	uçların	"edge"
son	sonların	"end"
öç	öçlerin	"vengeance"
gül	güllerin	"rose"
ek	eklerin	"junction"

a. What are the two forms of the genitive suffix in this data?
   1.   2.
b. What determines where you find each suffix?
   • Suffix (1.) occurs...
   • Suffix (2.) occurs...

Recall that we wondered if the genitive marker in the genitive plural needed to be encoded differently from that in the singular, since the former shows up in only two forms, whereas the latter has the four combinations of NON-BACK/BACK and ROUND/NON-ROUND discussed above. The genitive marker in the plural has only the NON-ROUND variants. What do you think—are there two genitive markers, one for singular and one for plural, or can the two patterns, a four-way contrast and a two-way contrast, all be derived from a single underlying form?

We propose that there is a single genitive suffix underlyingly. To see how this works, consider the system of morphology and phonology that we are proposing. The morphology takes roots and suffixes as they are stored in memory and puts them together. That will give us structures like the following for a form that exits the grammar as *öçler*, with the vowels expressed in terms of features. We use phonetic symbols for the consonants for ease of presentation.

| 6.22 | Input to the phonology for *öçler* |

$$
\text{INPUT:} \quad
\begin{bmatrix}
\text{V} \\
\text{NON-BACK} \\
\text{ROUND} \\
\text{NON-HIGH}
\end{bmatrix}
\text{ç-l}
\begin{bmatrix}
\text{V} \\
\text{NON-ROUND} \\
\text{NON-HIGH}
\end{bmatrix}
\text{r}
$$

Since the suffix vowel is lacking a specification for NON-BACK/BACK, it looks to its left and copies the first one it finds—in this case the NON-BACK of the vowel *ö*.

6.23   Output of the phonology for *öçler*

$$\text{OUTPUT:} \quad \begin{bmatrix} V \\ \text{NON-BACK} \\ \text{ROUND} \\ \text{NON-HIGH} \end{bmatrix} \text{çl} \begin{bmatrix} V \\ \text{NON-BACK} \\ \text{NON-ROUND} \\ \text{NON-HIGH} \end{bmatrix} r$$

A mapping from the combination of stored forms to the output generated by the phonology is called a *derivation*. For the genitive of the same root we have the following derivation, again with missing values copied from the left:

6.24   Derivation of *öçün*

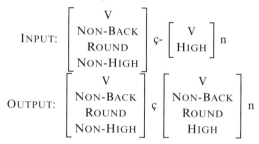

$$\text{INPUT:} \quad \begin{bmatrix} V \\ \text{NON-BACK} \\ \text{ROUND} \\ \text{NON-HIGH} \end{bmatrix} \text{ç-} \begin{bmatrix} V \\ \text{HIGH} \end{bmatrix} n$$

$$\text{OUTPUT:} \quad \begin{bmatrix} V \\ \text{NON-BACK} \\ \text{ROUND} \\ \text{NON-HIGH} \end{bmatrix} \text{ç} \begin{bmatrix} V \\ \text{NON-BACK} \\ \text{ROUND} \\ \text{HIGH} \end{bmatrix} n$$

Now, let's see what happens when we add both suffixes to the same root. Now we have two vowels in a row that are missing values for some features.

6.25   Input representation of *öçlerin*

$$\text{INPUT:} \quad \begin{bmatrix} V \\ \text{NON-BACK} \\ \text{ROUND} \\ \text{NON-HIGH} \end{bmatrix} \text{ç-l} \begin{bmatrix} V \\ \text{NON-ROUND} \\ \text{NON-HIGH} \end{bmatrix} r \begin{bmatrix} V \\ \text{HIGH} \end{bmatrix} n$$

We assume that a vowel that is missing values for any feature pair like ROUND/NON-ROUND looks to its left and copies the first value it finds. Both suffixes have to look all the way to the root vowel to get a value for NON-BACK/BACK. This is the only feature missing for the plural marker. The genitive marker, however, also needs a value for ROUND/NON-ROUND. In the genitive singular, the first such value to the left was on the root, but, in this case, the plural marker has a relevant feature, and the genitive suffix copies it. Thus, we end up with the following:

6.26   Output representation of *öçlerin* with features for the vowels

$$
\text{OUTPUT:} \quad
\begin{bmatrix}
\text{V} \\
\text{NON-BACK} \\
\text{ROUND} \\
\text{NON-HIGH}
\end{bmatrix}
\text{çl}
\begin{bmatrix}
\text{V} \\
\text{NON-BACK} \\
\text{NON-ROUND} \\
\text{NON-HIGH}
\end{bmatrix}
\text{r}
\begin{bmatrix}
\text{V} \\
\text{NON-BACK} \\
\text{NON-ROUND} \\
\text{HIGH}
\end{bmatrix}
\text{n}
$$

We now see that we can derive the genitive alternations in the singular and plural from the same abstract stored form. There are fewer surface forms of the genitive suffix in the plural because the genitive suffix always gets its ROUND/NON-ROUND value from the plural suffix. The latter is always NON-ROUND since it is underlyingly specified as such. We also see that the form of the suffixes is determined phonologically—the computations depend on the preceding vowel, not on what root the suffix is attached to. This is clear, because different forms of the genitive surface with a given root, depending on what intervenes. The root *öç-* takes a genitive suffix *-ün* if the suffix follows the root directly, but it takes the form *-in* if a NON-ROUND vowel like that of the plural comes between the root and the genitive.

Now, we have just illustrated the computational nature of vowel harmony in Turkish. Getting back to our story, it turns out that the vowels of Turkish roots tend to be harmonic as well, especially with regard to the features NON-BACK/BACK. Here are some examples:

6.27   Harmonic Turkish roots

BACK	boru	"pipe"
	arı	"bee"
	oda	"room"
NON-BACK	inek	"cow"
	dere	"river"
	güzel	"beautiful"

There are some exceptions, especially in recent borrowings like *pilot* "pilot," but for the most part all the vowels in a root will be either NON-BACK or BACK. This is how Charles knew that *Ozel* was a very unlikely name, and that *Özel* would conform to the general pattern of the language.[20]

---

[20] Paul did manage to visit our venerable doctor, who inadvertently squirted some anesthetic into his eye, and then diagnosed him as having a case of trenchmouth that eventually cleared up on its own. This story is not meant to denigrate the Turkish medical profession—after all, Dr. Özel worked at the *American* hospital in Istanbul.

So, like our analyses of syntactic structure and the allophones of /t/, we once again end up positing very abstract symbols—this time the partially specified vowels of Turkish—to account for complex sets of linguistic data. We turn in the next section to yet one more analysis, from the domain of morphology, that demonstrates just how abstract the equivalence classes are over which grammatical computations apply.

6.5 Words are not derived from words

Recall the discussion of Warlpiri and Samoan from Chapter 1. In those examples, we assumed that the plurals were built from the singulars. Similarly, we saw that the Turkish nominative plural, genitive singular, and genitive plural seem to be formed from the nominative singular form by adding suffixes and providing them with the appropriate values for missing features. So far, it always appeared to be the case that complex words are built out of simple words. However, in some languages, even for simple categories like singular and plural, it is necessary to recognize a complication—it may be the case that both singular and plural need to be expressed as a function of some unit that, by itself, is neither singular or plural. In fact, this unit cannot ever appear as a word on its own. An example will help to clarify.

Here are some singular/plural pairs from the language Swahili, spoken in Tanzania and other countries in eastern Africa (the letter š is pronounced like *sh*). Swahili is the native language of about one million people, but is used as a second language by about 30 million.

| 6.28 | Swahili singular/plural pairs |

singular	plural	meaning
mtoto	watoto	"child/children"
mtu	watu	"person/people"
mpiši	wapiši	"cook/cooks"
mgeni	wageni	"stranger/strangers"

Note that each singular/plural pair shares something—for "child/children" it is *toto*; for "person/people" it is *tu*, and so on.

If we want to revive our mathematical analogies from Chapter 1, where we expressed the plural in Warlpiri as a function of the singular, then we can treat the Swahili singular and plural forms as being generated by two different functions of the same independent variable. If we refer to the shared part of each pair as the ROOT, then the functions can be expressed as follows:

- SINGULAR = m⌢ROOT
- PLURAL = wa⌢ROOT

The singular is a function of the root computed by placing *m* before the root. The plural is a function of the root computed by placing *wa* before the root.

In order to highlight the fact that we are dealing with the computation of two dependent variables, SINGULAR and PLURAL, from the same independent variable ROOT, we can rewrite this as follows.

- One function of ROOT = m⌢ROOT
- Another function of ROOT = wa⌢ROOT

These examples introduce a convention commonly used in math. An equivalent notation to, for example, $y = 2x + 3$ is $f(x) = 2x + 3$. This just means "There is some function of the independent variable x, computed by $2x + 3$, and we will call this function $f(x)$. This is read as "f of x."

If we want to distinguish this function of x from another one, we can just assign it another letter. For example, we can refer to $f(x)$ and $g(x)$, two functions of the same variable, just as the Swahili singular and plural are two functions applied to the same set of roots. An alternative notation is to use always f, but with indexes that distinguish functions: $f_1(x)$ is one function and $f_2(x)$ is another.

Using our Swahili example, we could express the two functions by assuming that x is a variable standing for the members of the set of roots. Then we would have, say, the following:

6.31   a. $f(x) = m⌢x$
b. $g(x) = wa⌢x$

Similarly in math, we can have two functions of a variable like, say, the following:

6.32   a. $f(x) = 2x - 3$
b. $g(x) = 4x$

What's the point? Well, there are two. First, we want to remind you once again why we focus on the theme of computation. The application of mathematical notions like variables and functions, if it gives us insight, supports our contention that language, at least some aspects of language, are amenable to scientific inquiry.

The second point is to illustrate, once again, the abstract nature of the symbolic elements over which grammatical computations occur. As we have seen, words are highly abstract entities, but now we have found evidence that words actually have to be analyzed in terms of even more abstract elements. These elements, roots, and prefixes and suffixes cannot be used on their own without occurring in combination with other elements—for example, *toto*, without a prefix, is not a Swahili word.

6.6 Think negative

In the preceding sections we have given you a sample of linguistic topics that we find useful for illustrating notions like computation and equivalence class. Our examples thus far have been drawn from phonology, morphology, and syntax. In this section we introduce you to some semantic patterns, patterns related to meaning, drawing on very simple English data related to one of the puzzles introduced in Chapter 3. We expect that you will be surprised at the regularities that emerge.

Before we delve into the data, we would like you to ask yourself how much you know about basic set theory. Many people will say that they know almost nothing. If you do know some basic set theory, then think about when you learned it. We assume that, unless you have deviant parents, it was sometime after the age of six. Now hold those thoughts. . . .

Consider the following sentences:

- Sami wasn't wearing clothes
- Sami wasn't wearing footwear
- Sami wasn't wearing socks
- Sami wasn't wearing white socks

Notice that we can insert a word like *any* in these sentences as indicated below and the result is grammatical:

6.34

- Sami wasn't wearing any clothes
- Sami wasn't wearing any footwear
- Sami wasn't wearing any socks
- Sami wasn't wearing any white socks

However, the examples become ungrammatical if we remove the negation:

- *Sami was wearing any clothes
- *Sami was wearing any footwear
- *Sami was wearing any socks
- *Sami was wearing any white socks

The generalization seems to be that there is some relationship between negation and the presence of *any*. This is confirmed by the fact that, if we remove *any* from the ungrammatical strings above, the result becomes grammatical.

6.36

- Sami was wearing clothes
- Sami was wearing footwear
- Sami was wearing socks
- Sami was wearing white socks

What's interesting is that there are other lexical items, apart from *any*, that are sensitive to whether the sentence in which they occur is affirmative or negative, in other words to the polarity of the sentence in which they occur. Such items include *ever*, *yet*, *at all*, *anything*, and others. Just like *any*, such items are grammatical in negative sentences but ungrammatical in affirmative ones.

6.37

a. Sami wasn't *ever* wearing clothes
b. Sami wasn't wearing clothes *yet*
c. Sami wasn't wearing clothes *at all*
d. Sami wasn't wearing *anything*

a. *Sami was *ever* wearing clothes
b. *Sami was wearing clothes *yet*
c. *Sami was wearing clothes *at all*
d. *Sami was wearing *anything*

The technical name for such words is *negative polarity items* (NPIs). NPIs thus form an equivalence class of semantic computation, a class of items that share the property of being sensitive to the (negative) polarity of the sentence in which they occur. These observations would be enough to make you aware of the fact that linguistic computation operates on equivalence classes at all levels, including the semantic one. However, it turns out that not only are items like *any*, *ever*, *yet*, or *at all* members of a class that can be consistently defined in a semantic way but the negative **environment** in which these items occur grammatically is itself a member of a larger equivalence

class which can be defined semantically. In order to see that, consider again
the negative sentences in (6.33):

 • Sami wasn't wearing clothes ⇒
• Sami wasn't wearing footwear ⇒
• Sami wasn't wearing socks ⇒
• Sami wasn't wearing white socks

Observe that the meanings, the propositions expressed by these sentences,
have certain entailment relations among them, as shown by the arrows. In
particular, the meaning of the higher elements in the list entails the meaning
of the lower ones. If we know that a higher one is true, we know that the
ones below it are true as well. It is impossible that a higher one be true and
a lower one false. For example, if Sami wasn't wearing footwear, then it is
necessarily the case that he was not wearing socks, including white socks. In
(6.39), the objects are in a *downward-entailing environment*.

   In contrast to the sentences we just examined, those in (6.36), which do
not constitute a proper environment for the occurrence of *any*, have the
entailment relations reversed, as indicated below. The lower sentences entail
the higher ones—if Sami was wearing white socks, then it is necessarily the
case that he was wearing socks, footwear, clothing.

 • Sami was wearing clothes ⇐
• Sami was wearing footwear ⇐
• Sami was wearing socks ⇐
• Sami was wearing white socks

In (6.40), the objects are in an *upward-entailing environment*.

   Now think about what these entailment relations mean. Every white sock
is a sock. And every sock is a piece of footwear. And every piece of footwear
is an article of clothing. The terms we have used refer to nested sets: the set
of clothes is a superset of the set of footwear, or, equivalently, the set of
footwear is a subset of the set of clothes. The claim we want to make is that
NPIs are not actually sensitive to the polarity of the sentence in which they
occur but to the directionality of the entailment relations that the respective
sentences license. More specifically, NPIs are a class of lexical items that
occur in downward-entailing environments like (6.39). Such environments
include negative contexts, but are not reduced to the latter. In other words,
negative contexts are just one member of a larger equivalence class—that
of downward-entailing contexts. That this is the right generalization is
supported by the following data showing various contexts in which NPIs
like *any* can occur.

6.41 More entailment switches

*any	any
*Sami *always* wears any socks	Sami *never* wears any socks
*Sami *often* wears any socks	Sami *hardly* wears any socks
*Sami left *with* any socks	Sami left *without* any socks
*_Many_ cats wear any socks	*Few* cats wear any socks
*Sami smiles *after*	Sami smiles *before*
he puts on any socks	he puts on any socks

You can confirm that *never* behaves just like the negative marker *n't* with respect to entailment: if Sami never wears socks, then we know that he never wears white socks. This is perhaps unsurprising since *never* so transparently contains negation. The same is true about *hardly* and *without*. However, you may be surprised to see that *few* and *before* also create downward-entailing environments, in spite of the fact that it is hard to maintain that they contain negation in any way. For example, if Sami smiles before he puts on socks, he clearly smiles before he puts on white socks; and if it is the case that few cats wear socks, it is also the case that few cats wear white socks.

You may have already thought of some difficulties with what we have presented so far. First of all, you may be thinking about uses of NPIs that clearly do not appear in downward-entailing environments. For example, the word *anything* seems to be an NPI, as shown above, yet sentences like (6.42) are perfectly grammatical.

6.42 He'll eat anything

This is a so-called "free-choice" usage, and we will assume that it is actually a different item from the NPIs we have been looking at. We cannot provide full justification here, but we just note that the two types of sentences are translated with very different elements in many languages, for example, French.

6.43

	English	French
Negation:	He won't eat anything	Il ne mange rien
Free Choice:	He'll eat anything	Il mange n'importe quoi

Since there are languages that do not treat free-choice meanings and NPIs identically, we will assume that they correspond to distinct representations, even in English where they are homophonous. In other words, simplifying a bit, we assume that English actually has two different words pronounced *anything*, one corresponding to French *rien* and one to *n'importe quoi*.

A second issue that you may have noticed is that NPIs also occur in Yes/No questions:

 6.44   NPIs in questions
   • Did you kick anyone?
   • Have you ever been to Timbuktu?
   • Has anybody seen my girl?

It is hard to say what a question means, and thus it is hard to say what a question entails—it is not clear that it even makes sense to ask if *Does Sami wear socks?* entails *Does Sami wear white socks?* Informally, we just note that if the answer to the first question is "no," this entails that the answer to the second is the same, so perhaps this is the way to interpret entailment in questions. This is a topic of current research that we leave aside.

Recall our question about your knowledge of set theory in the beginning of this discussion. Not only English but all languages make use of NPIs; they all require analysis in terms of entailments, implications that can be understood as set theoretic relations. Thus, in a sense, everybody who speaks a language has knowledge of set theory. Every human language makes implicit use of notions like *subset* and *superset* well before formal schooling begins. Downward-entailing environments make up an equivalence class that turns out to be defining for a class of lexical items—the class of NPIs. These two equivalence classes do not have correlates outside of the semantics—they are pure semantic categories. Notice in this sense that the syntactic correlates of NPIs do not make up a coherent syntactic category—NPIs like *any* are determiners, *ever* is an adverb, while *at all* is a prepositional phrase. We will come back to NPIs in later chapters to study their syntax, and also to discuss some differences in NPI patterns across dialects of English.

6.7 Summing up

In this chapter, we first saw that it is necessary to appeal to a very abstract notion of syntactic structure—we can't understand the patterns of possible sentences by just considering sequences of sounds or words. We then argued for the abstract notion *phoneme* in order to account for the patterns of distribution and alternation of speech sounds like plain and aspirated [t], flap, and glottal stop. In the next section, we showed that a reasonable analysis of Turkish vowel harmony leads us to posit forms stored in memory that are not even pronounceable since some of the features that determine pronunciation are filled in by the computational system. Then we argued that, at least in some cases like Swahili nouns, the building blocks of words are abstract roots, elements that cannot be used in isolation. It is not always possible to analyze complex words as consisting of simple words. Finally, we examined the set theoretic conditions on the distribution of certain words and phrases.

In each phenomenon we looked at, contracted copula, allophones of /t/, Turkish vowel harmony, Swahili nouns, and English NPIs, we saw that we could make an explicit formulation of the relevant pattern. We saw that the output of the grammar can be *computed* by explicit rules. These rules apply to equivalence classes of abstract symbols, or complex structures of symbols, that are related to the physical manifestations of speech in only very indirect ways.

6.8 Exercises

Exercise 6.8.1. Do grammars avoid ambiguity? When we present the *Mary's* data in class, we have found that there are always some students who insist that the unacceptability of *I know Mary's* in the sense intended in (6.1d.) must be somehow connected to the fact that the string has another, acceptable reading. In other words, these students suggest that we, or our grammars, somehow refuse to allow strings that are ambiguous.

There are several problems with such a view, the most obvious being that it is trivial to find examples of ambiguity, of all types. The string *I saw the man with a telescope* has two obvious readings, one in which the man who was seen had a telescope and one in which the device used for seeing was a telescope. Of course, there is also another pair of readings that can be paraphrased as *I regularly use a telescope to cut (to saw) the man* and *I regularly cut the man who has a telescope*. The second problem with the explanation that appeals to ambiguity is that grammars, which are just computational systems, have no way to avoid generating ambiguous structures—they just produce outputs from inputs mechanically, and, furthermore, grammars have no reason to care about ambiguity. People communicate, grammars do not.

In any case, it is still useful to come up with examples where the issue of ambiguity does not arise. We can find such cases by making our subject plural as in (6.45a.). In spoken English, there is also a reduced or contracted form of the plural copula, although there is no standard orthographic convention for writing this—we have used *'er*. We see that the patterns of grammaticality are exactly the same as in the previous sentences.

> **6.45**   *Do you know if anyone is here yet?*
> a. I know Sami and Bill are here.
> b. I know Sami and Bill 'er here.
> c. I know Sami and Bill are.
> d. *I know Sami and Bill 'er.
> e. *I know Sami and Bill 'er, but Mary's not.

Explain how these examples help to show that avoidance of ambiguity is irrelevant to an explanation of the distribution of the contracted copula forms that we developed in this chapter.

Exercise 6.8.2.   English allophones: Using Praat record the following sets of words, making a separate file for each set. The Praat manual or our mini-manual will tell you how to do this.

- *leaf, feel*
- *bead, bean*
- *pit, spit, bit*

a. Using the symbols of the International Phonetic Alphabet, one might transcribe the first set as [lif] and [fi]. In Praat, open (using READ) the first file, select it in the object list, and then choose EDIT. Play the file. Then select the file in your Praat object list and choose **Modify > Reverse**. Play the waveform again. Based on the transcription, one would expect the reverse of *leaf, feel* to sound like the original. Does it? Record other examples of words that begin with *l* and words that end with *l*. Try to select the part corresponding to *l* in the waveforms. Is there a consistent difference between the initial and final pronunciation of this letter?

b. Open the file containing *bead, bean*. One might expect the two words contain the same vowel since one might transcribe the words [bid] and [bin]. Isolate the vowel part of each word in the waveform and play it. Do they sound the same? Try to find other examples of each of these two types of vowel. Try to find other vowel pairs that differ in the same way, such as those in these words: *lode, loam, lone, lobe*. Does English have twice as many vowels as you thought? Hint: It depends on what you mean by "a vowel." Think of equivalence classes.

c. Like /t/, the phoneme /p/ has a plain and aspirated variant. Open and play the file containing *pit, spit, bit*, then select and play the aspirated and unaspirated allophones of /p/ by selecting parts of the waveform. Then select all of *spit* except the /s/. Play what remains—how does it sound?

Exercise 6.8.3.   Guaymí: This language is spoken in Panama and Costa Rica by about 128,000 people. Use the notation we developed for Swahili to express Guaymí verbs as a function of two variables, based on the following table:

present	past	meaning
kuge	kugaba	burns/burned
blite	blitaba	speaks/spoke
kite	kitaba	throws/threw
mete	metaba	hits/hit

Exercise 6.8.4.   Nahuatl: An expression like $z = 5w - 2x + 3y - 6$ represents z as a function of three independent variables. Come up with a function of three variables to generate the form of possessed nouns in Nahuatl, spoken by about 1.5 million people in Mexico. List the full set of possibilities for each variable.

nokali	my house	nokalimes	my houses
mokali	your house	mokalimes	your houses
ikali	his house	ikalimes	his houses
nopelo	my dog	nopelomes	my dogs
mopelo	your dog	mopelomes	your dogs
ipelo	his dog	ipelomes	his dogs
nokwahmili	my cornfield	nokwahmilimes	my cornfields
mokwahmili	your cornfield	mokwahmilimes	your cornfields
ikwahmili	his cornfield	ikwahmilimes	his cornfields

Further Readings

The first of these readings is not only very funny in places but is also a foundational document of the cognitive revolution. The second is a classic of psychology, and is also very entertaining. As you read these articles think about how they illustrate the necessity of positing abstract representations in order to understand human and rat behavior. The third selection is Roberts's discussion of the sense of time in rats—it is fairly long and difficult, but definitely a worthwhile read. The author publishes widely, both in academic journals and in popular media such as *Spy* magazine.

- Review of Skinner's *Verbal Behavior* by Noam Chomsky (1959).
- "Cognitive maps in rats and man" by E. C. Tolman (1948).
- "The mental representation of time: Uncovering a biological clock" by Seth Roberts (1998).

7

Some details of sentence structure

In previous chapters we argued that the input to operations involved in linguistic computation must be abstract entities, i.e. classes of words, or roots, or sounds, in other words, *equivalence classes*. In Chapter 1 we hinted at the existence of some abstract *syntactic* categories, such as noun and verb, and in Chapter 6 we illustrated another equivalence class that is relevant for syntactic computation, namely the class SENTENCE. In this chapter we offer more details on equivalence classes in syntax and the computations involving them.

7.1 Basic syntactic categories

Consider the following examples:

7.1
    a. This fat cat is red with white spots
    b. This fat chicken is red with white spots
    c. This fat pencil is red with white spots
    d. *This fat goes is red with white spots

In (7.1a.), the word *cat* can be substituted by certain other words, say, *chicken* or *pencil*, and grammaticality is preserved, as in (7.1b.c.).

However, if a word like *goes* is substituted for *cat*, as in (7.1d.), the result is ungrammatical. Crucially, when we substituted *cat* for *chicken* or *pencil*, we left the rest unchanged and the result was still a grammatical sentence. This suggests that *cat*, *chicken* and *pencil* share some property that *goes* does not share, and thus that they are members of a syntactic equivalence class. As members of the same equivalence class they have the same syntactic distribution. The syntactic distribution of the equivalence class that includes *cat*, *chicken*, and *pencil* but excludes *goes* can be identified by the (immediate) contexts in which these words can occur, as in (7.2):

7.2   This fat ... is

We will take the fact that certain words, *cat*, *chicken*, and *pencil*, can occur in this context to be an indication that they share a property to the exclusion of other words. We will refer to the class of words that have this property as nouns, Ns. Since *goes* cannot occur in this context, it does not have the same syntactic distribution, and thus it appears not to belong to the category, the equivalence class, N.

Now, just as we replaced *cat* by *chicken* and *pencil* in (7.1) to discover the class N, we can replace other words in the same sentence to discover other syntactic categories. For example, we can replace the first word, *this*, with *that*, *the*, or *a*, as illustrated in (7.3b.–d.). Each of these replacements yields a grammatical sentence, which suggests that *this*, *that*, *the*, and *a* are all members of the same syntactic category. We call this the category of determiners, D. However, replacement of the same word, *this*, with a word like *away*, as in (7.3e.), is ungrammatical, which suggests that *away* is not part of the same class as *that*, *the*, or *a*, and thus that it is not a determiner.

7.3   a. This fat cat is red with white spots
         b. That fat cat is red with white spots
         c. The fat cat is red with white spots
         d. A fat cat is red with white spots
         e. *Away fat cat is red with white spots

The category of determiners, then, is defined by the context given in (7.4) below.

7.4   ... fat chicken

The same substitution test can be applied not only for *cat* and *this* but for all words in (7.1a.). Each of the words in (7.1a.) belongs to a certain syntactic category that can be defined by a minimal context in the manner illustrated in (7.2) and (7.4). Apart from the category determiner and noun, (7.1a.) also contains words belonging to categories like verb (V), preposition (P), and adjective (A).

7.5   *This$_D$ fat$_A$ cat$_N$ is$_V$ red$_A$ with$_P$ white$_A$ spots$_N$.*

Given that (7.1b.c.) are identical to (7.1a.), with the exception of the fact that a different noun is substituted for *cat*, (7.1b.c.) contain words that belong to exactly the same syntactic categories as (7.1a.).

7.6   *This$_D$ fat$_A$ chicken$_N$ is$_V$ red$_A$ with$_P$ white$_A$ spots$_N$.*

7.7   *This$_D$ fat$_A$ pencil$_N$ is$_V$ red$_A$ with$_P$ white$_A$ spots$_N$.*

In other words, (7.1a.-c.) can be seen as particular instantiations of the same string of syntactic categories and, conversely, one and the same string of syntactic categories can be instantiated by different words. To further illustrate this latter point, consider the following sentence.

7.8   That blue fish got skinny despite strong warnings.

Even though (7.8) obviously means a different thing than (7.1a.-c.), at a certain level they are all the same, they are all definable by the same string of syntactic categories.

7.9   *That$_D$ blue$_A$ fish$_N$ got$_V$ skinny$_A$ despite$_P$ strong$_A$ warnings$_N$.*

Just as in (7.1a.) we replaced *cat* by other nouns, such as *chicken* and *pencil*, in (7.8) we replaced each of the words in (7.1a.) with other words in the same syntactic categories. What is crucial is that the words that we substitute for our initial words should keep the sentence grammatical. Grammaticality is preserved whenever the word we substitute belongs to the same category as the one we replace.

We can now go back to the minimal distributional contexts we provided for nouns and determiners. It should be obvious by now that we could express these contexts at a higher level of generality, by using syntactic categories instead of just words. So, the distributional context for nouns is [D A...V], rather than just [*This fat...is*], and for determiners is [...A N], rather than [...*fat cat*]. This captures the fact that a noun, for instance, can occur not only in the context [*This fat...is*] but also in a context like [*that blue ...grows*], [*a redundant...gets*], or any other context that represents an instantiation of [D A...V]. Similarly, expressing the distributional context in terms of categories rather than words captures the fact that a determiner would be any word that occurs in the context [...*fat cat*], or [...*smiling face*], or [...*implausible excuse*], in fact in any context that contains words representing instantiations of the A and N categories that are part of [...A N]. Last, but not least, expressing the distributional context in terms of categories also allows us to treat all members of a particular category alike. For example, the distributional context [D A...V] can accommodate any noun, irrespective of whether it is singular or plural, masculine or feminine, third person or first or second. This is closely related to the fact that the D, A and V, which are part of the distributional context, can themselves potentially be instantiated by any D, A, and V, regardless of whether they are singular or plural, masculine or feminine, third person or first or second. Clearly, expressing the distributional context in terms of lexical items or words would fail to capture that singular and plural nouns, for instance, share the same distribution at some level. To see that, notice that plural nouns cannot be inserted into the context [a fat...is], since in English, the noun has to agree with the form of the D (*this* as opposed to *these*, for example) and of the V (*is* as opposed to *are*). In contrast, plural nouns can easily be inserted in a context like [D A...V], as for instance in "these fat cats are," or "some tall students left."

The careful reader will surely have noticed that the substitution methods we have suggested are not formal proofs of, or even foolproof tests for, category membership. They are *heuristics*, tests that build on our intuitions and seem to help us develop formal models, but strictly speaking they are not themselves part of the theory of grammar. They are techniques for building a model that have proven to be useful.

7.2 Syntactic constituents

Let us now consider a string like (7.10).

7.10   *I spotted that rodent with a telescope.*

There are two meanings associated with such a string.[21] One interpretation is that the rodent in question was spotted, in some unspecified manner, but that the rodent is specified as having a telescope—in this case, *with a telescope* tells us something about the rodent, not about the event of spotting. The second meaning could be paraphrased as "Using

---

[21] Actually, there are more: we are taking the verb *spot* in the sense of "see" and leaving aside the meaning "to put spots on."

a telescope, I spotted that rodent." In other words *with a telescope* may be understood as specifying something about the verb that describes the action involved.

Clearly, these two interpretations cannot be distinguished from each other just by using categories like noun, verb, etc., since both interpretations correspond to the same string of such categories, the string in (7.10). The two interpretations can, however, be distinguished by grouping together the categories in this string in two different ways. One crucial difference is indicated in (7.11a.b.).

7.11   a. I_N [spotted$_V$ [that$_D$ rodent$_N$ with$_P$ a$_D$ telescope$_N$]]
        b. I_N [[spotted$_V$ that$_D$ rodent$_N$] with$_P$ a$_D$ telescope$_N$]

The difference between the two consists in whether *with a telescope* is grouped together with *that rodent* (to the exclusion of *spotted*) or not. If it is, as in (7.11a.), then we will say that the string *that rodent with a telescope* makes up a *phrasal category*. Otherwise, if the grouping is as in (7.11b.), then *that rodent* and *with a telescope* are part of separate phrasal categories. Each of the two groupings of the atomic categories N, D, A, and so on, gives rise to a distinct organization into phrasal categories.

The general term that covers both simple and phrasal categories is *constituents*, since categories constitute the structure of the sentence. In (7.11a.) above, the sequence of simple syntactic categories D, N, P, D, N make up a constituent instantiated by *that$_D$ rodent$_N$ with$_P$ a$_D$ telescope$_N$*, whereas in (7.11b.) the sequence *that$_D$ rodent$_N$* makes up a constituent with *spotted$_V$*, rather than with *with$_P$ a$_D$ telescope$_N$*.

A question that might come to mind is "How do we come up with the grouping in (7.11a.b.)?" One answer is that our native speaker intuitions support the grouping of the simple categories involved in the way indicated in (7.11a.b.). Our intuition tells us that the string *that$_D$ rodent$_N$ with$_P$ a$_D$ telescope$_N$* in (7.11a.) has a certain cohesion, acts as group. In addition to this intuition, we can test this cohesion of syntactic constituents in various ways. One test consists of replacing a string of words with certain simple lexical items. If the replacement yields a grammatical result, then the string of words that was replaced is a constituent; if not, it is not a constituent. Under the interpretation in (7.11a.), shown again in (7.12), for example, *that rodent with a telescope* can be replaced by a pronoun like *it*.

7.12   *I spotted [that rodent with a telescope], and Mary spotted [it], too.*
([it]=[that rodent with a telescope])

The pronoun *it* can also replace a sequence of words in (7.11b.), but, crucially, it cannot replace the whole string *that rodent with a telescope* but only part of it, namely *that rodent*.

7.13   *I spotted [that rodent] with a telescope and Mary spotted [it] with a magnifying glass.* ([it]=[that rodent])

Another way of showing the same thing is to look at it from the other end. If a pronoun like *it* shows up in an example like (7.12), where it replaces the sequence *that rodent with a telescope*, then the only possible interpretation for the string *I spotted that rodent with a telescope* is the one in which the rodent had the telescope. If, on the other hand, *it* replaces *that rodent*, to the exclusion of *with a telescope*, as in (7.13), then the only possible interpretation is the one in which the telescope was used as an instrument to spot the rodent.

Turning now to (7.11b.), we can apply the same kind of substitution test to show that *spotted that rodent* makes up a constituent, to the exclusion of *with a telescope*.

7.14   *I [spotted that rodent] with a telescope and Mary [did] with a magnifying glass.* ([did]=[spotted that rodent])

The pro-verb *did* can also replace a sequence of words in (7.11a.), but, crucially, it cannot replace just the string *spotted that rodent*, but only the larger string *spotted that rodent with a telescope*.

7.15   *I [spotted [that rodent with a telescope]] and Mary [did], too.* ([did]=[spotted that rodent with a telescope])

Now let's try to work our way to providing the complete constituency of (7.11a.b.). In order to do that, notice that the phrasal categories that we have identified so far, such as *that rodent with a telescope* and *spotted that rodent with a telescope* in (7.11a.), and *that rodent* and *spotted that rodent* in (7.11b.), are complex not only in the sense that they contain a sequence of simple syntactic categories. Each of these phrasal categories can be broken down into subconstituents that are themselves complex. For example, the constituent *that rodent with a telescope* in (7.11a.) contains a subconstituent *rodent with a telescope* that is itself complex, that is made up of several simple syntactic categories. That *rodent with a telescope* does make up a (sub)constituent can be shown by the fact that this sequence can be replaced by a pronoun like *one*.

7.16
- [*that* [*rodent with a telescope*]]
- [*that* [*one*]]

Moreover, even this subconstituent, *rodent with a telescope*, can be further broken down into its own subconstituents. One such example is the string *with a telescope*, which can be replaced by some other modifying word, such as *there*:

7.17
- [*that* [*rodent* [*with a telescope*]]]
- [*that* [*rodent* [*there*]]]

Finally, the phrase *a telescope* can also be identified as a (sub)constituent, as shown by the fact that it can be replaced by the pronoun *it*:

7.18
- [*that* [*rodent* [*with a telescope*]]]
- [*that* [*rodent* [*with* [*it*]]]]

So, in (7.11a.), *a telescope* is a phrasal category; *with a telescope* is a phrasal category; *rodent with a telescope* is a phrasal category; and *that rodent with a telescope* is a phrasal category.

A sentence is thus made up of simple syntactic categories that contain a single word of the types we have seen, N, V, and so on, and of phrasal categories that are successively embedded within each other. The arrangement of these categories constitutes the structure of the sentence. This structure can be illustrated either by using brackets, as we have been doing, or else by using tree diagrams, as in (7.19) and (7.20). We give you the complete constituency of both sentences (7.11a.b.). The first exercise at the end of the chapter will provide you with more tests that you can use in order to check the constituency of sentences. You can go through this exercise and convince yourself that the grouping we indicate below corresponds to the actual syntactic constituents of our string.

7.19   Tree structure for (7.11a.):
[*I* [*spotted* [*that* [*rodent* [*with* [*a telescope*]]]]]]

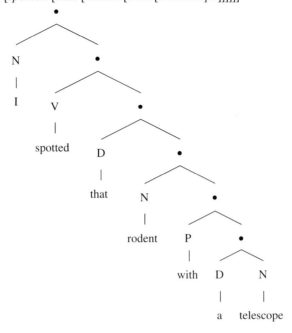

7.20   Tree structure for (7.11b.):
[*I* [*spotted* [*that rodent*]] [*with* [*a telescope*]]]

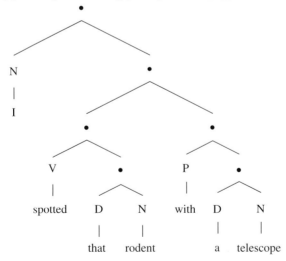

Nodes that are combined to form a higher-level node are called sisters. Notice that each of the nodes in these trees above the level of the word is the result of joining together exactly two constituents. In other words, each node above the word-level terminal nodes is *binary branching*. We assume that this is the case for all trees in all languages. We will not provide a full justification for this position, and we acknowledge that many linguists disagree with it. However, since we suppose the basic operation of syntax to be grouping of two elements to form a constituent, binarity follows automatically.[22]

7.3 Labels and phrasal categories

Now, the nodes in these trees could be labeled. The labeling of each non-terminal node is not random—it inherits the label of one of its components. We call the component that provides the label to the resulting node a *head*. For example, the label of the category resulting from syntactically merging a nominal element like *books* and an adjectival one like *interesting* will have to be either nominal or adjectival, since the two components are a nominal element and an adjectival one. Now let us take a look at the meaning of the phrase *interesting books*—it denotes a type of *books* and not a type of *interesting*, so it is reasonable to assume that the head is the nominal element *books*. The semantic relationship between the head *books* and the non-head *interesting* is one of *modification*: we say that *interesting* is a modifier of *books*. Semantically, the modification relation in our example is a set-intersection relation: if we assume that *books* denotes the set of all books and *interesting* denotes the set of all interesting entities, we may say that the denotation of *interesting books* is the intersection of the set of books and the set of interesting entities. In other words, *interesting books* denotes a subset of the set of books, namely the subset of books that also have the property of being interesting.[23]

---

[22] Trees are binary, not because there is a rule of Universal Grammar that says they must be, but because of the nature of the basic operation that constructs trees, known as *Merge* in current syntactic theory. In many cases, there is clear evidence that trees are binary-branching; in other cases, there is not clear evidence for say, binarity versus ternary (three-way) branching. We assume that the more elegant model adopts the position that all trees are consistently binary, since the number of branches is actually a consequence of how they are constructed.

[23] The modification relation between an adjective and a noun is not always set inter-section. An example of a non-intersective adjective is *fake* as in *fake gun*.

Categories other than adjectives can also serve as modifiers. Some mod-ifiers are prepositional, for example, as in *books on the table*. On the other hand, not all modified categories are nouns. Verbal expressions can also be modified, as in *run with a duck*, or *run fast*.

Apart from its semantics, there are other ways of identifying the head of a construction. Morphologically, the features of the phrase are inherited from the head. For instance, the phrase *books on the table* is plural, just as its head noun *books*, and unlike *table*. Syntactically, a phrase always has the same distribution as its head. In our example, *interesting books* has the same distribution as *books*, not as *interesting*.

7.21
- He has many [interesting books].
- He has many [books].
- *He has many [interesting].

The modification relation is not the only relation that a head might have with the non-head. Another possible relation is a selection relation: apart from being modified by a phrase, the head can select for a certain phrase. A verb like *gather*, for instance, must be accompanied by a noun, as in *gather peanuts*. If this noun is missing, the result is ungrammatical, as in **Peter gathered*.[24] When an element, like *gather*, requires another element, like *peanuts*, we say that the former selects for the latter. So, it appears that the verb *gather* selects for the noun *peanuts*. Notice that this is completely different from the semantic relation between a head and a modifier; the modifier can be missing, and the phrase without the modifier would still be well formed.

Now, as they stand, the two phrases—*interesting books* and *gather peanuts*—seem to be built out of simple lexical, word-like categories, as in the following diagrams. These diagrams indicate not only the internal constituency of our phrases, but also the fact that *interesting books* is syntac-tically more complex than the simple noun *books*, and that *gather peanuts* is syntactically more complex than *gather*. This is captured by assigning a phrasal label to the resulting node: *XP*, rather than a simple terminal node *X* (with *P* for "Phrase"). The term X here is a variable ranging over the set of primitive categories, so there are NPs, VPs, and so on.

---

[24] We set aside the so-called "collective" use of *gather*, as in *The family gathered in New York each winter*.

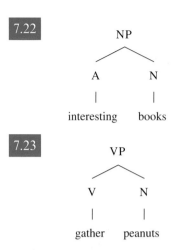

7.22

NP

A   N

interesting   books

7.23

VP

V   N

gather   peanuts

These diagrams are not entirely accurate, however. Notice that the simple noun *peanuts* in *gather peanuts* could be replaced with a more complex syntactic object, like *blue peanuts*, and the replacement would not disturb the relation with the verbal head *gather*—*gather* would still be the head and *blue peanuts* would be the selected syntactic phrase. Crucially, *blue peanuts* is of the same nature as *peanuts*—they are both nominal. In order to capture both possibilities, we might say that the head *gather* always takes a noun phrase as a complement, and that this noun phrase could be instantiated either by a complex phrase, like *blue peanuts* or by a simple lexical item like *peanuts*. In other words, the simple noun *peanuts* is just a particular case of a more general pattern, which is indicated in the diagram below.

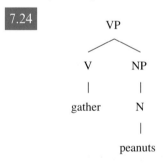

7.24

VP

V   NP

gather   N

peanuts

Likewise, in *interesting books*, *interesting* could be replaced with a more complex phrase like *very interesting*, and the simple noun *books* could be replaced with a more complex phrase, like *books on linguistics*. The relation between the two components would still be one of modification: *very interesting* would still be a modifier of *books on linguistics*. In order to capture both possibilities, we might say, as in the case of *gather peanuts* above, that *interesting books* is just a particular case of a more general pattern, the one given below.

7.25

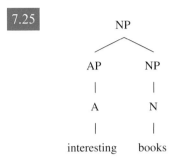

With this in mind, let us now look again at the trees above for the two interpretations of our rodent example, but this time let's label the nodes that show up in the tree. Let's begin with the first interpretation, that is, the one under which the rodent has the telescope.

7.26

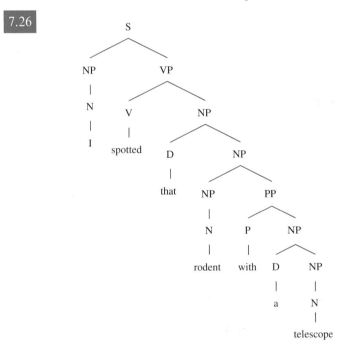

A first observation is that the labels we used are somewhat simplified. For instance, we assumed that the result of merging together a determiner and a noun is a nominal phrasal category—a NP, and therefore that the head is the noun rather than the D. In this, we glossed over an important distinction between functional categories, like determiners, and lexical categories, like nouns and verbs. Our aim here is not to provide you with the latest syntactic model for analyzing the structure of sentences but to convince you that sentences do have a structure, and that the building blocks of this structure are syntactic constituents.

Let us go through the labeling in this tree from the bottom up. The label of the node immediately dominating the P *with* and the NP *a telescope* is a PP. In other words, we assumed that the head is the preposition *with*. The relevant subtree is given below.

7.27

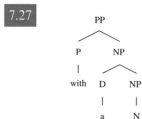

A preposition expresses a relation—in our rodent example a relation either between the N *rodent* and the NP *a telescope* or between the V *spotted* and the NP *a telescope*. By choosing the P as the head, rather than the NP, we capture the fact that it is the P that establishes the relation in question. The arguments of the relation depend on the P head.

Going on with the labels we used in (7.26), notice first that we grouped together the noun *rodent* and the PP *with a telescope*, and only then did we put together the resulting constituent with the determiner *that*. This is supported by the fact that we can replace the whole string *rodent with a telescope* with a word like *one*. This indicates that *rodent with a telescope* makes up a phrasal category to the exclusion of *that*. Moreover, our representation assigns to *rodent* the label NP. In fact, what (7.26) says is that *rodent* is a N, which in turn is a possible way in which NPs can be analyzed. In order to see why we analyze *rodent* as a NP, compare the following two strings:

7.28   a. that rodent with a telescope
        b. that inquisitive rodent with a telescope

It is clear from these examples that the simple noun *rodent* could be replaced with a phrase, something like *inquisitive rodent*. This points to the fact that the simple noun *rodent* is just one of the possible instantiations of a noun phrase. This is why the structure we proposed in (7.26) contains a NP label that dominates an N label.

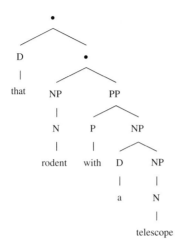

Now, we indicated in (7.26) that the label of the constituent formed by joining together the NP *rodent* and the PP *with a telescope* is nominal—a NP. This is because our familiar semantic and distributional tests clearly point to this conclusion. Semantically, *rodent with a telescope* is a type of rodent and not a type of telescope or a type of *with*-ness, and, distributionally, *rodent with a telescope* occurs in the same environments as *rodent*.

   a. [A rodent with a telescope] is all we need in this house.
   b. [A rodent] is all we need in this house.

Moving on upwards to higher nodes in (7.26), the NP *that rodent with a telescope* is joined together with the verb *spotted*. We assumed that the verb is the head that selects a NP as a complement. To show that it is the verb that is the head of the newly created phrase *spotted that rodent with a telescope*, consider the fact that this whole phrase can be replaced by a simple verb like *did* in (7.15), and therefore that it has the same distribution as a verb. The phrase that results from joining together the verb *spotted* and the NP *that rodent with a telescope* is thus a VP, as indicated in (7.31).

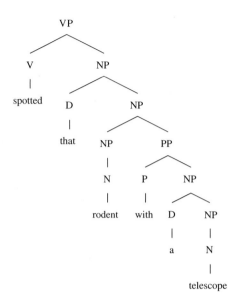

Finally, the highest node is the sentential node S, which is the result of joining together the VP *spotted that rodent with a telescope* and the NP *I*. Regardless of whether the relation between the two phrases that combine is one of modification or of selection, the principle we have adopted so far is that the resulting node should inherit the category of one of the two subconstituents: either N or V. However, labeling the resulting node as S is obviously inconsistent with this principle. This inconsistency is unavoidable given the incompleteness of our presentation and its resolution would require a discussion of so-called *functional categories*, something that we will not address in this book. For our purposes it is sufficient to note that a sentence S has two immediate syntactic constituents: a NP—the subject of the sentence, and a VP—the predicate. You should bear in mind, though, that the example under discussion illustrates only one possible instantiation of the two major constituents of a sentence. It turns out that the subject of a sentence can be any phrasal category, not just a NP. It is true that in most cases the subject of a sentence is a NP, just as in our example. However, the subject of a sentence can also be a prepositional phrase, as in (7.32a.), an adjectival phrase, as in (7.32b.), or even another sentence, as in (7.32c.).

7.32   a. [Under the table] is Oonagh's favorite place.
        b. [Fortunate] is what we consider ourselves to be.
        c. [That Davey always talks about Sami] is something we all got used to.

Likewise, the predicate can be something more complex than a VP, such as an auxiliary phrase. We'll come back with more details about auxiliary phrases in the next section.

Both readings of (7.10) correspond to a simple sentence. Sometimes, however, one can put two or more sentences together as in (7.33) and build a complex sentence. One example is in (7.32c.). Other examples are provided below:

7.33   a. Mary thought [I spotted that rodent with a telescope].
             b. I believe [Mary thought [I spotted that rodent with a telescope]].
             c. I scorn the man [who thought [I spotted that rodent with a telescope]].

In (7.33a.) our initial sentence *I spotted that rodent with a telescope* is selected as a complement by the verb *thought*. The verb *thought* together with *I spotted that rodent with a telescope* make up a VP which in turn combines with a subject NP *Mary*.

Furthermore, in (7.33b.) this resulting sentence—*Mary thought I spotted a rodent with a telescope*—is itself selected as a complement by the verb *believe*. The resulting VP—*believe Mary thought I spotted that rodent with a telescope*—combines with the NP *I*, and a new sentence is formed. Thus, (7.33b.) contains three sentences: the all-encompassing one—*I believe Mary thought I spotted that rodent with a telescope*; another one which is a sub-component of it—*Mary thought I spotted that rodent with a telescope*; and a third one which is a subcomponent of the latter, namely *I spotted that rodent with a telescope*.

Example (7.33c.) contains again the sentence *I spotted that rodent with a telescope* which is selected by the verb *think*, but it also contains a sentence—*who thought I spotted that rodent with a telescope*, that is not selected by any head. This sentence is immediately related to the noun *man*, and its relation to the latter is one of modification. The meaning of (7.33c.) is that the object of my scorn is an individual who has both the property of being a man and the property of being someone who thought I spotted that rodent with a telescope.

We will call sentences like *I spotted that rodent with a telescope*, and *who thought I spotted that rodent with a telescope*, that occur as part of a larger sentence, as in (7.33), *embedded sentences* or *embedded clauses*. Non-embedded sentences are called *main sentences* or *main clauses*. We will return to the notion of embedded clause in the next chapter.

Let us now focus on the tree of (7.11b.), which represents the reading in which *with a telescope* indicates the instrument of spotting.

7.34

```
                                S
              ┌─────────────────┴─────────────────┐
             NP                                   VP
              │                      ┌────────────┴────────────┐
              N                     VP                         PP
              │              ┌──────┴──────┐           ┌───────┴───────┐
              I              V            NP           P              NP
                            │         ┌───┴───┐        │          ┌────┴────┐
                         spotted      D       N      with         D        NP
                                      │       │                   │         │
                                    that    rodent               a         N
                                                                           │
                                                                        telescope
```

We labeled the constituent resulting from merging the verb *spotted* and the nominal constituent *that rodent* as VP. In other words, we assumed that the head is the verb.

7.35

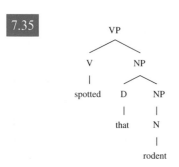

This assumption can be justified both on semantic grounds and with distributional arguments. Semantically, *spotted that rodent* denotes a particular type of event that is a subclass of the event denoted by the verb *spotted*. In other words, spotting a rodent is a type of spotting event, rather than a type of rodent. Distributionally, *spotted that rodent* can be substitued with a simple verb like *did*, for instance.

7.36   I [spotted that rodent] with a telescope, and Mary [did] with a magnifying glass.

Moving on, we assumed that the result of joining together the VP *spotted that rodent* and the PP *with a telescope* is a verbal constituent.

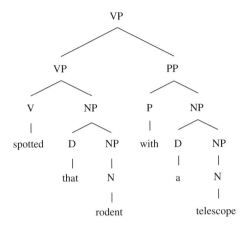

Semantically, *spotting a rodent with a telescope* is a specific type of *spotting a rodent* event. Distributionally, *spotted that rodent with a telescope* occurs in the same contexts as *spotted that rodent*.

7.38   a. I spotted that rodent with a telescope.
        b. I spotted that rodent.

The highest label in (7.34) should make sense by now, as we have already justified it for (7.26). See the exercise at the end of the chapter for more practice.

Let us wrap up this discussion. Sentences are not just strings of words. What is crucial for a string of words to be a sentence is structure. The structure is actually a reflection of how words are grouped together into constituents. One way of representing a sentence is in the form of the tree diagram. Each node in the tree is a constituent. The identity of a node is provided not only by its label, since there can be several VPs or NPs in the same sentence, for instance. Clearly, the two instances of VPs or NPs are different from each other. Apart from the label, which provides information about the nature of that node, the hierarchical position of the respective node is also important for identifying a particular constituent. The constituent *a telescope*, for example, is the NP which is sister to the preposition *with*, whereas *that rodent with a telescope* is the NP which is sister to the verb *spotted*. The hierarchical position of nodes will turn out to be crucial in the next chapter.

Given our new understanding of what a sentence is, it is now clear that in everyday speech, we might say "The sentence *I spotted that rodent with a telescope* is ambiguous," but, as linguists, we would say the following: "The string *I spotted that rodent with a telescope* corresponds to two sentences" since a sentence is a string of words with a particular arrangement of elements, a structure among the words.

7.4 Predicting syntactic patterns

You are probably still skeptical about the utility of drawing these trees, the utility of thinking of sentences as structures. You might just be saying to yourself "What's the big deal? Strings of words like *I spotted that rodent with a telescope* have two meanings, and I just figure them out because they both make sense. Why do I need all this complicated syntactic structure to understand something about meaning?"

Even with these simple examples, we can demonstrate the usefulness of syntactic structure—we'll give more complex applications later. One motivation for positing structure as part of the representation of a sentence is that, as we saw in the previous chapter, a notion of structure is required to make predictions about the grammaticality or ungrammaticality of strings. Remember that we needed to refer to a unit of structure—the sentence—in order to understand when the contracted form of the copula could appear. In order to further illustrate this point, consider the string *The fish will hit the chicken with the belt*. This string is made up of several simple syntactic categories, like D, N, V, P, some of which occur several times. This string also contains a category that we haven't yet introduced: the auxiliary (Aux). Auxiliary verbs like *might, will, can, have, be* precede lexical verbs like *hit* or *smile*.

7.39   The$_D$ fish$_N$ will$_{Aux}$ hit$_V$ the$_D$ chicken$_N$ with$_P$ the$_D$ belt$_N$

In fact, the relation between the auxiliary and the lexical verb is more than just simple precedence; the auxiliary *selects* a lexical verb of a particular form. To convince yourself of this, think of examples like *Peter has broken the ice* or *Peter will break the ice*, where it is clear that the morphological form of the lexical verb—*broken* versus *break*—is dictated by the choice of the auxiliary. An auxiliary like *has* selects a past participle form like *broken*, whereas *will* selects the short infinitive form *break*. Given that the auxiliary is the item that selects and that the lexical verb is selected, we will assume that the auxiliary is a head and that the verb is part of the VP complement selected by the auxiliary.[25] In other words, our string contains a verb phrase *hit the chicken with the belt* headed by the lexical verb *hit* and an auxiliary phrase *will hit the chicken with the belt* headed by the auxiliary *will*. This is represented in (7.40), with the triangle representing structure that we are not yet specifying, apart from the claim there is a node that contains exactly everything under the triangle—the VP is a constituent.

7.40

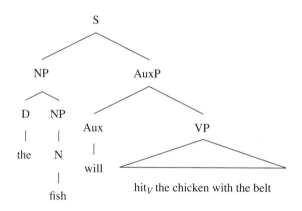

There are, of course, several other phrasal categories in this string, such as the noun phrases *the fish*, and *the chicken with the belt*, and *the belt*, and the prepositional phrase *with the belt*.

Let's focus on this PP *with the belt*. The head of the PP is the preposition *with*, while *the belt* is its (non-head) sister. The relation between the two is one of selection: the P head *with* selects a NP that in this case is instantiated by *the belt*. What this means is that if there is no NP following the preposition *with* the result is ungrammatical, as in (7.41).

7.41   *The fish will hit the chicken with.*

You might have noticed that the string *The fish will hit the chicken with the belt* can have two interpretations: one in which the belt is an instrument with which the fish hit the chicken and one in which the belt is a fashion accessory of the chicken.[26] Crucially, the prepositional phrase *with the belt*

---

[25] These assumptions can be justified, but it would take us too far afield to do so here.

[26] The two readings are exactly parallel to those of the *rodent* sentences in the previous section—we just want to give you some practice in abstracting away from particular lexical items.

is a constituent under both interpretations. In fact, the difference between the two is whether the prepositional phrase *with a belt* is grouped together in a larger constituent with *the chicken* or not. The two ways of grouping the simple syntactic categories into phrasal categories that correspond to the two interpretations are given below:

7.42
    a. The$_D$ fish$_N$ [will $_{Aux}$[hit$_V$ [the$_D$ chicken$_N$ [with$_P$ the$_D$ belt$_N$]]]]
    b. The$_D$ fish$_N$ [will $_{Aux}$ [[hit$_V$ the$_D$ chicken$_N$] [with$_P$ the$_D$ belt$_N$]]]

Now suppose we ask the following question:

7.43
    What will the fish hit the chicken with?

Note that this can only be a question about what hitting utensil was used, not about what was holding up the pants of the chicken who got hit. In other words, this question can only correspond to the grouping in (7.42b.), and not to the one in (7.42a.). Notice there is nothing wrong with the other meaning—we can express it by saying something like one of the following:

7.44
    Asking about the chicken
    a. *The fish will hit the chicken with what?*
    b. *What was the chicken that the fish will hit wearing?*
    c. *For what x is it the case that the fish will hit the chicken and the chicken was with x?*

The problem is just that the question in (7.43) cannot be interpreted as paralleling any of these questions in (7.44). One striking difference between questions (7.43) and (7.44a.) is the position of *what*. In (7.43) it is at the beginning of the sentence, whereas in (7.44a.) it is at the end. However, in both instances, *what* is interpreted as the noun phrase selected by the preposition *with*. In both cases, *what* replaces a NP constituent—*a belt* in (7.42a.b.), which is a sister of the preposition *with*. Clearly, the preposition *with* is the same in both (7.43) and (7.44a.). More specifically, in both (7.43) and (7.44a.) the preposition *with* selects a noun phrase that must follow the preposition. In (7.44a.) this noun phrase is where we expect it to be—it follows the preposition. However, in (7.43), the noun phrase selected by the preposition *with* does not show up in the expected place but at the beginning of the sentence.

How can we relate these two facts? On the one hand, *what* is selected by the preposition *with* and thus should be next to the preposition, and on the other hand, *what* occurs at the beginning of the sentence in spite of the fact that it is interpreted as the noun phrase selected by the preposition *with*.

We will assume that *what* in (7.43) occupies both positions at the same time, that there is a copy of *what* in each position. We will refer to these two positions as the base position and the derived position. We will assume that the base position of *what* is the position where we would expect *what* to be by virtue of the fact that it is selected by the preposition *with*—namely right next to the preposition. The other position—the one at the front of the sentence—will be assumed to be a derived position, in the sense that we will consider that the copy that shows up there is the result of what is called a movement or dislocation operation. Thus, *what* originates in its base position, as a sister to the preposition and then it "moves" to a derived position, at the left edge of the sentence. This particular process of putting question words in the front of the sentence is called *wh*-movement since it affects words like *who, what, when, where, why*. The process is also called *wh*-movement when referring to questions beginning with *how*, and linguists even refer to the process as *wh*-movement when talking about other languages where the question words do not begin with *wh*. *Wh*-movement is a very common process in the languages of the world, maybe even common to all languages in some sense.

There are processes that move other constituents in addition to *wh*-words. For example, you might have noticed that in order to ask a *wh*-question in English, there are two constituents that must move: the *wh* and the auxiliary. We will come back to auxiliary movement at the end of this section.

Let us now go back to (7.43). Remember that (7.43) can only be a question about what hitting utensil was used, not about what was holding up the pants of the chicken who got hit.

Why should this be? One way of describing these facts is to say that movement of *what* correlates with a particular interpretation. Alternatively, we may say that movement is impossible if what we want is the second interpretation.

Notice that, in general, there is no restriction on how far a word like *what* can be displaced to get to the beginning of the sentence. We have added an index on the *what* and inserted a copy of *what* in the base position to show where the *what* must be interpreted, as the object of the preposition *with*. The strikethrough indicates that this copy is not pronounced.

| 7.45 | What$_i$ will the fish who kissed the rat who bit the kitty who licked the turtle who scratched the pony's eyes out hit the chicken with ~~what$_i$~~? |

So why can the *what* in (7.45) move so far to the front of the sentence, but it cannot do so to form a question from (7.43) corresponding to the meanings expressed in (7.44)?

Instead of answering this question, we'll give you another case of the impossibility of asking a question by putting *what* or *who* at the beginning of a sentence.

| 7.46 | Two simple sentences |

    a. *You will see John.*
    b. *You will see Bill and John.*

Note that a *wh*-question in which the *wh*-item corresponds to *John* is grammatical only for (7.46a.), but not (7.46b).

| 7.47 | Only one *wh*-question possible |

    a. *Who will you see?*
    b. **Who will you see Bill and?*

Despite the fact that we find it trivial to assign an interpretation to (7.47b.), we have clear judgments that it is ill formed. (In fact, this example again illustrates Chomsky's point from *Syntactic Structures* about the independence of meaning and syntax.) Why should this be? Since the meaning is fairly easy, the reason for the ungrammaticality cannot have anything to do with the fact that we use language for communication.

More surprising, perhaps, is the fact that this conclusion about *wh*-questions does not appear to be a fact only about English—it seems to be a fact about all languages, and, thus, it appears to reflect in some way a fundamental property of the human language faculty. We won't worry about how to formalize this in more general terms, but note that we need to refer to our abstract structures and equivalence classes just to formulate the issue.

How does this relate to our previous sentences about a fish hitting a chicken? Well, recall that we could not front a *wh*-element that was inside a PP that modified the object noun, in other words something like the following structure does not allow *wh*-elements to be fronted:

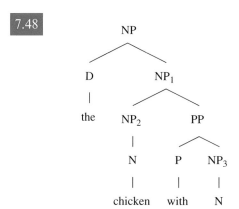

7.48

The tree in (7.48) shows the case where the PP *with what* is inside of NP₁ headed by *chicken*. We can ask a so-called *echo question* with this structure, like (7.44a.), leaving *what* in place, but we cannot move it to the front.

At this point, the generalization can be stated in fairly simple terms. It appears to be the case that *wh*-words like *what* and *who* cannot be moved to the front of the sentence when the position where they are interpreted falls inside of another noun phrase. In (7.48), we see that *what* is NP_3, which is inside the PP, which is inside of NP_1. NP_3 thus is inside of NP_1.

A phrase like *Bill and John* or *Bill and who* is a NP that itself contains two NPs—one is *Bill* and the other is *John* or *who*.[27] For reasons not relevant to our point here, we do not want to present the internal structure of the top level NPs, and so we adopt again the standard convention of abbreviating structure with a triangle. In other words, everything under the triangle belongs to the same constituent, but we are not making any claims about the internal structure and subconstituents, other than the fact that *Bill* and *John* and *who* are also NPs.

7.49

---

[27] The reason why we assume that *Bill* and *John* are NPs, rather than Ns should be obvious by now. It is true that *Bill* and *John* are simple nouns, but clearly each of them could be replaced, in the same construction, by a more complex nominal phrase, as for instance in *the teacher and the student*.

Again we see that the *wh*-element is a NP inside another NP, and that seems to make it impossible to place it at the front of the sentence. It appears to be the case this kind of constraint on *wh*-questions holds in all languages. This appears to be a constraint on the kind of computations that the human language faculty is capable of. *People* can pronounce strings like **Who did you see Bill and?*, but *grammars* do not generate structures corresponding to these strings—they are not sentences.

The most important point that we want to make, however, is only partly related to the universality of such constraints. The other part is that such constraints can only be understood—in fact they can only be stated—in relation to the structure that we assign to strings. This dependency on the structure transcends meaning and interpretation: it is not simply the case that we assign two interpretations to a string and that those two interpretations can be related to two different structures. Even though it is clear that the two interpretations of a string like *I spotted that rodent with a telescope* or *The fish hit the chicken with the belt* can each be related to two different structures, one can make the claim that this relation between meaning and structure is not a necessary one. After all, we haven't shown that the meaning and structure must be related, but we have made only the weaker point, that they *can* be related. On the other hand, the discussion above about the restrictions on *wh*-movement makes a stronger point: certain patterns can only be understood by appeal to models of syntactic structure.

We have discussed the movement possibilities for the equivalence class of *wh*-elements, a category that appears to be present in all languages. However, English *wh*-questions involve an additional instance of movement, apart from the movement of the *wh*-constituent. There is also movement of the auxiliary—copies appear in two positions. The auxiliary occupies a position immediately preceding the verb in *The fish will hit the chicken with the belt*, and we assume that this is the base position. However, in *What will the fish hit the chicken with?*, the auxiliary is separated from the verb by the subject *the fish*, and we will assume that the auxiliary undergoes movement. Its base position is in between the subject and the lexical verb, as in (7.40), whereas its derived position is in front of the subject *the fish*. So, both the auxiliary and the *wh*-element are pronounced in a derived position before the subject. Furthermore, the relative position of the auxiliary with respect to the *wh*-constituent is also important. Thus, (7.50a.), in which the *wh*-constituent precedes the auxiliary, is grammatical, but (7.50b.), in which the *wh*-constituent follows the auxiliary, is ungrammatical.

a. What will the fish ~~will~~ hit the chicken with ~~what~~?
b. *Will what the fish ~~will~~ hit the chicken with ~~what~~?

This suggests that the derived positions for both *wh-* and auxiliary-movement are not just "anywhere in front of the subject," but such that the dislocated *wh-*constituent precedes the dislocated auxiliary. We won't provide the arguments here, but it turns out that what is relevant is not simply precedence but a hierarchical relation called c-command, defined in Section 8.2—the dislocated *wh-*constituent must c-command the dislocated auxiliary. The structure we propose is that in (7.51). We have labeled the node resulting from joining together the moved copy of the auxiliary with the S node as S′ in order to capture the fact that the resulting phrase is still sentential, but nevertheless different from the S node that does not contain any fronted constituents.

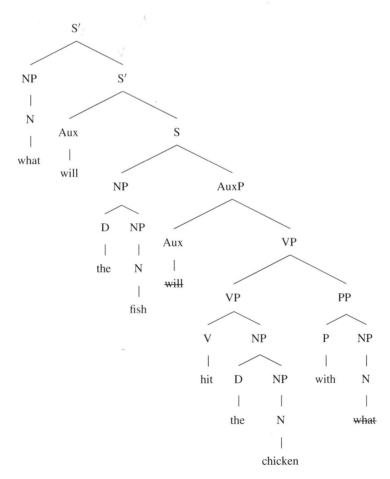

Looking at the tree in (7.51), you may have the intuition that the *wh*-word ends up in a higher position than the Aux. Similarly, the derived position of each moved item seems to be higher than its base position. The definition of c-command developed in the next chapter formalizes this notion of "higher in the tree," a fundamental component of structure dependence in syntax.

There is a third structure-dependent aspect to these examples, this one relevant to the properties of the base position of a moved item. We have already seen that there are certain restrictions on the kind of environment from which a *wh*-constituent can be moved. We have shown that a *wh*-constituent like *what* cannot be moved from inside a NP like *the chicken with what* or *Bill and who*. Before we proceed to show a similar constraint on the base position of Aux movement, we need to demonstrate that this process is independent of *wh*-movement. The examples in (7.52) show this:

> 7.52   a. The fish will hit the chicken with the belt.
> b. What will the fish ~~will~~ hit the chicken with ~~what~~?
> c. Will the fish ~~will~~ hit the chicken with the belt?
> d. I wonder who the chicken will hit ~~who~~.

Example (7.52b.) has both kinds of movement, but you can get Aux movement without *wh*-movement, as in (7.52c.); and you can also get *wh*-movement without Aux movement, as in (7.52d.).

We can now return to the structural constraint on the base position of Aux movement. It turns out that only the Aux of the highest level S is fronted in questions. Movement of an auxiliary to the front of a main S is impossible if that Aux is embedded under another S. Consider the following:

> 7.53   The boy who can dance will kiss the dog that should whine.

What Yes/No sentence corresponds to this sentence? Which of the three auxiliaries gets copied to the front of the sentence? Here are the options.

> 7.54   Which Aux gets fronted?
> a. *Can the boy who ~~can~~ dance will kiss the dog that should whine?
> b. Will the boy who can dance ~~will~~ kiss the dog that should whine?
> c. *Should the boy who can dance will kiss the dog that ~~should~~ whine.

Only (7.54b.) is grammatical. The reason is apparent if we look at the (abbreviated) tree for (7.53), which shows the base positions of all the auxiliaries in (7.54b.).

7.55   Tree for (7.53)

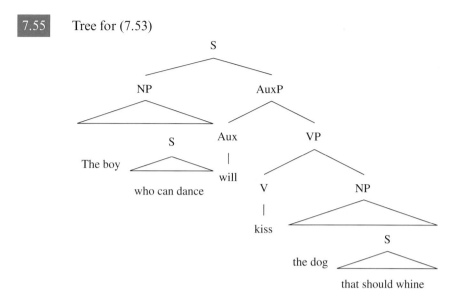

Of the three auxiliaries, only *will* is not contained in an additional S, other than the main S. So, *will* can move to form a question.

7.56   Tree for (7.54b.)

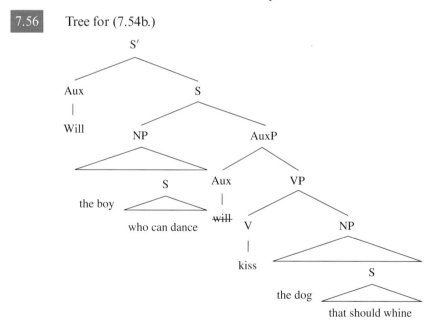

You can confirm for yourself that this result generalizes—it is always the Aux of the main S that is fronted to make a question. In this case, it happens to be the second Aux in declarative sentences, but linear position is not relevant. You will be asked to demonstrate this in an exercise.

To sum up, there are restrictions both on the base position and on the derived position for the movement of the auxiliary. These restrictions concern the hierarchical position of these elements—movement of the auxiliary is structure-dependent.

We are now in a position to further discuss one of the puzzles we mentioned in Chapter 3—the one concerning Yes/No questions. When we introduced this puzzle, we pointed out that in spite of the fact that English speakers have no problem generating grammatical Yes/No questions when given a declarative, they typically cannot formulate the rule for doing so. Without having any *conscious* knowledge of what an Aux is or what a syntactic tree looks like, every English speaker can quickly generate a question when prompted with a declarative sentence.

In contrast, it is trivially simple to state a rule for reversing the order of words in terms that the average person will understand, and, yet, when prompted with a sentence, it is impossible for people to quickly reply with the string of words in reverse order—they need time, and perhaps a pencil and paper. Why is there such a discrepancy in performance of these tasks?

The grammar itself does not form questions from declarative sentences, but it appears that people can use their grammar to construct sentences that meet certain explicitly provided criteria, like "Give the question corresponding to this statement." We can harness the computations of the grammar, which are fast and inaccessible to consciousness, to perform this task. We do not have any such system for reversing words, and so we have to perform the string reversal task consciously and methodically, thus slowly.

7.5 Using trees to predict reaction times

If you like laboratory procedures and statistics, you will be pleased to learn that the syntactic structures we have been positing can also be used to make testable predictions in a laboratory setting. If sentences were just strings of words, then we would expect that the time it takes to recognize a written sentence would be a function of its length and the words it contains—it takes longer to process more words than fewer, and common words are typically recognized faster than less common words.

It turns out, however, that sentence structure, as modeled by our trees, is an important factor in the time it takes speakers to recognize a sentence as well formed. The following sentences are about the same length and they use most of the same words:

7.57   a. *The rat the cat the dog worried chased ate the malt*
         b. *The dog worried the cat and the rat ate the malt*

You may have a hard time realizing that sentence (7.57a.) is even grammatical. It is easier to grasp the structure if you realize that it is basically the same as this:

7.58   *The rat that the cat that the dog worried chased ate the malt*

There is a dog that worried a cat, and that cat chased a rat, and that is the rat that ate the malt. Sentence (7.57a.) would be assigned a structure like this:

7.59   Structure with a lot of embedding

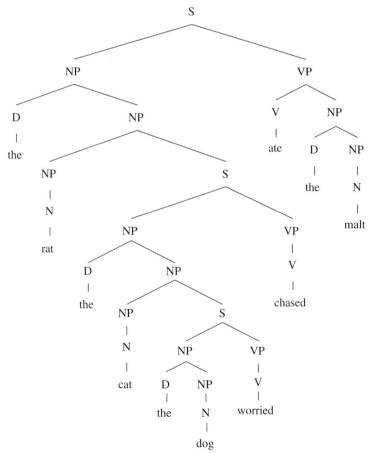

What this structure shows is first of all that the main VP of the sentence is *ate the malt*. This is captured by the fact that the top S node splits into a NP, the subject of the sentence, and a VP.[28] This VP *ate the malt* which is sister of the subject NP is called the main predicate of the sentence. Now, the subject is rather complex syntactically. First, the NP subject node splits into a determiner and a NP. This NP contains two nodes: a NP and a S. One of them must be the head and the other one the non-head. Given that it is the NP *rat* that provides its label to the higher node, it must be that the NP *rat* is the head. The sister of this NP node is obviously a modifier of the NP *rat*. In other words, the subject of this sentence is not just any rat but one that has the property expressed by this modifier—the property of having been chased by some entity. Notice now that this latter entity itself is expressed by a rather complex syntactic phrase. The NP denoting this entity again expresses a modification relation—the head is a NP—*cat*—that has the property expressed by the S modifier, namely the property of having been worried by the dog. In contrast, sentence (7.57b.) has less complex structure:[29]

7.60   Structure with less embedding

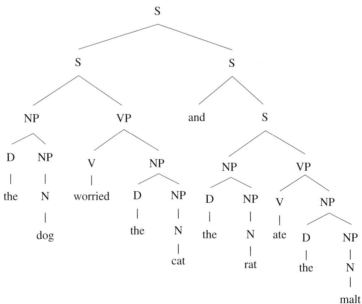

[28] We will be forced to complicate this below with the introduction of auxiliary verbs in Chapter 10.

[29] We are not going to justify this structure for conjoined sentences here.

You can tell that sentence (7.57a.) has a much deeper level of embedding than sentence (7.57b.). Sentence (7.57a.) has a NP subject that contains two successively embedded modifiers. Both of these modifiers are expressed syntactically by a S node. The most deeply embedded S is a modifier of the noun *cat*, whereas the next, higher embedded S is a modifier of the noun *rat*. Moreover the S modifying *cat* is embedded within the S modifying *rat*, which is itself embedded under the main sentence. When we ask subjects to read strings of words and press a button if the string corresponds to a grammatical sentence, we find that sentences with more embedding require a longer response time than those with less embedding. So a sentence like (7.57a.) would require more time than a sentence like (7.57b.) in such a task.

Thus, the syntactic structures that we represent in tree diagrams have the same status as any other scientific models—they give us insight into phenomena and can be used to make experimental predictions that can be replicated.

7.6 To sum up

If you remain skeptical about the "reality" of these trees, the validity of positing them, consider the following points:

- These abstract derivations can only be stated in terms of abstract trees, which in turn are abstract structures described in terms of relations among words. However, as we saw, even the notion of word is an abstraction, one that has no consistent physical correlates.
- If we reject derivations we fail to account for very strong intuitions and patterns such as the fact that the verbs in *Pat broke the door* and *What did Pat break?* are the same verb. In one sentence the verb is followed by an object and in the other it is not, yet it seems extremely uninsightful to consider them as two different verbs.
- Like the components of any scientific model, trees and derivations give us insight into observed data and allow us to make predictions in replicable experiments. One can be a methodological dualist by stipulation—deny the reality of cognitive phenomena—but there does not seem to be any good reason to do so, since the models of physics

and chemistry, say, have exactly the same status as those of linguistics—they afford us an understanding of phenomena in ways that can be made mathematically explicit.

- There are no competing explanations of *wh*-movement or the distribution of the reduced copula that even come close to the account provided using syntactic structure. Many questions remain, but scientific explanations are always incomplete and open to improvement.

In the following chapters, one of our goals will be to apply our model of syntactic structure to explain some very puzzling patterns of English syntax.

7.7 Exercises

Exercise 7.7.1. Tree Practice: For more practice of how words are grouped together into constituents, and for the labeling of these constituents, consider the following string.

7.61   *The fish with the hat hit the chicken with the belt.*

Draw the tree for the meaning in which the chicken's pants won't fall down. What is *with a belt* modifying? What does this PP attach to? What does *with a hat* modify? What does this PP attach to?

Now draw the tree for the reading in which the fish uses a fashion accessory as a chicken-hitting implement. How does this tree differ from the previous one?

Exercise 7.7.2. Aux movement: In the tree in (7.55) there are three distinct auxiliaries, and it is the one whose base position is second that is fronted.

i. Give a Yes/No question which also contains three auxiliaries, but in which the Aux whose base position is first undergoes Aux movement. Draw the tree showing base and derived positions.

ii. Give another Yes/No question in which the Aux whose base position is last of the three is fronted. Draw the tree showing base and derived positions.

iii. Without drawing a tree, give a Yes/No question in which there are nine auxiliaries (you can reuse them—for example, you can use *should* more than once) and the one that is moved is the seventh in base position.

iv. What do these examples tell us about linear order and structure?

Further Reading

- The chapters on syntax by H. Lasnik (The Forms of Sentences) and sentence processing by J. D. Fodor (Comprehending Sentence Structure) in Osherson (1995) complement the discussion in this chapter.

8

Binding

This chapter is concerned with one of the puzzles introduced in Chapter 3 concerning the distribution of reflexives, also called anaphors, like *himself* and *herself*, as opposed to regular pronouns like *he, him, she*, and *her*. We will be studying a fairly narrow range of data and ignoring some difficult issues,[30] but the analysis will be challenging, nonetheless. One point that will hopefully come through by the end of the chapter is an old one—the distribution of these items is structure-dependent. In other words, the generalizations concerning the distribution of reflexives or of regular pronouns can only be expressed by referring to the structure of the clause that contains these items. In addition, we hope that you will be once more intrigued by the complexity of the phenomena underlying the grammar of natural languages, and implicitly by the complexity of your knowledge— your knowledge of language, that is. In a way, what follows, and in fact all of the rules we have described so far, are things you already know. You may

---

[30] For example, we are not interested here in the form that is used for emphasis, as in *Mary, herself, killed the snake*—this is probably a different *herself* from the one we are interested in, since in other languages it is expressed as a completely different word from the reflexive.

be not aware of them, but you know them, since you have absolutely no problem producing and understanding sentences that represent the output of these rules. So let us now tell you what you know about words like *herself* or *himself*, and about words like *her* or *him*.

8.1 Preliminaries

Before we begin, we need to introduce some notational conventions. If we asked you if the string *Mary saw her* corresponds to a grammatical sentence in your dialect of English, you would probably say that it does. However, when you make this decision you clearly have in mind a certain interpretation of the individual words and their relations. For example, if you interpret *saw* not as the past tense of *see* but as a form of the verb *to saw*, then the string cannot be said to correspond to a grammatical sentence. The grammatical string in this case would be *Mary sawed her*, and it would contain the past tense form of the verb *to saw*.

Another condition on your acceptance of *Mary saw her* as grammatical is that you must not interpret *her* as referring to the same individual as *Mary*. One notation for expressing the distinctions we are interested in is the use of indices on nominal expressions. Informally, we will say that two NPs that have the same index "refer to the same individual" and two nominal expressions that bear different indices "refer to different individuals." So the grammatical reading of *Mary saw her* corresponds to something like (8.1).

8.1	Mary$_i$ saw her$_j$

Mary bears the index i and *her* bears the index j, so the two refer to different individuals. In contrast, the ungrammatical reading corresponds to something like (8.2).

8.2	*Mary$_i$ saw her$_i$

This string is marked with an asterisk, which means that the string is ungrammatical under the reading in which *Mary* and *her* refer to the same individual.

For ease of presentation, and in order to save space, it is customary to use an abbreviatory convention to present the contrast between (8.1) and (8.2), as shown in (8.3).

8.3   Mary$_i$ saw her$_{*i/j}$

This means that the string *Mary saw her* corresponds to an ungrammatical sentence if *her* is indexed identically to *Mary*, but it corresponds to a grammatical one if they are indexed differently. Of course, the values of the indices are arbitrary, and what is important are the labeling relations among nominal constituents, NPs. Thus, (8.4) has the same interpretation as (8.3):

8.4   Mary$_j$ saw her$_{i/*j}$

Finally, note that the labeling relations that correspond to grammatical sentences change when we substitute reflexives for regular pronouns:

8.5   Mary$_i$ saw herself$_{i/*j}$

In this case, the string corresponds to a grammatical sentence only if *Mary* and *herself* have the same index.

We hedged a bit above when we said that indices informally are understood to relate to the individuals or entities that nominal expressions refer to. The reason for this is that we want to avoid a slew of issues that arise in situations like the following. Suppose that you and Bob Dylan went into a wax museum on different days and each saw a wax statue labeled "Bob Dylan." Our judgment is that the following strings would both correspond to grammatical sentences expressing true propositions if uttered after these museum visits:

8.6   a. You saw Bob Dylan at the wax museum.
b. Bob Dylan$_i$ saw himself$_i$ at the wax museum.

Clearly Bob Dylan, the museum guest, and the wax statue of Bob Dylan are different entities in the world—one has a digestive system and one does not, for example. So, the indices clearly cannot be denoting identity of objects in the world. For now, all we will say is that the relation between words and things in the world is not simple, and we will avoid dealing with it at this point by devising a theory of pronoun and reflexive distribution that refers just to the indices on nominal expressions. How these relate to objects in the world is not a matter of syntax, although we will have something to say about the issue in a later chapter.

8.2 Anaphors

What we want to do now is to account for the distribution and interpretation of anaphoric (reflexive) pronouns like *herself*. We will then relate our findings to aspects of the model of syntax that we have been developing in previous chapters. The first important requirement that we should keep in mind is that the model we develop should not *overgenerate*—it should not predict the grammaticality of structures that are clearly ungrammatical according to our native speaker judgments. It is equally important that the model also should not *undergenerate*—it should not treat as ungrammatical, or fail to generate, structures that our judgment tells us are perfectly well formed. We don't want our model to be too lax or too strict—we want it to generate all and only the grammatical forms.

Consider first the following strings.

8.7   a. *Mary$_i$ sees herself$_j$.
       b. Mary$_i$ sees herself$_i$.
       c. *Herself$_i$ sees Mary$_i$.

Comparing (8.7a.) and (8.7b.) we might conclude that the right generalization is something like (8.8).

8.8   Hypothesis I: *herself* must appear in a sentence that contains a
        coindexed nominal expression, a phrase bearing the same index
        as *herself*.

This condition is not satisfied in (8.7a.) because *herself* is indexed *j*, but *Mary* is labeled *i*. This explains why (8.7a.) is ungrammatical. In (8.7b.) the two nominal expressions are both indexed *i*, and therefore the condition for the occurrence of *herself* is met, and the sentence is grammatical, as expected. Sentence (8.7c.) however suggests that mere co-occurrence with a coindexed nominal expression is not sufficient—apparently the coindexed expression must precede the reflexive. Such a simple data set may lead you to modify our initial hypothesis concerning the distribution of *herself* in English sentences, along the lines of Hypothesis II.

8.9   Hypothesis II: *herself* must be preceded by a coindexed nominal
        expression, a phrase bearing the same index as *herself*.

You might already suspect that it is unlikely that Hypothesis II would be correct. In previous chapters we have seen a number of syntactic phenomena that are sensitive to the *structure* of a sentence and neither mere co-occurrence nor linear precedence rely on structural notions.

In order to check the validity of Hypothesis II, we should look at more data and see whether Hypothesis II can account for it. Consider (8.10):

 a. *Mary$_i$ knows that Jane$_j$ loves herself$_i$.
b. Mary$_i$ knows that Jane$_j$ loves herself$_j$.

Example (8.10a.) is ungrammatical even though, as required by Hypothesis II, *herself* is preceded by a coindexed NP, namely *Mary*. Thus, Hypothesis II overgenerates—it wrongly predicts the grammaticality of (8.10a.).

Example (8.10b.) is consistent with Hypothesis II, since *herself* is preceded by coindexed *Jane* and the example is a grammatical sentence. But we need a hypothesis that works for all and only the grammatical sentences. In other words, even if Hypothesis II is successful in generating (8.7b.), as well as (8.10b.), therefore for all the grammatical strings in our sample, it does not generate only the grammatical strings, since it would also generate (8.10a.).

Let's try something else then:

 Hypothesis III: *herself* must be preceded by a coindexed nominal expression, and no other nominal expression may intervene between *herself* and the coindexed preceding nominal expression.

The first thing to do is to check whether this new Hypothesis actually works for the examples that we have already looked at, (8.7a.-c.) and (8.10a.-b.). This is something that you can do by yourself at this point. Once you have convinced yourself of this, consider the following.

 a. *A friend$_j$ of Mary's$_i$ flogs herself$_i$.
b. A friend$_j$ of Mary's$_i$ flogs herself$_j$.
c. *I flog herself$_i$.
d. *Mary$_i$ knows that I/we/they/you flog herself$_i$.

Examples (8.12a.) and (8.12b.) are doubly problematic for Hypothesis III. First, it looks like (8.12a.) should be grammatical, since no nominal constituent intervenes between *herself* and the coindexed *Mary*. But the example is ungrammatical according to our native speaker judgments. Thus Hypothesis III *overgenerates*: it generates strings that are not grammatical for the mental grammar being modeled.

Hypothesis III also fails when we look at example (8.12b.). We judge it to be grammatical from the point of view of our mental grammar. However, it is not generated by Hypothesis III since *Mary* intervenes between *herself* and coindexed *friend*. This means that Hypothesis III also *undergenerates*: it fails to generate sentences that are grammatical in the mental grammar being modeled.

Hypothesis III has to be rejected because it both undergenerates—does not generate *all*—and overgenerates—does not generate *only*—the sentences of the language being modeled.

Example (8.12c.) suggests that *herself* definitely needs to occur with some preceding coindexed nominal expression and that this expression needs to agree with respect to properties like person, gender, and number. Sentence (8.12d.) shows us that we cannot appeal to the need for clarity to explain the distribution of *herself*—this anaphor denotes an individual that is third person singular and female, and the only thing in the sentence it agrees with for these features is *Mary*. Yet, the anaphor cannot be licensed in this sentence. This suggests that avoidance of ambiguity has no bearing on the analysis of anaphor distribution, since there is only one plausible antecedent for *herself*, and yet the string is ungrammatical.

Anyway, we know that many sentences are ambiguous. Let's consider some sentences with a regular pronoun like *her* rather than a reflexive.

8.13 $Mary_i$ told Sue_j that $Jane_k$ likes $her_{i,j,*k,l}$.

The indexing in (8.13) indicates that we get a grammatical sentence from this string if *her* is coindexed with *Mary*, *Sue*, or some other nominal expression referring to a human female, but not *Jane*. Some ambiguities are possible and others are not.

So, here is the final Hypothesis we will make:

8.14   Hypothesis IV: an anaphor, like *herself*, must be bound in its minimal clause.

You should not yet be able to understand this—we need some definitions first.

8.15   Some definitions:
   • **Clause**: this is a notion we have already introduced in the previous chapter. We defined a clause as a syntactic phrase that contains two constituents: an XP functioning as the subject of the clause and a VP or AuxP. We also mentioned that some clauses may be complex and may include several embedded clauses that are dependent on various constituents in the main clause. For example, *John thinks Mary left Montreal yesterday* is a complex clause that contains a main clause and one

embedded clause. The embedded clause contains the VP *left Montreal yesterday* and its subject *Mary*, and is dependent on the verb *thinks*, which selects this clause as a complement. The main clause contains its subject NP *John* and its VP *thinks Mary left Montreal yesterday*.

- **Binding**: A constituent α of a sentence *binds* another constituent β just in case α and β are coindexed and α *c-commands* β.
- **C-command**: α c-commands β just in case α does not contain β, but every category that contains α contains β. (This is most easily seen if we draw trees for our sentences and translate *contain* to *dominate*.)

To get a feel for c-command consider the following tree:

8.16   What are the c-command relations in this tree?

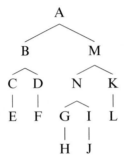

You should be able to see that node C c-commands nodes D and F, and nothing else. Node A doesn't c-command anything, since it contains or dominates all the other nodes. Node K c-commands nodes N, G, I, H and J.

If we call two nodes immediately dominated by the same node "sisters" then each node c-commands its sister and all nodes dominated by its sister. The relationship of c-command is not relevant only to binding phenomena. It is a relationship that pervades syntax, as we will see in subsequent chapters.

Now that we have the definition of c-command, let's go back to Hypothesis IV which says that *herself* must be bound in its minimal clause. In the sentence *John thinks Mary left Montreal yesterday*, both clauses contain *Mary*, but the embedded clause is the minimal clause containing *Mary*. On the other hand, the minimal clause of *John* is the main clause.

Let's check that Hypothesis IV actually works. We need to check three conditions on the relationship between *herself* and a potential antecedent.

8.17   Three conditions in Hypothesis IV
- Is there a nominal constituent that is coindexed with *herself*?
- Does that nominal constituent c-command *herself*?

Those two conditions constitute binding—*herself* is *bound* if those conditions hold.

- Is that nominal constituent in the same minimal clause as *herself*?

This is referred to as a *locality* condition—the binder must be local to the bindee.

Let's apply Hypothesis IV to examples (8.7a.b.). Examine the following tree that represents the structure that would be assigned to these strings by our grammar.

| 8.18 | Trees for (8.7a.b.) |

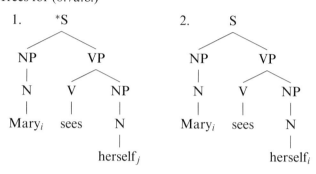

These trees have the same structure and the same lexical items, but the indexing on *herself* differs. If we select the index *j* for *herself* the form is ungrammatical; if we select the index *i* for *herself*, we have a grammatical sentence.

Actually, we now have to admit to having purposely led you astray. Thus far we have indexed the examples in a misleading way. First, we need to point out that indices are part of the abstract representation that we assign to a string and not part of the string itself. Thus, the index should not show up on the lexical item *herself* in the diagrams above, but on one of the syntactic nodes which are part of the tree.

Second, whatever theory of reference one ultimately adopts, it seems clear that Ns themselves are not referential. Bare nouns, nouns that are not preceded by any determiner, do not in fact refer to individuals but rather to sets of individuals.[31] Thus, a bare noun like *car*, for example, does not refer to a particular individual car but to any car, to the set of all cars. On

---

[31] Just to be clear, we are not referring to individuals out in the world but rather to mental representations. We remind you that a theory of reference will probably not correspond in a straightforward way to commonsense notions, and for present purposes you will have to accept some of our stipulations concerning indexation.

the other hand, if a noun like *car* is preceded by a determiner like *this*, then the whole NP *this car* refers to a single individual car, in contrast to the bare noun *car*. It appears, then, that (some) NPs can refer to individuals, but Ns cannot, and thus we propose that indices are a feature that can only belong to NPs, but not to Ns. Let us return now to our trees, and fix our indices.

8.19   Revised trees for (8.7a.b.)

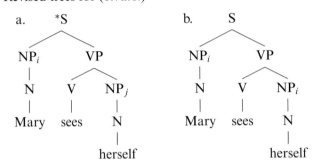

Now we can confirm that Hypothesis IV works for these examples. Example (8.7a.), in which herself$_j$ is not coindexed with *Mary*$_i$ obviously does not satisfy Hypothesis IV. The tree in (8.19a.) shows that the two NPs that dominate *herself* and *Mary* are in the same minimal clause, and that NP$_i$, which dominates *Mary*, does c-command NP$_j$, which dominates *herself*, but the two are not coindexed so binding fails. Thus (8.7a.) is predicted to be ungrammatical by Hypothesis IV. This is consistent with our intuitions.

The labeling that makes *herself* coindexed with *Mary* leads to a grammatical sentence corresponding to (8.7b.) above. This is consistent with Hypothesis IV:

- There is a nominal constituent, NP$_i$ *Mary*, that is coindexed with NP$_i$ *herself*.
- NP$_i$ *Mary* c-commands NP$_i$ *herself*.
- Given that the two conditions above are met, NP$_i$ *herself* is bound.
- Since there is only one clause in this example, it is clear that NP$_i$ *herself* and NP$_i$ *Mary* are in the same minimal clause.

The string in (8.7c.) clearly is ungrammatical since the NP$_i$ *herself* appears in subject position, and the coindexed NP$_i$ *Mary* cannot c-command it, and thus cannot bind it.

So, (8.7a.) is ungrammatical because of a failure of the coindexation requirement and (8.7c.) is ungrammatical because of a failure of the c-command requirement. To see an example of the failure of locality, the requirement that binding of a reflexive should hold within the minimal clause containing the reflexive, we need to examine structures with more than one clause, such as examples (8.10a.b.). We have labeled each S in a tree with a distinct subscript so that we can refer to it.

8.20   Trees of (8.10a.b.) with correct labeling

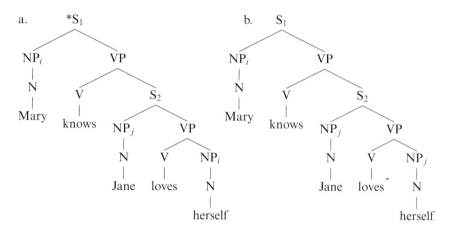

In (8.20a.) the NP anaphor *herself* is c-commanded by both the NP *Mary* and the NP *Jane*, but only the NP *Mary* is coindexed with the NP *herself*. Thus, only the NP *Mary* binds the NP *herself*. So, the NP *herself* is bound, but the minimal clause containing the NP *herself* is S_2, and the NP *Mary* is not contained in S_2. Therefore the locality condition for binding of reflexives is not satisfied and (8.20a.) is ungrammatical.

In (8.20b.), on the other hand, the NP *Jane* is coindexed with the NP *herself*; and at the same time it c-commands the same NP *herself*. Moreover, the NP *Jane* is in the same minimal clause with the NP *herself*. All the conditions necessary for Hypothesis IV to apply are met, so we have a grammatical sentence.

We now turn to the more complex cases, the ones that Hypothesis III could not handle. At this point we will start making use of our abbreviatory convention for indexation by presenting a single tree with both indexes listed, one of which will be marked with an asterisk to show that this choice represents an ungrammatical structure.

Examples (8.12a.b.) involve the embedding of one NP inside another, as the following tree makes clear.

8.21   Trees for (8.12a.b.) NP within NP

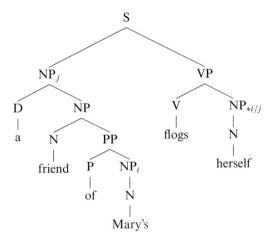

For (8.12a.) the NP *Mary's* is indexed i, and it is contained in the NP *a friend of Mary's*, which itself is indexed j. Since the NP *Mary's* cannot c-command the NP *herself*, it cannot bind the latter, and so (8.12a.) is ungrammatical.

You can see that the NP *a friend of Mary's* is the sister of the VP, and thus c-commands everything in the VP, including the NP *herself*. If the NP *a friend of Mary's* is also coindexed with the NP *herself*, it will bind it, and since there is only one clause, it will bind it in the minimal clause that contains the NP *herself*. All the conditions that are necessary for Hypothesis III to apply are met, and thus example (8.12b.) is a grammatical sentence.

The reasons for the ungrammaticality of (8.12c.d.) should now be obvious. The first person pronoun *I* has incompatible features with the third person female *herself*, so we will assume that the two NPs that dominate them cannot be coindexed.

In (8.12d.) the NP *Mary* is the only nominal expression that is featurally compatible with the NP *herself*, and yet, because the NP *Mary* does not bind the NP *herself* locally, the conditions for Hypothesis IV to apply cannot be met, and all the listed options are ungrammatical.

Hypothesis IV will thus account for a wide range of data. There are a few cases, however, where it appears to fail, and it is a question of current research how to deal with such cases. We are not going to discuss such cases here, but see if you can come up with any data that poses a problem for

Hypothesis IV on your own. In any case, take a moment to ponder how difficult it has been to study even the very simple English data examined thus far. Of course, the solution itself is not difficult to understand—coindexation, c-command, and locality are all simple notions.

8.3 Pronouns and "referential expressions"

We have come up with an analysis for the distribution of anaphors like *herself, themselves*, and so on. Anaphors have turned out to be nominal expressions with a deficient referential potential, in the sense that they need another (coindexed) NP in order to acquire the ability to refer to an individual. Crucially, this other NP must occupy a position that is subject to well-defined structural conditions. Apart from anaphors, nominal expressions can also be of two other types from the point of view of their referential potential: *pronouns* and *referential* or *R-expressions*. Both of these types of expressions are subject to their own "binding" conditions. We will not provide the details of these conditions here. You will be asked to try to find the conditions for the distribution of regular pronouns like *her, him*, as well as for R-expressions like *Mary, the cat*, or *those three blind mice* in the exercises at the end of the chapter.

8.4 Some implications

We argued earlier that a sentence is not just a string of words but rather has a structure that relates certain words to each other to form constituents. If our approach to binding phenomena is valid, it suggests that sentences, which are members of an equivalence class used by the syntax, are not only structured but also must encode indexing on NPs. Even a well-structured representation will be ungrammatical if the coindexation relations among parts are not licit.

Just like sentence structure, binding relations (c-command and indexation) have no physical correlates in the speech signal; thus, they must be constructed, or computed, by the language faculty. Since, as we have argued, syntactic relations are always structure-dependent, it appears to be the case that the human language faculty can only construct patterns that are sensitive to structure, and not, for example, linear order notions like "x intervenes between y and z." Notions like binding and the differences between pronouns, R-expressions and anaphors also appear to recur over and over again in the languages of the world, thus suggesting that they are part of the primitive resources that constitute the language faculty.

8.5 Binding and *wh*-movement

In this section we want to consider one apparent counterexample to our hypothesis about the distribution of anaphors, namely the hypothesis that anaphors must be bound in their minimal clause. The relevant example is given below:

8.22   I wonder who$_i$ John$_j$ thinks squashed himself$_{i,*j,*k}$

This example initally appears problematic. Our intuition tells us that the anaphor *himself* must be interpreted as referring to the same individual as *who*. However, the position of *who* seems to be outside of the minimal clause containing *himself*. Notice that *who* is outside of the clause containing the verb *think*, since it precedes the verb *think*, as well as its subject *John*. If this is so, then *who* is clearly outside of the embedded sentence containing the verb *squashed* to which *himself* is related. Now, if our hypothesis about the distribution of anaphors is correct, then *himself* must be coindexed with a local c-commanding NP. However, the problem is that *who* does not seem to satisfy the locality condition, since it is out of the minimal clause containing the anaphor.

In order to solve this problem, notice that *squashed* seems to be missing a subject. An English clause containing a transitive verb like *squashed* also contains an object and a subject, in the order subject-verb-object, as in (8.23).

8.23   a. [Peter]$_{SU}$ [squashed]$_V$ [the squirrel]$_{OBJ}$.
          b. [Peter]$_{SU}$ [squashed]$_V$ [himself]$_{OBJ}$.

In (8.22), the object of *squashed* occurs in the expected position, that is after the verb, but the category immediately preceding the verb *squashed* is another verb—the verb *think*, which clearly cannot be the subject of *squashed*. Notice at the same time that we do interpret one of the NPs in (8.22) as being the subject of *squashed*. This NP is precisely the NP *who*, which is coindexed with our anaphor. To convince yourself of this, compare (8.22) with (8.24) below.

8.24   a. John thinks Peter squashed the squirrel
          b. I wonder who John thinks squashed the squirrel?

In (8.24b.), it should be obvious that the subject of *squashed* is *who*. The answer to the question in (8.24b.) is *Peter* and *Peter* is the subject of *squashed* in (8.24a.). Yet, the only difference between (8.22) and (8.24) is the anaphoric vs. non-anaphoric nature of the object of the verb *squashed*. The relation of *who* to the verb *squashed* is the same in both instances: *who* is the subject of *squashed*. If this is so, the clause that contains the anaphor *himself* in (8.22) seems to contain all the constituents that normally occur with a transitive verb like *squashed*, but one of these constituents, the subject, occurs in a dislocated position relative to the verb *squashed*. Why is that? The answer lies in the somehow special properties of constituents like *who*, which were briefly described in the previous chapter.

There are several ways to formalize this property of *wh*-expressions. The analysis we have adopted in this book is to assume that sentences that contain *wh*-expressions like *who*, *what*, *what student*, *which*, *which student*, *why*, *for what reason*, etc., can be assigned a tree-like representation that indicates both the base position and the derived position of the *wh*-expression. Continuing an older terminology, we will say that the *wh*-constituent *moves* from the base to the derived position, and that as a result of movement a copy of the *wh*-constituent appears in a dislocated position.

The appearance of *wh*-phrases in two positions occurs not only in complex strings like (8.22), which contain a main clause and two embedded clauses, but also in simple clauses like (8.25).

8.25   a. John squashed Mike.
            b. Who did John squash?

Let's assume that the order subject-verb-object corresponds to the base positions of the subject and object of a clause. Sentence (8.25a.) transparently reflects this order. In other words, the subject *John* and the object *Mike* occupy their base positions. In (8.25b.), however, the subject *John* is in its base position, but the object of the verb is not. The object of *squash* in (8.25b.) is *who*, and *who* does not follow the verb, as expected under the subject-verb-object order, but precedes it. In other words, the object of the verb *squash* in (8.25b.) is pronounced in its derived position.

The representation that we assign to (8.22) and that includes both the base and the derived positions of *who* is given in (8.26). There are three S nodes in this representation: the higher one corresponds to the main clause, the middle one to the clause immediately selected by the verb *wonder* of the main clause, and the lowest one to the most deeply embedded clause, the clause selected by the verb *think* of the middle clause. In addition, the middle clause is dominated not only by an S node, but also by an S′ node, which actually contains the S and the NP *who*. We will not offer any details about the S′ node. For our purposes, S′ should be seen as an extension of the S node. Each of the three S nodes is analyzed as containing a subject NP and a VP, the verbal predicate.

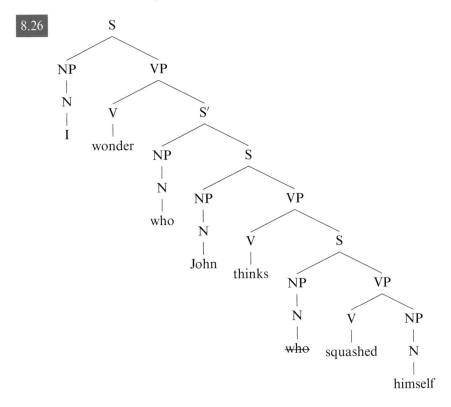

Given that *who* is the subject of the verb *squashed,* the base position of *who* is to the left of the verb *squashed.* Structurally, this corresponds to the NP position in the embedded clause that is sister to the VP that contains the verb *squashed* and the object *himself.* The derived position of *who,* on the other hand, is higher than the S node whose subject is *John.*

At this point you might wonder how all this can help with the problem we pointed out at the beginning of this section related to the distribution of *himself.* Remember that the problem posed by (8.22) was that *himself* is coindexed with *who* in spite of the fact that our theory predicts that (8.22) should be ungrammatical, since *himself* and *who* do not seem to be in the same minimal clause—the locality condition appears not to be satisfied.

However, (8.22) is grammatical and coindexation between *himself* and *who* is possible. How can this be?

Given what we now know about *wh*-expressions, it is easy to account for examples like (8.22). In order to see this, let us first point out that the two copies of *who* in (8.26) must be coindexed by virtue of their being copies of the same lexical item. The representation in (8.26) that also contains the indexes on *who* is shown below.

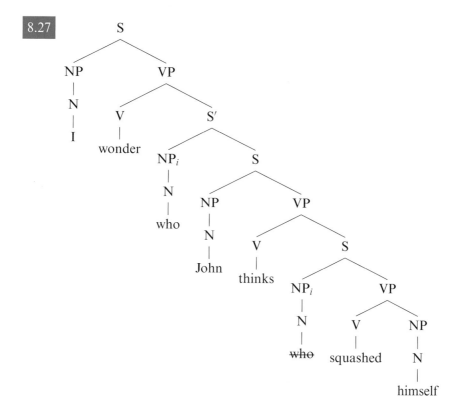

Now, even if the copy of *who* that occupies a derived position is not in the same minimal clause as *himself*, the base copy of *who* clearly is. The tree representation in (8.26) shows that the base copy of *who* and *himself* are dominated by the same *S* node. Notice that a sentence like *Who squashed himself?* is grammatical and the interpretation that we assign to it is one in which *himself* and *who* are coindexed. This shows that a *wh*-expression like *who* can be a binder for an anaphor. So, on the one hand, the two copies of *who* must be coindexed, as discussed above, and, on the other hand, *himself* must be coindexed with the base copy of *who*. The only way in which both these coindexation conditions can hold simultaneously is if all three of these NPs bear the same index, as in the representation below.

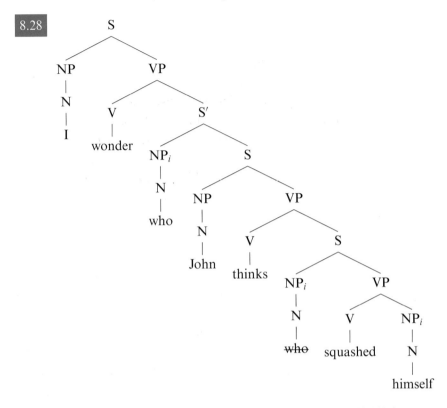

8.28

This representation now accounts both for the fact that (8.22) is grammatical in spite of the fact that *himself* does not have a *pronounced* local binder, and for the fact that *himself* is interpreted as being coindexed with a distant NP, namely with the higher copy of *who*. The grammaticality of (8.22) can be explained by the presence of the lower copy of *who*, the one in the base position, which acts as a local binder for *himself*. The coindexation between *himself* and the higher copy of *who* is simply a side effect of the coindexation between the local binder for *himself* and the higher copy of *who*. This latter coindexation follows in turn from the fact that the lower *who* and the higher *who* are copies of the same NP constituent—one that corresponds to its base position and one that corresponds to its derived position.

We hope you find this example as impressive as we do—it allows us to bring together the notions of *wh*-movement and binding, which we argued for independently, in an elegant manner. This is an example of the benefits of precise formulation mentioned in the quotation from the Preface of

Syntactic Structures in Section 5.1.1—our model of *wh*-movement was not "explicitly designed" to make our account of binding work out right, and, yet, the model of *wh*-movement "automatically provides" a solution for an apparent counterexample to the binding generalizations.

Once again, we need to step back and appreciate what this teaches us about basic issues like the nature of sentences. A sentence is not just a string of words but rather a string of words with a structure—we posited structural relations in part to account for ambiguous strings. However, in addition to structure, we need to assume that indexation is also part of a sentence's representation. Furthermore, a sentence is not just an indexed structural arrangement of words but rather a representation that contains the derivational history of constituents that are subject to syntactic movement—it contains both the base position of constituents that move, and their derived position, where they are pronounced.[32] We now appreciate that the computations involved in evaluating the binding conditions appear to refer to the base position of the binder.

Once again, we see that linguistic computation involves construction by the mind of very abstract structures involving equivalence classes with no grounding in the categories of physics. Just as our minds construct triangles and words and auditory streams and phonemes, it constructs syntactic representations and derivations over which c-command relations and indexations can be evaluated. All of this computation and representation goes on *in* our minds and thus can only be considered under the I–language approach.

8.6 Non-structural factors in interpretation

We have tried to maintain a distinction between the output of the grammar and the production and comprehension behavior of speakers. Our binding conditions involve precise formal models, but when looking at actual behavior, whether speech, comprehension, or even the behavior of providing grammaticality judgments, "there are all those other ways in which the winsome mess of what we call real life encroaches on the austere simplicity of a mathematical abstraction" (to quote mathematician Vašek Chvàtal). In

---

[32] Remember that *movement* is one of the possible metaphors used to describe the relationship among the relevant positions in a tree.

some cases the issue is obvious, for example, it is easy to understand why a speaker will have difficulty with judgments about the grammaticality of a sentence that takes three minutes to utter. However, other cases are not so simple and warrant further discussion.

Let's now consider the interpretation of the possessive form *her* in (8.29). Example (8.29a.) has at least the two interpretations shown by the indexing. The bicycle could belong to either the asker, Janie, or the askee, Loretta. The same holds for sentence (8.29b.)—we get the two readings, one in which it is the asker's bicycle and one in which it is the askee's. (We can also interpret *her* in each sentence as neither the asker nor the askee, but this possibility does not concern us here.)

  Parallelism in interpretation

a. Janie$_i$ asked Loretta$_j$ to fix her$_{i,j}$ bicycle—*at least two readings.*
b. Rayette$_k$ asked Eve$_l$ to fix her$_{k,l}$ bicycle—*at least two readings.*
c. Janie$_i$ asked Loretta$_j$ to fix her$_{i,j}$ bicycle and Rayette$_k$ asked Eve$_l$ to fix her$_{k,l}$ bicycle—*how many of the following readings are possible: i & k; i & l; j & k; j & l?*

Given the two possibilities under consideration for each sentence, one would expect the conjunction of the two sentences to have four possible interpretations, since there are four combinations provided by the two simple sentences—*her* is the asker in both cases; *her* is the askee in both cases; *her* is the asker in the first case and the askee in the second case; and *her* is the askee in the first case and the asker in the second. However, speakers of English report that only the first two options are possible readings of the sentence—either *her* is the asker in both cases or it is the askee in both.

Although it is not entirely clear what the explanation is for why the other two readings are not acceptable to speakers, linguists have decided that the necessity of interpreting both instances of *her* in parallel reflects a property of how we process sentences in real time, and not a fact about the interpretations of pronouns made available by the grammar. In other words, we recognize that many factors other than binding theory enter into people's speech comprehension and production behavior.

Many people initially judge the following string to be ill formed:

  The pilot called the flight attendant into the cabin because she needed his help.

However, as soon as it is pointed out that the pilot can be a woman and the flight attendant a man, those who judged the sentence ill formed revise their opinions. It appears that when a *person* interprets pronoun reference, he or she calls on many diverse aspects of cognition, including (possibly false) presuppositions about the gender of individuals in certain professions. We would never make any progress in linguistics, or any other science, if we did not recognize that various factors can interact to produce an observed behavior.

So, binding theory determines a range of possibilities for pronoun interpretation that may be further constrained by other factors, such as a bias to interpret parallel strings in parallel fashion when they occur in sequence, or general knowledge or suppositions about the nature of the world. Just like the hypothetical physiologist from Chapter 3 who limits study to a very narrow range of human behavior related to arm raising, the linguist must limit study to those aspects of pronoun interpretation that seem to offer the promise of being formalizable. We further discuss this issue of isolability of the grammar in Chapter 14.

8.7 Exercises

Exercise 8.7.1. Show with trees that the following examples a. and b. show exactly the same problems for Hypothesis II as (8.12a.) and (8.12b.), respectively.

   a. *The teacher$_j$ who Mary$_i$ likes flogs herself$_i$.
   b. The teacher$_j$ who Mary$_i$ likes flogs herself$_j$.

Exercise 8.7.2. R-expressions and binding theory: Consider the following data and confirm that these examples are compatible with the claim that R-expressions cannot be bound at all, even at a distance. The opposite of bound is "free," so we can say "R-expressions must be free."

   a. She$_i$ loves Mary$_{*i/j}$.
   b. She$_i$ says that John loves Mary$_{*i/j}$.
   c. John says that Jim thinks that she$_i$ promises to tell Bill to beg Sam to force Mary$_{*i/j}$ to eat better.
   d. The woman$_i$ who loves her$_{j/k}$ told Mary$_j$ to leave immediately.

Draw a tree for each example and explain why each indexed R-expression is or is not bound by other indexed NPs.

Exercise 8.7.3. Pronouns and binding theory: The point of this exercise is to reinforce the idea that syntactic phenomena are structure-dependent. In the text we examined the conditions on the appearance of anaphors (like *himself* and *herself*) and in the exercise (8.7.2) the conditions on regular referring expressions. You will now go through similar steps of reasoning to discover conditions on the distribution of non-reflexive pronouns like *him* and *her*.

Some data:

    a. Tom_i sees him_j.

    b. *Tom_i sees him_i.

1. Propose a Hypothesis I that relies exclusively on linear order to account for the grammatical vs. ungrammatical indexing of *him* and *Tom* in (a.) and (b.):

More data:

    c. Tom_i knows that $Fred_j$ loves him_i.

    d. *Tom_i knows that $Fred_j$ loves him_j.

Explain:

2. Why is (c.) a problem for Hypothesis I?
3. Is (d.) a problem for Hypothesis I? Explain.
4. Propose another linear order Hypothesis II using the notion of intervention (x comes between between a and b) to account for just (a.b.c.d.):

More data:

    e. The $aromatherapist_j$ Tom_i likes flogs him_i.

    f. *The $aromatherapist_j$ Tom_i likes flogs him_j.

    g. A $friend_j$ of $Tom's_i$ flogs him_i.

    h. *A $friend_j$ of $Tom's_i$ flogs him_j.

    i. He_i flogs him_j.

Explain:

5. Why is (e.) a problem for Hypothesis II?
6. Why is (f.) a problem for Hypothesis II?
7. Why is (g.) a problem for Hypothesis II?
8. Why is (h.) a problem for Hypothesis II?
9. Is (i.) a problem for Hypothesis II?

Draw trees and show indexing on the noun phrases for sentences p.-t. Use the trees in the chapter to help you.

10. e:

f:

g:

h:

i:

A constituent α of a sentence *binds* another constituent β just in case these two conditions are satisfied:

11. i.

ii.

Give the letter of an example from the sentences above in which:

12. *him* is bound, and the sentence is grammatical:_____

13. *him* is not bound, and the sentence is grammatical:_____

14. Formulate a Hypothesis III for the distribution of *him* that uses binding and accounts for all of (a.-i.):

Consider the grammaticality of the three sentences represented by the following string and indexation: Who$_i$ does Annie$_j$ think loves her$_{*i/j/k}$.

15. Explain only the reason why the following reading is ungrammatical. Your answer should include a tree (tell us what it is a tree of) and one sentence.

Who$_i$ does Annie$_j$ think loves her$_{*i}$.

9

Ergativity

As we indicated in Chapter 1, experts in all sorts of fields are willing to make proclamations about the acquisition, use, and evolution of language without anything like the depth of knowledge about what language is that you now have from reading this book. In this chapter we survey some less familiar language data—partly just for the fun of it; partly to reinforce a sense of humility about the complexity of language, a sense that we wish was more widely shared by non-linguists; and partly to further illustrate the following:

- how linguists reason about data patterns;
- the tension that arises from the complementary goals of developing a theory of Universal Grammar and accounting for the diversity of the world's languages; and
- once again, the idea that our minds construct linguistic representations—the analysis is not "in the signal."

To construct these representations, a grammar needs a set of symbolic equivalence classes. A theory of Universal Grammar must specify a set of primitives—the fundamental representational primitives that constitute the equivalence classes of all grammars, and the computational primitives that constitute the computations of possible individual grammars. Linguistics is still a long way from this goal, and in this chapter we will content ourselves with a fairly superficial description of some complex phenomena. There do exist several well-articulated analyses of the data we present, but our aim is not to bring you to the cutting edge of linguistic research in this area but rather to attain the goals sketched above, especially the goal of increasing a sense of humility.

We will examine a phenomenon called *ergativity* found in many languages spread all over the world, but not present in obvious form in the major languages of science and culture such as English, German, French, Japanese, Chinese, Arabic, or Spanish. The "exoticness" of the phenomena we discuss is just a reflection of our particular point of view given the languages we happen to speak—there is nothing inherently strange about these patterns and, in fact, modern linguistics has been able to abstract away from much of the superficial differences among languages to find some underlying unity.

We have already applied similar reasoning in the domain of phonology. In our discussion of English allophones in Chapter 6, we saw that English integrates the mental representations plain [t] and aspirated [t^h] into a single equivalence class, the phoneme /t/. In contrast, a language like Thai treats the two kinds of *t* as belonging to separate phonemes. So, the phoneme equivalence classes of English phonology differ from those of Thai. We will see in Chapter 11 that the two languages must construct their equivalence classes from a universal set of innate, atomic building blocks, but the languages differ in the combinations that are made from these atoms. The atomic building blocks are entities like the vowel features we used to account for Turkish vowel harmony in Chapter 6—the features themselves correspond to equivalence classes. In the course of language acquisition each language treats certain bundles of features as higher-order equivalence classes. The human language faculty thus has some plasticity with respect to which equivalence classes can enter into computations. In English the learner abstracts away from the difference between [t] and [t^h], whereas in Thai the learner does not. What better illustration could one want for Sapir's statement quoted in Chapter 1 that "no entity in human experience can be adequately defined as the mechanical sum or product of its physical properties"? Both English and Thai have aspirated and unaspirated consonants, but they pattern completely differently in the two types of grammar.

In the following sections, we will illustrate a similar kind of plasticity, not in the domain of phonology but in morphosyntax, the interface of morphology and syntax, of a variety of languages.

9.1 Preliminaries

As we proceed, we will make use of three distinct sets of terminology to refer to syntactic phrases, and it will become apparent that we need all three. Consider a sentence like (9.1):

9.1   He kicked the frog.

The element *he* can be described in several ways:

9.2   Describing a constituent like *he*
  - it is a PRONOUN, which is a kind of NP
  - it is the SUBJECT of the sentence
  - it is in the NOMINATIVE CASE, as opposed to a form like *him*

In this chapter we will be examining the relationships among these three ways of describing constituents of a sentence.

The first categorization we used was NP. NPs, VPs, and so on are phrases built from elements called lexical categories like N and V. A more traditional term for "lexical category" is *part of speech*.

The second categorization includes categories like subject and object. In the model of syntax we developed earlier, these labels were just names for positions in a syntactic tree—the subject is the NP that is the direct daughter of the sentence node and c-commands the rest of the sentence. The object is just the name of the NP that is the daughter of the VP and sister of the V.

Notions like subject and object are called *grammatical functions* or *grammatical relations*. In some syntactic theories, grammatical functions are actual theoretical primitives, not just names for positions in the tree. In this book, we use the terms only in a descriptive way to indicate syntactic positions. You will soon see that the status of these notions is more complex than you may have realized. There are many difficult issues that arise when studying these topics, some of them not yet resolved. For our purposes we will assume that every sentence in every language has a subject, which means that every sentence has an NP as a direct daughter of S.

If there is only one argument of a verb, we assume it is the subject and say that the sentence is *intransitive*.[33] If the verb has both a subject and an object, we will say that it is *transitive*. A *ditransitive* has a subject as well as two arguments within the VP.

 9.3   Transitivity
- *Mary yawned* (no arguments within the VP) = Intransitive
- *Mary kicked him* (one argument within the VP) = Transitive
- *Mary gave him the cold shoulder* (two arguments within the VP) = Ditransitive

In the following discussion, we won't worry about ditransitives, or about which NP is the object of the verb *give*, but we mention them just to make it clear that our sketch is far from complete.

In English the subject and verb sometimes show agreement:

9.4   Agreement in English

	PRESENT	PAST
SINGULAR	*He sees John*	*He saw John*
PLURAL	*They see John*	*They saw John*

The verb marker *-s* occurs only on present tense verbs with a third person singular subject like *he*. Thus *sees* is said to agree with *he*, and *see* agrees with *they*. In the past tense, however, there is no overt marking of agreement.

Some languages show much richer agreement systems, with different forms for each person and number of the subject, with the differences marked in all tenses. Latin is such a language, as shown by the following forms for the verb *amāre* "to love":

9.5   Subject-verb agreement in two Latin tenses

	PRESENT		FUTURE	
	SG	PL	SG	PL
1st	amō	amāmus	amabō	amabimus
2nd	amās	amātis	amabis	amabitis
3rd	amat	amant	amabit	amabunt

Each of the three persons in the singular and plural has its own endings in both the present and future tenses. Aside from a failure to distinguish

---

[33] More sophisticated readers will see that we are glossing over the subcategories of intransitive verbs, *unergatives* and *unaccusatives*, and assuming that all intransitives end up with a NP in subject position, although the base position of this NP may differ from its derived position.

singular and plural in the second person form *you*, English pronouns mark the same person and number distinctions as do the Latin verb suffixes.

Many languages mark categories that English does not mark at all. For example, the English form *we write* corresponds to four distinct forms in Mohawk, an Iroquoian language, and also in Tok Pisin, an English-based Creole, one of the official languages of Papua New Guinea. Mohawk marks the differences with verbal morphology, whereas Tok Pisin does it with pronoun morphology. The four-way contrast corresponding to English *we* is shown in (9.6).

9.6   First person, non-singular forms in three languages

	Mohawk	Tok Pisin	English
1, DU, EXC	iakenihiá:tons	mitupela raitim	we write
1, PL, EXC	iakwahiá:tons	mipela raitim	we write
1, DU, INC	tenihiá:tons	yumitupela raitim	we write
1, PL, INC	tewahiá:tons	yumipela raitim	we write

First of all, these two languages differentiate plural from dual, which is used for subjects that have exactly two members. Second, these languages distinguish forms that are inclusive of the person addressed ("me and you"), from forms that are exclusive of the addressee ("me and her, but not you").

Note that these languages make more distinctions than English in person and number categories, but, like French and German, they do not distinguish what is rendered in English as *we write* and *we are writing*. So, it is not the case that we can say that either English or Mohawk is more complex than the other. We can find a contrast that is overt in the morphology of each language but not the other. The notion of complexity appears to be irrelevant to the comparison of languages.

In addition to the subject-verb agreement patterns we have looked at, some languages show agreement of a verb with its object as well. Hungarian has very rich subject-verb agreement, but as the following forms show, there is also some agreement with objects.

9.7   Hungarian has some nice suffixes on verbs:

Verb	I V an X	I V the X	I V you
send	küldök	küldöm	küldelek
watch	lesek	lesem	leslek
await	várok	várom	várlak

Having read the discussion of Turkish in Chapter 6, you surely recognize that there is some kind of vowel harmony in Hungarian as well—we won't analyze it here. Focus instead on the difference in endings between a verb with an indefinite third person object (such as *a boy*), a definite third person object (such as *the boy*), and a second person (singular or plural) object (*you*). The verb suffixes thus encode features of both the subject and object in Hungarian—a different form of the verb is used for *I send a boy, I send the boy* and *I send you*.

We have already introduced lexical categories like N, V, and their phrasal counterparts, NP, VP, and so on. These are assumed to be based on proper-ties or features that define equivalence classes in the mental dictionary, the lexicon of a grammar. We have also seen grammatical function terms like subject and object that are defined, at least in some approaches, as names for positions in syntactic trees. The last categorization we discuss is not lexical or syntactic but rather morphological. Terms like nominative case refer to the form taken by the elements in NPs, especially their head nouns. Case is very limited in English, only showing up in the pronoun system in distinctions like *I*/*me*, which are both first person singular pronouns, or *we*/*us* which are both first person plural pronouns, or *she*/*her* which are both third person singular female pronouns. In other languages, case may be marked on all nouns, and sometimes on the determiners and adjectives that modify them. We will see an example below from Latin. The remainder of this chapter is about verbal agreement patterns and case systems—the markers on verbs and nouns (or NPs) that show their relationship to each other.

9.2 A nominative-accusative system

We are now ready to examine some data following a very useful survey presented by Payne (1997). Consider the Latin sentences in (9.8). Sentence (9.8a.) is intransitive since it has a subject, *dominus* "master," but no object. Sentence (9.8b.) has exactly the same structure, but with a different subject, *servus* "slave." Notice that *dominus* and *servus* both end in -*s*—that is not an accident. Note that in the transitive sentences (9.8c.) and (9.8d.) we also get forms ending in -*s* serving as subjects, as the translations show. In addition to the subject *dominus* in (9.8c.) we also get a form of the word for slave, but with the ending -*m* instead of -*s*, that is *servum*. This NP is the object of sentence (9.8c.). Likewise, in (9.8d.) *servus* is the subject and *dominum* is the object.

 Latin nominative-accusative system

    a. dominus venit   "the master is coming"
    b. servus venit   "the slave is coming"
    c. dominus servum audit   "the master hears the slave"
    d. servus dominum audit   "the slave hears the master"

The traditional name for a morphological case form in a language like Latin, one that treats subjects of transitives and subjects of intransitives alike, is nominative. So, in our examples, *-s* is the nominative ending, and we say that *dominus* and *servus* are "in the nominative case." The suffix *-m* that appears on the objects of transitive verbs marks the accusative, so *dominum* and *servum* are in the accusative case.

Note that English uses the same pattern, at least for pronouns:

 English pronoun case

    a. **I** am coming
    b. **She** is coming
    c. **I** hear **her**
    d. **She** hears **me**

The forms *I* and *she* are used for subjects, whereas *me* and *her* are for objects.[34] A language that uses the Latin or English case pattern is called a *nominative-accusative* language. Of course, it is not the names of the cases that make a nominative-accusative language but rather the pattern of having subjects all sharing the same form in opposition to the form of objects.

9.3 An ergative-absolutive system

At this point you may be wondering how else a case system could be organized. Some languages do not show any overt morphological case at all. Aside from the pronouns, English NPs have no case[35] and the grammatical

---

[34] Of course things are actually more complex if you consider real colloquial English of many dialects. Like many speakers of English, we use *me* as a subject form in sentences like *Me and John left early.*

[35] That is, no nominative/accusative distinction. The possessive form, as in *John's book*, is sometimes treated as a case called *genitive*, which we met in the Turkish discussion of Chapter 6.

functions correspond only to positions in the sentence. Even among English pronouns the second person form *you* does not distinguish nominative from accusative.

A very different kind of case system is manifested in the Yup'ik Eskimo language of Alaska. Find the subjects of sentences (9.10a.-d.). You will note that there are two sets of suffixes. In (9.10a.) and (9.10c.) the subject is marked with -*aq*, but in (9.10b.) and (9.10d.) the subject is marked with -*am*. What is the difference between the sentences? Note that (9.10a.) and (9.10c.) are intransitives, there is a subject but no object, whereas (9.10b.) and (9.10d.) are transitive, there is a subject and an object of the verb.

9.10 Ergative-absolutive system

Yup'ik Eskimo (Alaska)

a. Doris-aq ayallruuq	"Doris traveled"
b. Tom-am Doris-aq cingallura	"Tom greeted Doris"
c. Tom-aq ayallruuq	"Tom traveled"
d. Doris-am Tom-aq cingallura	"Doris greeted Tom"
e. Ayallruu-nga	"I traveled"
f. Ayallruu-q	"He traveled"
g. Cingallru-a-nga	"He greeted me"

If we look at the markings on the objects in (9.10b.) and (9.10d.), we see that the suffix is -*aq*, the same as the *subjects* in (9.10a.) and (9.10c.). Here is a summary of the patterns in (9.10a.-d.) for Yup'ik and (9.8a.-d.) for Latin:

9.11 Two case-marking patterns

	Yup'ik	Latin
Subject of transitive (ST)	-*am*	-*s*
Subject of intransitive (SI)	-*aq*	-*s*
Object (O)	-*aq*	-*m*

A case form that is used to mark objects (O) and subjects of intransitives (SI), as opposed to subjects of transitives (ST) is called an *absolutive* case. The form used to mark transitive subjects in such a system is called the *ergative* case. Yup'ik is called an *ergative-absolutive* (or sometimes just *ergative*) system.

The table in (9.12) shows us that a nominative-accusative system treats all subjects the same with respect to morphological case, whereas an ergative-absolutive system treats objects the same as subjects of intransitives. The three-way distinction of grammatical relations is divided up in two different ways:

9.12   Two case-marking patterns

Yup'ik		Latin
ERGATIVE	ST	NOMINATIVE
ABSOLUTIVE	SI	
	O	ACCUSATIVE

As you can see, we have chosen the abbreviations O, SI and ST for object, subject of intransitive and subject of transitive. It is worth pointing out that a more standard set of abbreviations is O (for "object"), S (for "subject") and A (originally for "agent"), respectively—these labels exemplify a potentially confusing mixing of categories (grammatical functions and semantic notions).

Thus far, we have discussed ergative-absolutive and nominative-accusative patterns solely as a property of NPs. Now examine sentences (9.10e.f.g.). In particular, look at the suffixes on the verbs. Unlike English verbs which can only mark agreement with the subject, Yup'ik verbs are somewhat like Hungarian in that they can mark both subject and object agreement. We have a limited data set, but you can see that the first person agreement marker *-nga* in (9.10e.) corresponds to an intransitive subject (which need not be expressed by an independent NP), and in (9.10g.) it corresponds to the object of a transitive verb.

You can also see that the third person subject agreement markers in (9.10f.) and (9.10g.) are different. Perhaps at this point you are not surprised by this—after all, the *-q* in (9.10f.) marks the fact that the subject is subject of an intransitive verb, whereas the *-a-* in (9.10g.) marks agreement with a subject of a transitive verb.

To summarize, the marking on both nouns and verbs in Yup'ik treats the subject of an intransitive and the object of a transitive alike, in contrast with the subject of a transitive. The marking on nouns parallels that on verbs. Keep this in mind as we proceed.

For some reason, it typically takes students a while to be able to keep straight the ergative-absolutive vs. nominative-accusative contrast. Here is an informal example to help you. Consider the following sentences involving transitive and intransitive uses of the verb *grow*.

9.13   English transitive alternation

TRANSITIVE	INTRANSITIVE
a. Davey and Sami grow pansies there	Pansies grow there
b. They grow *them* there	*They* grow there

English uses different pronoun forms to correspond to the word *pansies* in the two (9.13b.) sentences—*they* as opposed to *them*. However, from the point of view of meaning, it is clear that both sentences describe a situation in which pansies blossom. So you can imagine a language, English', which marks the argument that has the same relationship to the verb in a consistent fashion, as in (9.14).

9.14   Hypothetical English' transitive alternation

TRANSITIVE	INTRANSITIVE
a. Davey and Sami grow pansies there	Pansies grow there
b. They grow *them* there	*Them* grow there

This hypothetical English' shows an ergative-absolutive pattern, since the form *they* is only used for subject of transitive, and *them* is used for both objects and intransitive subjects.

9.4 A tense-split system

The next language we examine is Georgian, spoken in the Republic of Georgia, in the Caucasus region. You can see from sentences (9.15a.b.) that Georgian seems to have a nominative case marker -*i* that shows up on the subject in both sentences, both SI and ST, and an accusative case marker -*s* on the O in (9.15b.). However, examination of (9.15c.) and (9.15d.) shows a patterning of the SI in (9.15c.) and the O in (9.15d.), both marked by -*i*, as opposed to the ST in (9.15d.) marked by -*ma*. The other difference between the sentences is their tense—Georgian is an example of a tense-split language. It has the nominative-accusative pattern in the present, and the ergative-absolutive pattern in the past tense.

9.15   Tense-split system in Georgian
  a. student-i midis   "The student goes"
      student-NOM goes
  b. student-i ceril-s cers   "The student writes the letter"
      student-NOM letter-ACC writes
  c. student-i mivida   "The student went"
      student-ABS went
  d. student-ma ceril-i dacera "The student wrote the letter"
      student-ERG letter-ABS wrote

There is a potentially disturbing aspect of this analysis. The subjects of (9.15a.) and (9.15c.) look exactly the same—*studenti*, and they are both subject of a form of the verb that we translate by "go." However, in (9.15a.) the suffix -*i* must be analyzed as nominative, due to its occurrence on the subject in (9.15b.); and in (9.15c.), the -*i* must be analyzed as absolutive, given its occurrence on the object in (9.15d.). Recall, however, that cases are categorized by virtue of patterns of relations, not, for example, on the basis of their phonological content. The NPs in Georgian show one pattern in the present tense and another in the past.

This example once again illustrates the necessity for abstract symbolic equivalence classes in linguistic analysis, since the patterns force us to posit two distinct case markers of the form -*i*. The form *studenti* is a subject in all of our sentences above, but it can also be an object. Can you give an English sentence that you think would be rendered into Georgian with the word *studenti* as an object?

9.5 A nominal-verbal mismatch

Recall from the discussion of Yup'ik that the ergative-absolutive pattern on NPs was echoed in the verb agreement markers. For example, the sentences translated "I traveled" and "He greeted me," with a first person singular SI and O, respectively, both had verbs marked with -*nga*. Similarly, there are languages with nominative-accusative case marking on NPs and subject and object agreement on the verb following the same pattern of grouping together SI and O in contrast to ST.

With these patterns in mind, look at the Managalasi data in (9.16). The first two sentences are intransitive, and so you can see that the SI forms of "you" and "I" are *a* and *na*, respectively. Sentence (9.16c.) shows that the O form of "you," *a*, is the same as the SI form in (9.16a.); and (9.16d.) shows that the O form for "me" is the same as the SI form in (9.16b.). Thus, the pronouns show the ergative-absolutive pattern.

9.16   NP vs. V marking split in Managalasi (Papua New Guinea)

a. a vaʔ-ena   "you will go"
   2SG go-FUT:2SG

b. na vaʔ-ejo   "I will go"
   1SG go-FUT:1SG

c. nara a an-aʔ-ejo   "I will hit you"
   1SG 2SG hit-2SG-FUT:1SG

d. ara na an-i?-ena   "you will hit me"
   2SG 1SG hit-1SG-FUT:2SG

Compare this system of pronouns with the so-called agreement markers on the verbs in Managalasi. We see that the verb root meaning "go" is *va?* and the one meaning "hit" is *an*. There are suffixes on these roots that agree with the subject and object pronouns. The suffix *ena* in (9.16a.) marks a second person singular subject (in the future tense), and the suffix *ejo* in (9.16b.) marks a first person singular subject (again in the future tense). These sentences are intransitive, so the subjects are both SI. However, we see in sentences (9.16c.d.) that transitive subjects are marked the same as intransitive ones. In (9.16c.) the subject is "I" and the verb again is marked with *ejo*, as in (9.16b.). There is a second person singular marker *a?* agreeing with the object that differs from the *ena* SI marker in (9.16a.). Sentence (9.16d.) does have *ena* but as a ST, and it has an object marker *i?*.

9.17   Two patterns in a single language—Managalasi first singular

Pronouns		Verb Markers
nara	ST	*ejo*
	SI	
na	O	*i?*

The first exercise at the end of this chapter asks you to make a similar table to show that the same pattern holds for the second person singular forms.

Managalasi provides another example of why it is not useful to classify languages as nominative-accusative or ergative-absolutive. In Georgian, the case system of NPs depended on the tense of the verb. In Managalasi, the pronouns pattern one way and the verb agreement markers pattern the other way. This suggests that the distinction between these systems cannot be stated at the level of the language (the grammar) as a whole. In Georgian it depends on tense; in Managalasi it depends on the pronoun-verb contrast. Think about the implications of these findings for a theory of Universal Grammar.

9.6 A NP-split system

We now consider data from an Australian language called Dyirbal that illustrates yet another kind of split between a nominative-accusative and an ergative-absolutive system.

First, examine the Dyirbal sentences below. We have provided both an English paraphrase with pronouns in order to show case distinctions that are not present on other English NPs and a translation of the Dyirbal words. The typeface coding (bold and italics) both highlights the correspondences in words in Dyirbal and English and corresponds to consistent case forms across the three Dyirbal sentences.

9.18   Some simple Dyirbal sentences

English	Dyirbal	gloss
a. **he** saw *her*	*yabu* **ɲumaŋgu** buran	"**father** saw *mother*"
b. *she* returned	*yabu* banaganʸu	"*mother* returned"
c. **she** saw *him*	ɲuma **yabuŋgu** buran	"**mother** saw *father*"

We see that the meaning "mother" is expressed consistently by *yabu*. When this form occurs as the object of a transitive in (9.18a.), the form is just *yabu*. When it is the subject of an intransitive in (9.18b.), the form is again *yabu*. When it is the subject of a transitive verb in (9.18c.) it occurs with the suffix *-ŋgu*. We can call this the *ergative* marker; the *absolutive* forms are unsuffixed.

9.19   Ergative-absolutive case pattern

ɲuma	yabuŋgu	buran	"**mother** saw *father*"
father	**mother**	saw	
ABSOLUTIVE	ERGATIVE		
yabu		banagan	"*mother* returned"
mother		returned	
ABSOLUTIVE			

The same pattern applies to the words for *father*—so how do you say in Dyirbal "Father returned"?

Here is a table showing the case forms for the Dyirbal word for "mother" in contrast to the pattern shown by the English third singular female pronoun:

9.20   Case patterns for English pronoun and Dyirbal noun

	English	Dyirbal
Transitive subject	**she**	**yabuŋgu**
Intransitive subject	*she*	*yabu*
Object	*her*	*yabu*

So far, Dyirbal just looks like Yup'ik, or Georgian in the past tense, or the pronouns of Managalasi. Now look at sentences that contain first and second person plural pronouns corresponding to *we / us* and *you*.

9.21   Dyirbal pronouns

    a. ŋana banaganʸu   "we returned"
       we-all returned.NON-FUT

    b. nʸurra banaganʸ   "you returned"
       you-all returned.NON-FUT

    c. nʸurra ŋanana buran   "you saw us"
       you-all we-all see.NON-FUT

    d. ŋana nʸurrana buran   "we saw you"
       we-all you-all see.NON-FUT

If we arrange these forms in a table we see that the pronouns behave according to a nominative-accusative pattern.

9.22   Lexical NPs vs. pronouns in Dyirbal

ROOT	"mother"	"father"	"we all"	"you all"
ST	yabuŋgu	ɲumaŋgu	ŋana	nʸurra
SI	yabu	ɲuma		
O			ŋanana	nʸurrana

It thus appears that NPs with a lexical head like the word for "mother" or "father" follow the ergative-absolutive pattern, whereas the pronouns we have seen follow the nominative-accusative pattern. In Dyirbal the equivalence class of NPs has two subcategories that differ in terms of their case-marking properties.

Once again, we see that we cannot characterize grammars as ergative-absolutive or nominative-accusative. In Yup'ik, all nominals follow the ergative-absolutive pattern. In Dyirbal, there is a split between nouns and pronouns. In Georgian, the pattern depends on the tense of the verb. In Managalasi, there is a different patterning on NPs and verb agreement markers. In order to characterize these languages we would have to "look inside," below the level of the whole grammar to the behavior of individual morphemes. For example, the cases assigned by Georgian verbs appear to depend on the morpheme that marks tense. In Dyirbal, case patterns depend on the NPs that are involved.

At first blush, such patterns make the search for Universal Grammar appear to be a hopeless enterprise—it seems that almost anything goes. But this is far from true. In fact, some current approaches to syntax, especially the so-called Minimalist Program initiated by Chomsky, go so far as to suggest that all languages have the same syntax, including the mechanisms for case assignment. The different syntactic phenomena we observe are then attributed to differences in the properties of individual lexical items, including so-called *functional* items that express grammatical notions like tense and person.

Under this view, there is a single universal mechanism for treating the NPs that occur in various structural positions in syntactic trees. In Georgian, the tense morphemes differ in how they affect case marking. In Yup'ik, all tenses behave like the Georgian past. There are many details to be worked out and many controversial aspects of this approach, but the general idea is this: we know that languages differ with respect to the content of their lexicons—the English word *owl* covers both *chouette* and *hibou* of French. English, on the other hand, has a distinction in aspect in the present tense that is lacking in French: *I sleep* and *I am sleeping* would both be translated as *je dors* in French. We can characterize these differences as differences in the morphemes available in the two languages, a difference between the lexicons. Once we do this, the idea that all languages follow the same rules, at some abstract level, becomes more plausible.

9.7 Language, thought and culture

At this point you have certainly come to appreciate somewhat the complexity of human language. We actually suspect that you are less sure that you understand what language really is now that we have gotten you to accept that nothing about it corresponds to our pre-theoretical, everyday notions. With your new appreciation of ergativity and related phenomena, ask yourself what the implications would be for someone who wants to find a link between linguistic structures and the worldview, thought processes, or culture of a particular group. A tremendous problem immediately looms up—what are the elements of a worldview, thought, or culture that can be put into correlation with linguistic elements? Another question is: Is it even plausible to think that, say, all speakers of Dyirbal, Basque, Georgian, and other languages with ergative-absolutive systems share aspects of thought, worldview, or culture that are not shared by speakers of other languages that have no apparent ergativity? Finally, suppose that we could correlate aspects of culture with particular case-marking systems: What do we do about split systems? Do Georgians think and act like English speakers when they use the present tense, but think and act like Dyirbal speakers (using lexical nouns, not pronouns) when they (the Georgians) use the past tense? This all seems rather implausible, and in fact there appears to be no evidence for a correlation between aspects of linguistic structure and any cultural or cognitive property.

9.8 Exercises

Exercise 9.8.1.   Managalasi second person: Go back to the discussion of Managalasi and create a table like that in (9.11) for the second person singular forms from the data in (9.16).

Exercise 9.8.2.   Iyinû-Aimûn verbs: This exercise was prepared by our student Kevin Brousseau who is a speaker of this Algonquian language, a dialect of Cree spoken in Quebec, Canada.

Consider the following sentences:

  i. *nicî   tahcishkuwâu atimw*
     I-PAST kick   dog
     "I kicked the dog"
 ii. *nicî   tahcishken tehtapûn*
     I-PAST kick   chair
     "I kicked the chair"
iii. *cî   pahcishin an   atimw*
     PAST fall   that dog
     "That dog fell"
 iv. *cî   pahchihtin an   tehtapûn*
     PAST fall   that chair
     "That chair fell"

What seems to condition the form of the verb in the two transitive sentences (i.) and (ii.)? What seems to condition the form of the verb in the two intransitive sentences (iii.) and (iv.)? What do these facts together remind you of?

The words for "girl, woman, man, boy, moose" can all replace the word for "dog" in the sentences above; and the words for "sock, shoe, canoe" can all replace the word for "chair," but if we replace, say, "dog" with "canoe" or "chair" with "man," the sequences become ungrammatical. Note that the form *mishtikw* can mean both "tree" and "stick," but it is clear in each of the following which meaning is intended:

  i. *nicî   tahcishkuwâu mishtikw*
     I-PAST kick   tree/stick
     "I kicked the tree"
 ii. *nicî   tahcishken mishtikw*
     I-PAST kick   tree/stick
     "I kicked the stick"
iii. *cî   pahcishin an   mishtikw*
     PAST fall   that tree/stick
     "That tree fell"
 iv. *cî   pahchihtin an   mishtikw*
     PAST fall   that tree/stick
     "That stick fell"

Do the nouns in Iyinû-Aimûn appear to fall into different groups? How might you label those groups? Do you think it is plausible that a mental grammar, which we have been characterizing as a symbol-processing computational system, is sensitive to the kind of information you appealed to in characterizing the noun classes? How does the following bear on this issue?

  i. *nicî   muwâu âihkunâu*
     I-PAST eat   bread
     "I ate the bread"
 ii. *nicî   mîcham mîcim*
     I-PAST eat   food
     "I ate the food"
iii. *cî   pahcishin an   asinî*
     PAST fall   that stone
     "That stone fell"

What determines the nature of Iyinû-Aimûn noun equivalence classes—what the nouns mean or an abstract and arbitrary feature?

Exercise 9.8.3. Guugu Yimidhirr cases: Assume that *you* in a translation always refers to second person singular. Assume that word order is completely free in this language. Ignore any variation between long (double) and short (single) vowels.

1. Nyundu ganaa? Are you well?
2. Nyulu galmba ganaa. She is also fine.
    ★ What is the word for *well, fine*? a._____
    ⇒ The first two sentences have no verb—it need not be expressed in such sentences. You can also think of the adjective as serving as a verb.
    ★ What is the word for *you*? b._____
    ★ For *she*? c._____
3. Nyundu dhadaa? Are you going to go?
    ★ What is the verb in this sentence (in Guugu Yimidhirr)? d._____
4. Yuu, ngayu dhadaa. Yes, I am going to go.
5. Ngayu galmba dhadaa. I too am going to go.
    ★ What is the word for *also, too*? e._____
    ★ For *yes*? f._____
    ★ For *I*? g._____
    ★ For *she*? h._____
6. Ngali dhadaa gulbuuygu. You and I will go together.
    ★ If *gulbuuygu* means together, what does *ngali* mean? i._____
7. Nyundu ganaa. You are OK.
    ⇒ Note that a question does not have different word order from a statement—sentences 7. and 1. are the same in Guugu Yimidhirr.
8. Nyundu Billy nhaadhi. You saw Billy.
    ★ What is the word for *Billy*? j._____
    ★ For *saw*? k._____
9. Ngayu Billy nhaadhi. I saw Billy.
10. Nyundu nganhi nhaadhi. You saw me.
    ★ What does *nganhi* mean? l._____
11. Ngayu nhina nhaadhi. I saw you.
    ★ What does *nhina* mean? m._____
    ★ Using only the sentences above, find a transitive sentence (one with a subject and an object) with *you* (sg.) as the subject. n.# _____
    ★ Then find an intransitive sentence (no object) with *you* as the subject. o.# _____
    ★ Then find one with *you* as an object. p.# _____
    This gives us *you* as an ST, an SI, and an O.

* Fill in the following table:

	2 sg.
ST	q._____
SI	r._____
O	s._____

* Based on the entries in your table, does the 2 sg. pronoun follow the nominative-accusative pattern, the ergative-absolutive pattern, or some other pattern?

    t._____

12. Nyulu nganhi nhaadhi. He saw me.
13. Ngayu nhangu daamay. I speared him.
14. Nyundu nhangu nhaadhi. You saw him.
15. Nyulu nhina nhaadhi. He saw you.

    * How do you think you say *She saw you*?

        u. _____

    * Now fill in the table below:

	1sg.	2sg.	3sg.
ST			
SI			
O			

    * Do the first and third person forms show the same pattern as the second person form? _____

    Consider the further data below.

16. Billy ngayu nhaadhi. I saw Billy.
17. Nhina nhaadhi ngayu. I saw you.
18. Nhaadhi nhangu nyundu. You saw him.
19. Ngayu ganaa. I am well.
20. Wanhu dhadaara? Who is going?
21. Wanhdhu Billy nhaadhi? Who saw Billy?
22. Nyundu wanhu nhaadhi? Who did you see?
23. Nyundu buli? Did you fall down?
24. Wanhdhu nhina dhuurrngay? Who pushed you?
25. Billy-ngun nganhi dhuurrngay. Billy pushed me.
26. Nganhi dhuurrngay. I was pushed./Someone pushed me.
27. Billy dhadaa. Billy is going to go.
28. Ngayu Billy nhaadhi. I saw Billy.
29. Billy-ngun nganhi nhadhi. Billy saw me.
30. Yarrga-ngun nganhi gunday. The boy hit me.

31. Yugu-ngun bayan dumbi. The tree crushed the house.
32. Yarraman-ngun nhina dhuurrngay. The horse pushed you.
33. Yugu buli. The tree fell.
34. Ngayu yugu bulii-mani. I made the tree fall.
35. Nambal duday. The rock rolled away.
    ⋆ Complete the table:

	PERSONAL PRONOUNS			wh-PRONOUN	Name	Common NP
	1sg.	2sg.	3sg.	who	Billy	the boy etc.
ST				w.	z.	cc.
SI				x.	aa.	dd.
O				y.	bb.	ee.

⋆ How do names pattern? Ergative/absolutive or nominative/accusative?
  ff._____
⋆ How do regular noun phrases pattern?
  gg._____
⋆ How does the Guugu Yimidhirr word for *who* pattern?
  hh._____
⋆ How do you think you say *The boy rolled the rock away*?
  ii. _____
⋆ How do you think you say *The boy got pushed*?
  jj._____
⋆ Which sentence best shows that a ST need not be a volitional, conscious agent but rather just be the subject of a transitive sentence?
  kk.# _____

Exercise 9.8.4.   Lakhota: Do the agreement markers on the Lakhota verbs in the following data show a nominative-accusative pattern, an ergative-absolutive pattern, or something else? What seems to determine the forms of a marker agreeing with an intransitive subject? What categories do we need to refer to to predict the forms of a SI? Do you think it is consistent with our discussion thus far that the grammar should be sensitive to such issues? Can you propose any alternative accounts based only on structure?

a-ma-ya-phe   "you hit me"
DIR-1SG-2SG-hit

wa-0-ktékte   "I kill him"
1SG-3SG-kill

0-ma-ktékte   "He kills me"
3SG-1SG-kill

ma-hîxpaye   "I fall"
1SG-fall

ma-t'e'   "I die"
1SG-die

ma-čǎča   "I shiver"
1SG-shiver

wa-škate   "I play"
1SG-play

wa-nûwe   "I swim"
1SG-swim

wa-lowǎ   "I sing"
1SG-sing

Further Readings

Pullum's essay is not only entertaining but also very useful for preparing you for the inevitable moment when someone finds out that you have studied linguistics and asks about the massive number of words for "snow" in Eskimo. Mark Baker's highly accessible book provides an excellent overview of language variation in the context of a theory of Universal Grammar.

- *The Great Eskimo Vocabulary Hoax* by Pullum (1991).
- *The Atoms of Language* by Mark Baker (2001).

PART III

Universal Grammar

10

Approaches to UG: Empirical evidence

In previous chapters our main goal was to develop an understanding of what language is. The way we did that was by discussing many issue related to the concept of I-language, by drawing on examples from various individual I-languages. As mentioned in Chapter 1, however, even though elucidating aspects of individual languages is certainly an important task, one that should precede any other task, this is by no means the ultimate aim of linguistics. Linguistic theory has a goal that goes beyond the study of particular I-languages, namely to develop an understanding of the human language faculty itself. I-languages are fairly different from each other, sometimes in unexpected ways, but ultimately they are all human languages that can be equally well acquired by any human. This means that there must be something that all human languages share. The set of the shared properties of all I-languages and the study of this topic are both called Universal Grammar (UG). Universal Grammar is understood not only as a characterization of the core properties of all languages but also as the initial state of the language faculty. This latter view of Universal Grammar is intimately related to the way in which language acquisition is accounted for. Given that any human can acquire any human language, many linguists have concluded that there is an initial capacity for learning human languages, some innate knowledge, that all humans share.

In this chapter we provide an example of apparent innate knowledge outside of linguistics, in fact from another species, to help make the idea of domain-specific innate knowledge plausible. We then provide another data analysis as an indirect argument for specific content of an innate language faculty, a Universal Grammar. Here, as elsewhere in the book, we are less concerned with the details of specific analyses and specific claims in the literature concerning both linguistic facts and other phenomena than we are with demonstrating how linguists think and the kinds of evidence that they look for. We encourage you to remain skeptical concerning the claims we present, but we hope to convince you that the overall program is headed in the right direction.

10.1 On the plausibility of innate knowledge

As we pointed out in an earlier chapter, the notion of innate linguistic knowledge, or Universal Grammar, has generated a lot of controversy. Some of this controversy, we hold, arises from a failure to appreciate the I-language perspective. The example of Terry Deacon's work, discussed in Chapter 4, represents this problem: he has no reason to accept innate linguistic knowledge or Universal Grammar, since he appears to conceive of language as existing outside of the minds of speakers. However, there are also scholars who accept a fundamentally psychological approach to language yet are resistant to the idea that humans have innate knowledge specific to language. Their position is basically that we are able to learn and use language because of our general intelligence. Just as we can learn to read, play chess, dance the tango, or interact in social situations, we learn language using cognitive skills that are not specific to a single domain. It is unlikely that we evolved a tango faculty or a chess faculty, the argument goes, and it is equally improbable that we have a specific faculty dedicated to language.

There are two aspects to this view that we want to address in this section. First, we want to argue that general intelligence is not enough to learn just any skill. Second, we want to show that domain-specific innate knowledge does appear to exist elsewhere, and thus is at least plausible.

10.1.1 Is it enough to be very smart?

Humans have large brains and we like to think of ourselves as very smart. In general, though, we know that a larger machine or tool cannot always

Fig 10.1 Oonagh and Baby Z are raised in a very similar environment.

perform the functions of a smaller one—a large hammer cannot do what a small screwdriver can and most steamrollers do not allow you to send text messages as well as a compact cellphone does. If you want different functions, you need more than size, you need built-in specialized properties. Now the question becomes whether having and using a language is a fundamentally different type of function from dancing a tango—we'll explore this topic in the next chapter. For now we will make some suggestive remarks concerning domain-specific knowledge.

Consider the two organisms in Fig. 10.1. Baby Z (left) was about two years old when this picture was taken and Oonagh was about nine. There were many similarities in how they were treated:

- Baby Z and Oonagh often shared the same food.
- Baby Z and Oonagh went out on the mountain every day.
- Baby Z and Oonagh received a lot of physical attention, including hugs, caresses, and grooming.
- Baby Z and Oonagh both have heard people speaking to them and around them.

Of course, Oonagh had this wonderful upbringing for a lot longer than Z has—nine years as compared with two years. Perhaps this explains why Oonagh has certain skills that Z does not have. For example, when we take her onto the mountain, she knows where to find groundhogs and how to sneak up on them and catch them. However, when we think back, we realize that Oonagh already knew how to hunt when she was Z's age. One possibility is that Z is a slow learner; another is that he lacks Oonagh's innate knowledge that turned her into an expert hunter with no instruction.

On the other hand, at the time this picture was taken, after nine years of exposure to language, Oonagh appeared to understand and sometimes obey about five words in one language. Z, in contrast, appeared to understand several hundred words in three languages, and also to produce many strings of words in orders consistent with the language from which they were drawn.[36]

In the following year, Oonagh seemed not to progress at all, whereas Z's vocabulary expanded and his sentence structures become complex enough that we could make remarks like "Notice that he inverts subject and auxiliary verb in *wh*-questions like *Who did Sissy call?* but he doesn't invert in Yes/No questions, but rather begins with *if* as in *If Sissy can give me a cookie?* to mean 'Can Sissy give me a cookie?'." We also noticed that he started using negative polarity items in the way that we use them—*I don't want any*, instead of *I don't want some*—at around two years and nine months old. We have no evidence that Oonagh is sensitive to the difference between *some* and *any*.

Note that Oonagh has much better hearing than Z, including sensitivity to a wider frequency range. It seems to us that externalist perspectives on language, something like Deacon's view that posits that language is "out there" in the world, would lead us to expect that Oonagh's better hearing and longer experience would have given her better access to language. It has not. We can attribute her linguistic failure to a lack of intelligence, but then we should do the same with respect to Z's hunting failure. They are both well fed and coddled, so neither has any obvious survival motivation to either talk or hunt. They just seem to be endowed with different properties that develop as they grow up, one as a dog and one as a kid. One of the kid-properties seems to be a language faculty.

10.1.2 Bird brains

We will now move on to other animals, geese, in order to demonstrate the plausibility of innate knowledge in other species. If you cut out a cardboard

---

[36] In spite of his much more extensive linguistic knowledge, his obedience levels matched Oonagh's.

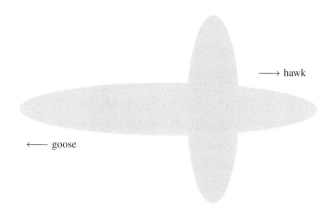

Fig 10.2 Instinct (Innate Knowledge) in goslings.

shape like that in Fig. 10.2 and move it right to left over a cage of newly hatched goslings, the baby birds do not react. However, if you move it left to right, the goslings appear to panic and run for cover. It just so happens that such a shape moving left to right resembles the silhouette of a hawk, a bird of prey that hunts goslings, whereas moving in the other direction, the shape resembles the silhouette of a goose or other non-predatory birds.

It is a commonplace to ascribe such reactions to "instinct." Clearly, the mother birds while sitting on the eggs (if they were indeed present in the laboratory where these birds were raised) did not tap a message on the shell of the egg in some kind of bird version of Morse code explaining to the unhatched gosling "If you see a shape like this, moving towards the long end, run like crazy, but if it moves the other way, you can relax." Somehow, God or evolution has arranged things so that the goslings have some kind of knowledge of shape and motion that underlies their behavior—it's not that they think "Hey, that looks like a hawk, I better find cover," but it seems reasonable to say that they know something about that shape, or rather an equivalence class of perceived shapes, and that their knowledge leads them to act in a certain way.

This knowledge is not learned, and thus is innate, and it is very domain-specific—it has to do with shapes and motion perceived visually. If we are willing to attribute this complex quality of domain-specific innate knowledge to bird-brained goslings, it seems unjustified to deny the possibility that humans, too, have innate domain-specific knowledge, perhaps for language.

10.1.3 An experiment of nature

If we want to claim that it is the structure of the human brain that allows the development of language and not just its size, then it is interesting to ask what would happen if an organism had a brain with human structure, but in miniature. Unfortunately, nature has performed this experiment in the genetic defect of Seckel syndrome, also called nanocephalic or bird-headed dwarfism.

Most cases of dwarfism result in a body that is disproportionate with the head. The head and brain are normal in size and intelligence is unaffected. Seckel syndrome, in contrast, results in a head that is proportionate in size to the body and thus is much smaller than that of normal humans. Subjects with Seckel syndrome suffer from severe mental retardation, but are reported to acquire language relatively normally—there is some delay in reaching developmental milestones, but the language acquired has normal syntax, morphology, and phonology. This suggests that the structure of the brain, not its absolute size, is what allows for the acquisition of human language. Perhaps it is more clear to say that a human brain will have a human language faculty, thus focusing on what is present from birth, rather than on the details of particular languages that may be acquired.

One implicit assumption of the preceding discussion is that knowledge is correlated with the physical properties of the brain. Given this assumption, our discussion thus far is meant to suggest the following:

- the existence of innate knowledge is plausible
- the existence of domain-specific knowledge is plausible
- the structure of the human brain results in or is correlated with human cognitive capacities including innate linguistic knowledge.

For some reason, such a claim tends to evoke much less controversy if we replace *human* with *canine* and *linguistic* with *hunting* knowledge. However, there seem to be no good reasons for this difference, aside from an emotional attachment to maintaining for humans a unique place in the world. For real understanding of what we are, we find it almost trivially obvious that we need to consider the human mind and brain as objects of the natural world.

10.2 More negative thoughts

In the previous sections we argued for the plausibility of innate knowledge arising from the structure of a normal human brain. In this section, we invoke a very different kind of argument for innate knowledge, but one that is also based on empirical considerations. Bear with us as we work through yet another data set—we return to the discussion of negative polarity items, a category introduced in Chapter 6. Our goal is to make explicit in syntactic terms what it means for a NPI to "be in" a downward-entailing environment. We will show you that the distribution of NPIs like *ever* or *anything*, as opposed to *sometimes* or *something*, can be accounted for by using the same kinds of primitives as the ones we need for describing the distribution of anaphors like *himself* or *herself*. The existence of such primitives, that turn out to be crucial for analyzing a number of apparently unrelated phenomena not only in English but in all languages, constitutes empirical evidence for the existence of Universal Grammar. Keep in mind that, although we may get mired in the details of analyzing specific English words, we are doing so with a much loftier goal—we are trying to discover some of the content of Universal Grammar.

Let's start with what we already know about the distribution of NPIs: their occurrence can be correlated with downward-entailing environments, that is, with environments that license an inference from supersets to subsets, like the following:

- If Davey is wearing (any) footwear, he is in trouble. ⇒
- If Davey is wearing (any) socks, he is in trouble.

The question we are asking now is whether this licensing relation has any syntactic correlates? In other words, is there any particular syntactic element that determines the downward-entailing properties of a particular sentence? And, correlatively, if downward entailment is related to such an element, what exactly does it mean to say that NPIs are licensed by this element? As usual, we will simplify the discussion—in this case by focusing on only one NPI—the adverb *ever*, and only one downward-entailing context—negative sentences. However, at the end of our demonstration based on negative sentences we will discuss ways of generalizing the conclusions to the other downward-entailing contexts as well.

You should now be an expert in the process of hypothesis formation and testing, so what we will do is to show you the relevant data and just provide some guidance. Consider the sentences in (10.2).

10.2   a. Nobody ever saw Davey.
        b. Sami didn't ever see Davey.
        c. Sami didn't see Davey ever.
        d. *Sami ever saw Davey.
        e. *Sami saw Davey ever.

Make a co-occurrence hypothesis about the distribution of *ever*. In other words, the grammatical sentences (10.2a.-c.) contain a certain kind of element lacking in the ungrammatical strings (10.2d.e.). Make an initial hypothesis:

10.3   Hypothesis I: *ever* can occur only if the sentence contains . . .

Here's another string that should be grammatical by Hypothesis I but is not.

10.4   f. *Davey ever sees nobody.

Propose an alternative to Hypothesis I that accounts for all the examples considered thus far. Refer to linear order in formulating this second hypothesis.

10.5   Hypothesis II: *ever* can occur only if . . .

Here again are some more examples.

10.6   g. *Mary claims that Sami ever sings.
        h. Mary claims that Sami doesn't ever sing.
        i. Mary doesn't claim that Sami ever sings. [= She does not claim "Sami sometimes sings."]

Is this data consistent with Hypothesis II? Explain how Hypothesis II applies to each of these examples.

Now consider the following:

j. *A man I don't know claims that Sami ever sings.
k. I never said that Sami ever sings.
l. *A man who never did anything nice said that Sami ever sings.

Is this data consistent with Hypothesis II? Explain how Hypothesis II applies to each of these examples.

Here are some more examples.

m. Davey does not believe Sami ever sings.
n. Davey agrees that Fred does not know that Trevor insists that Mary believes that Sami ever sings.

By now you should see that we need a new hypothesis. Formulate Hypothesis III that will account for all the examples seen so far. It must tell us why grammatical sentences are grammatical as well as why the ungrammaticals are ungrammatical. You will need to make a proposal concerning the position in the tree for negative words like *not* and *n't*—let's assume that they are in a position that c-commands the main VP. Here is the tree for sentence (m):

10.9   Position of negation

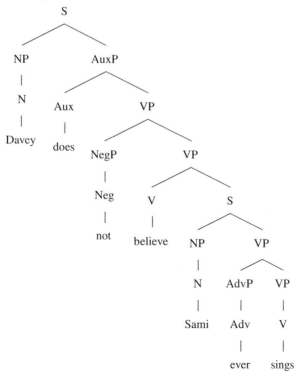

And here is another sentence with negation expressed by the NP *nobody*:

10.10   Nobody ever said Sami ever accepted the offer.

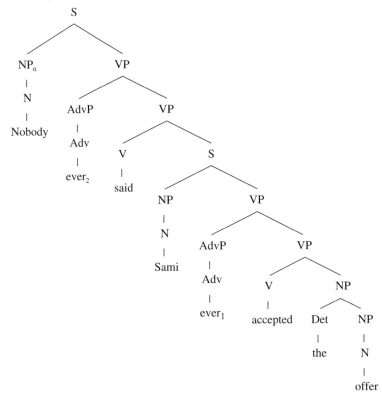

10.11   Hypothesis III: *ever* can occur only if . . .

First, confirm that your Hypothesis III works for the earlier cases as well (i.e. 10.2–10.8). Then use Hypothesis III to explain why each instance of *ever* in (10.10) is grammatical. You can see that the negative expression *nobody* that is NP$_a$ c-commands both *ever*$_1$ and *ever*$_2$.

Now use Hypothesis III to explain why each instance of *ever* in the following sentence is ungrammatical:

10.12   *A man who loves nobody ever said Sami ever accepted the offer.

Here is the tree:

10.13   No c-command

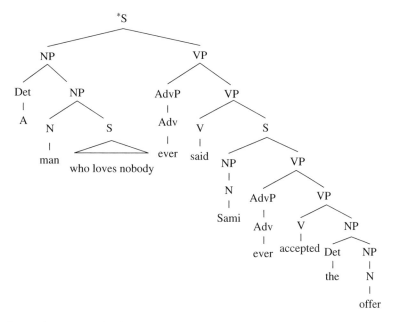

If you formulate Hypothesis III correctly you can now combine this result with our discoveries in Chapter 8 to construct a 2 × 2 table as in (10.14).

10.14   • *her*—must not be in a local c-command relation (may be c-commanded, but not locally)
• *herself*—must be in a local c-command relation
• *the girl*—must not be c-commanded
• *ever*—must be c-commanded

	Locality crucial	Locality irrelevant
Must be c-commanded	*herself*	*ever*
Must NOT be c-commanded	*her*	*the girl*

Some expressions, anaphors like *herself*, need to be in a local c-command relation with a coindexed antecedent; regular pronouns like *her* cannot be locally c-commanded by a coindexed antecedent; referring expressions like *the girl* must not be c-commanded at any distance by a coindexed antecedent; and we now have found that negative polarity items like *ever* must be c-commanded by a negative element, but that locality does not matter.

The conditions on the appearance of the word *ever* actually apply to the whole set (the equivalence class) of words known as negative polarity items

(NPIs). As we saw in Chapter 6, other NPIs include *any, anybody, anything, yet, at all*, etc. For now, we can assume that Hypothesis III generalizes as follows:

> 10.15   NPIs like *ever* must be c-commanded by a NEGATIVE word.

Before we conclude on NPIs, we want to address one more point. Hypothesis III takes care of NPIs occurring in negative contexts, but what about the other contexts that license NPIs? We know already that the right semantic generalization is that NPIs are licensed by contexts that are downward-entailing. Negative contexts are just a particular example of downward-entailing environments, but the latter are not reduced to the former. There are other downward-entailing contexts, such as the ones below, that also license NPIs.

> 10.16   a. Davey left without ever saying goodbye.
> b. Few people ever impressed Davey as much as Sami.
> c. Davey thinks before he ever says anything.
> d. If Sami ever calls, Davey dances gracefully.

How can we generalize Hypothesis III to these contexts? There are two crucial parts to consider: (1) each sentence has an item that triggers a downward-entailment context; and (2) in each case NPIs can only occur in the domain c-commanded by the trigger.

We can tease apart these two aspects by first replacing the trigger with an element that does not trigger downward entailment, as in (10.17). Compare each sentence to its correspondent in (10.16):

> 10.17   a. *Davey left *by* ever saying goodbye.
> b. **Many* people ever impressed Davey as much as Sami.
> c. *Davey thinks *after* he ever says anything.
> d. *Sami ever calls, if Davey dances gracefully.

In (10.16a.) the relevant item that renders the context downward-entailing is *without*; in (10.16b.) it is *few*; in (10.16c.) it is *before*; and in (10.16d.) it is *if*. The effect that these items have on the sentence in which they occur is the same as the effect that a negative element has. We call such items *downward-entailing operators*. In the corresponding examples in (10.17) we have replaced these items with ones that do not trigger downward entailments (10.17a.-c.), or we have moved the downward-entailing operator to the other clause (10.17d.). In each case the result is ungrammatical.

So, we need a downward-entailing operator to be present, but at this point you will not be surprised to know that the operator has to be in a particular position with respect to the NPI—it must c-command the NPI. Without going into all the details, you can probably see that the downward-entailing operator in the following examples clearly does not c-command the NPI, and thus the results are ungrammatical.

10.18 a. *Davey *ever* left *without* saying goodbye.
       b. *Davey *ever* impressed *few* people as much as Sami.
       c. *Davey *ever* thinks *before* he says anything.
       d. *Sami *ever* calls, *if* Davey dances gracefully.

Let's review by concentrating on the (c.) sentences of (10.16, 10.17, 10.18). In (10.17c.), *after* is not a downward-entailing operator and this cannot license the presence of *ever*, so the string is ungrammatical. In (10.18c.) we have a downward-entailing operator, *before*, but it does not c-command *ever*—(10.19) is the tree structure we propose, with *before* occupying what is called a complementizer (Comp) position at the beginning of an S', similar to the position of the connectors introduced in Chapter 6. The NPI c-commands *before*, but not vice versa.

10.19   Potential tree for (10.18c.)

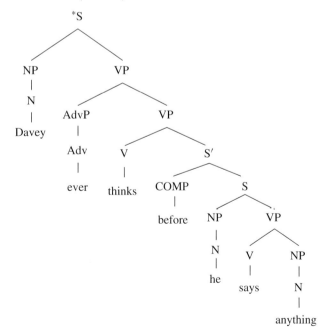

In contrast, the tree for the grammatical (10.16c.) has the NPIs *ever* and *anything* c-commanded by the downward-entailing operator *before*.

10.20 Tree for (10.16c.)

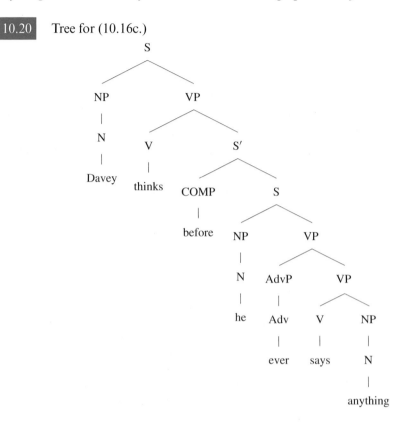

In this sentence, and the rest of the examples in (10.16), there is a downward-entailing operator present and it c-commands the NPI. We thus have found the general version of Hypothesis III:

10.21 NPIs must be c-commanded by a downward-entailing operator.

Note that a single operator can license more than one NPI, as shown by the occurrence of both *ever* and *anything* in this example.

To review, we have identified two equivalence classes, downward-entailing operators and NPIs, as well as the c-command relation, which is relevant to the relation between members of these two categories.

Imagine someone had asked you, before you studied any linguistics, if you thought there could be any significant generalization that governed the distribution of a pronoun like *anybody*, adverbs like *ever* or *yet*, and prepositional phrases like *at all*. Not only have we discovered that they are subject to the same condition—c-command by a downward-entailing operator, but we have also shown that their distribution can be captured by using the same primitives that are needed to explain the distribution of expressions like *her*, *herself*, and *the girl*.

At this point, you might be convinced that c-command is a primitive that is needed for the analysis of several phenomena, such as the distribution of anaphors and pronouns, or the distribution of NPIs, but you might still be skeptical about the actual universality of these categories and the c-command relation. After all, we have only shown you English examples.

Consider now the following examples from Modern Greek.

10.22   a. *I Ilektra enekrine *kanena* sxedhio.
             the Electra approved any plan
         b. I Ilektra *dhen* enekrine *kanena* sxedhio.
             the Electra not approved any plan
             "Electra didn't approve any plan."
         c. O papus pethane *xoris* na dhi *kanena* apo ta egonia tu
             the grandfather died without subj. see any from the grandchildren his
             "My grandfather died without seeing any of his grandchildren."
         d. O papus pethane *prin* na dhi *kanena* apo ta egonia tu
             the grandfather died before subj. see any from the grandchildren his
             "My grandfather died before seeing any of his grandchildren."
         e. *An* his tin Ilectra *puthena*, na tis pis na me perimeni
             if see the Electra anywhere, subj her tell subj me wait
             "If you see Electra anywhere, tell her to wait for me."
         f. *Elaxisti* fitites idhan *tipota*.
             very-few students saw anything
             "Very few students saw anything."

Just as in English, Greek NPIs must be c-commanded by a downward-entailing operator. In (10.22a.), the example includes no downward-entailing operator at all, and this explains why the occurrence of *kanena* in this context leads to ungrammaticality. In (10.22b.), *kanena* "any" is c-commanded by the downward-entailing operator *dhen* "not;" in (10.22c.) by *xoris* "without;" and in (10.22d.) by *prin* "before." The NPI illustrated in (10.22e.) is *puthena* "anywhere," and the latter is c-commanded by the downward-entailing operator *an* "if," while in (10.22f.), the NPI *tipota* "anything" is c-commanded by the downward-entailing operator *elaxisti* "very few."

We have not provided a proof that Greek works in exactly the same way as English with respect to NPIs, and, as usual, there are complicating factors as we look at NPIs cross-linguistically. Nonetheless it is striking that downward entailment and c-command should recur as necessary components of the explanations. It is at least plausible that this recurrence reflects a deep fact about the kinds of generalizations that the language faculty encodes.

So, c-command is clearly not restricted to English. We now show two new non-English phenomena which require appeal to c-command: noun incorporation and phonological "liaison."

Noun incorporation is a phenomenon in which a noun root appears inside of a complex verb form. Although we have presented word formation within the domain of morphology, in many cases, the distinction between morphology and syntax is still being explored in current research. In simplified terms, the generalization, due to Mark Baker (2001:90ff.), is

> **10.23** Noun incorporation: Incorporated nouns are copies of nouns that meet the following conditions:
>
> • they are *bare* nouns, nouns that occur without modifiers
> • their base position is that of the nearest NP to the verb which is c-commanded by the verb.

Consider the following Mohawk examples, where the slightly varying boldface form means "meat":

> **10.24** a. Owiraa wahrake ne **owahru**.
>   Baby ate the meat
>   b. Owiraa wah**awahr**ake.
>   Baby meat-ate
>   c. *Wahawirake ne **owahru**.
>   Baby-ate the meat

In (10.24a.) the noun is not a bare noun, since there is an article present in the NP, so incorporation cannot apply. In (10.24b.) the base position of "meat" would be the object position, which is c-commanded by the verb. Since the c-command condition is met, and since this is a bare noun, incorporation occurs. The subject noun cannot be incorporated, in (10.24c), since the subject NP c-commands the verb and is not c-commanded by it.

As a final dramatic example of the universality of c-command, consider the phenomenon of *liaison* in French. Liaison refers to the presence of certain consonants that are pronounced at the end of a word when the following word begins with a vowel. Before a consonant-initial word the consonant is not pronounced. The string *le marchand de draps anglais* corresponds to two meanings in French.

> **10.25**   *le   marchand de draps anglais*
> the merchant of cloth English

This can mean "the English merchant of cloth" or "the merchant of English cloth." When it has the first meaning, the *s* at the end of *draps* is not pronounced, but when it has the second meaning, the *s* is pronounced (as *z*).

Now examine the trees that correspond to these two meanings. If the meaning is "English merchant of cloth" then *anglais* modifies the NP *marchand de draps* and thus they are sisters in the tree, as in (10.26).

> **10.26**   • [Le [[marchand [de draps]] anglais]]
> • the English cloth seller

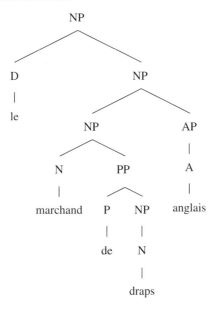

However, if *anglais* modifies *draps* then these two words must be sisters, as in (10.27).

10.27   • [Le [marchand [de [draps anglais]]]]
        • the seller of English cloth

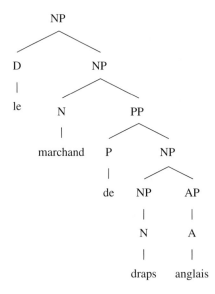

We are not going to attempt to prove that we have the correct analysis, but just note that in (10.27), the NP *draps* c-commands the adjective, and that is where we get the liaison consonant z. We suggest that the c-command relation is a necessary condition for liaison to occur. In (10.26) *draps* does not c-command *anglais* and liaison cannot occur.

If our suggestion is correct concerning c-command as a condition on liaison, then it now appears that this structural relation is found across constructions and across languages—it is a good candidate as a basic component of Universal Grammar. There is no logical reason why c-command should recur in construction after construction and in language after language. There is also no reason that relates the recurrence of c-command to the fact that we sometimes use language for communication. It just appears to be an arbitrary property of the language faculty that linguists have discovered—its very arbitrariness makes it most interesting.

Appealing to c-command really does allow us "to abstract from the welter of descriptive complexity certain general principles governing computation that would allow the rules of a particular language to be given in very simple forms" (Chomsky 2000b:122), which is the ultimate goal of linguistic theory. In addition, we must recognize that the relation of c-command is not present in the acoustic signal—it is a very abstract relation defined over the abstract tree structures that the mind constructs. The fact that c-command is not detectable in the signal and the fact that it is not taught to kids by their parents make it a good candidate for an aspect of innate knowledge.

In conclusion, we have provided two kinds of empirical evidence for the plausibility of innate knowledge. First, we have argued that innate knoweldge is found in animals, for example in the differential reactions shown to various shapes without any prior experience. Second, we argued that the recurrence of patterns like c-command relations across languages and across syntactic constructions suggests the use of a toolkit of primitives from which the patterns of language are constructed.

10.3 Exercises

Exercise 10.3.1.   Complex syntax of NPIs: Consider the following example. Draw a tree with as much detail of structure as you can argue for. Explain why each instance of *ever* is well formed in accordance with the final hypothesis developed in the chapter. Discuss any complications that this example presents.

10.28   Nobody who ever did anything nice ever said Sami sings.

Exercise 10.3.2.   "Mixed" languages: Mark Baker, author of *Atoms of Language*, proposes that Universal Grammar determines that languages should be *either* head-initial (with prepositions and verbs before their objects etc.) *or* head-final (with postpositions and verbs after their objects etc.). Amharic, however, shows properties of both types. To explain such mixed cases Baker says

Amharic, for example, is a Semitic language, related to pure head-initial languages like Arabic and Hebrew but spoken in Africa, in the environment of head-final Cushitic and Nilo-Saharan languages. The conflict of historical and geographic influences could partially explain why Amharic is a mixed case.

What do you think of Baker's proposal in the context of the I-language approach?

Further Readings

- Canty and Gould (1995) discusses the original goose/hawk findings from 1939 and 1948, as well as problems with attempts to reproduce the effect.

11

Approaches to UG: Logic

In Chapter 10 we argued that evaluation of c-command relations is a fundamental component of the human language faculty, on the basis of its recurrence in accounting for a wide range of phenomena in various languages. We did not actually address the issue of how individual languages are acquired, but instead implicitly adopted the approach that we have to first get an understanding of what language is *before* we ask how it is acquired or used.

It is common in discussions of Universal Grammar and innateness to refer to the speed and ease with which children learn language or the fact that the ability to learn languages appears to deteriorate as adulthood approaches. We have not based any arguments on such notions, since they seem to us to be imprecise—kids learn language fast compared to what? If it took twice as long as it does, would that be an argument against innateness? Also, it appears that much of what we impressionistically think of as language acquisition is really just maturation of the performance systems and acquisition of lexical items—young infants do not know any words and they spend a lot of time, as Melancholy Jacques says, mewling and puking, so it is hard to get much evidence about their underlying linguistic competence.

In this chapter we take a very different approach to arguing for the existence of Universal Grammar—we try to argue that it is a logical necessity that there exist some substantive knowledge specific to language prior to what we call language acquisition.

The idea that it is possible to develop a non-trivial Universal Grammar is not necessarily tied to the notion of innateness. Under non-internalist views of language, views that reject the I-language perspective we developed in Part I, there could potentially be universal aspects of language according to some other definition. For example, if one adopted the view of languages as Platonic ideals existing apart from speakers, then, presumably, it would be possible that all these P-languages could have some common properties, whatever it is that makes them languages, that nothing else has. However, the notion of Universal Grammar in the context of the I-language perspective seems to us to necessarily lead to what is sometimes called the Innateness (or Nativist) Hypothesis for language, the idea that (non-trivial) aspects of the linguistic competence of every human are derived from the genetic endowment that makes us human, just as aspects of our visual systems and our digestive systems are dependent on the human genome.

Basically, the Innateness Hypothesis for language states that a plausible source for those aspects of mental grammars that are universal and unlearnable is genetic inheritance. Human languages are constrained and partially determined by our genes. The same is true for the communication systems, visual systems, and digestive systems of whales, dogs, birds, and cockroaches, too.

It is hard to imagine how anyone could object to the Innateness Hypothesis, thus described. In some sense it could be taken as a description of a research topic, rather than a hypothesis: it is clear that there is such a thing as a human language faculty and it must have some initial state before the effects of individual experience; Universal Grammar attempts to understand that initial state. However, we want to take an even stronger position. We want to argue that it is a logical necessity that there be a body of innate knowledge that is specific to language (obviously not particular languages). We will demonstrate this by explicating a position we refer to as the *Innateness of Primitives Principle* (*IofPP*). One formulation of *IofPP* comes from Ray Jackendoff (1990:40): "In any computational theory, 'learning' can consist only of creating novel combinations of primitives already innately available."

We will demonstrate the logical necessity of *IofPP* with a set of model languages. The chain of reasoning we will pursue in explicating the *IofPP* can be summarized as follows. Intelligence (by which we mean merely cognition) consists of the construction and manipulation of symbolic representations. Interacting intelligently with the world requires the ability to *parse* input (assign it a representation). Learning is a form of intelligent interaction with the world, thus learning requires parsing inputs into representations. Without an innate set of representational primitives, learning cannot begin.

As you surely appreciate by now, actual human languages are quite complex, so we will discuss *IofPP* in light of a set of toy languages. In characterizing these languages we need to keep in mind the notion of equivalence classes corresponding to features like those we discussed in our characterization of vowels when we analyzed Turkish vowel harmony in Chapter 6. Linguists are far from agreeing on what the proper set of linguistic features are, and there are many kinds of feature systems proposed in the literature, for both syntax and phonology. In addition to our main point concerning innateness, we hope that the following discussion will also provide you with some insight into the various possibilities for feature systems that you may encounter as you learn more about linguistics.

In our discussion of vowels we introduced paired features like ROUND and NON-ROUND. More typically such pairs are described as valuations of a single binary feature [± ROUND]—vowels can be [+ROUND] or [−ROUND]. Another way to describe a symbol like [+ROUND] is as an attribute-value pair: ROUND is an attribute and it can have the value "+" or "−". Features can be binary or have more values, for example, some systems assign vowels any one of three values for height, as opposed to the HIGH vs. NON-HIGH contrast we set up in our discussion of Turkish. But our discussion also hinted at the possibility of privative features that are either present or absent, attributes that cannot take different values. In the following discussion you will see some of the implications of choosing one or another feature system. Finally, our discussion of Turkish implicitly made use of another tool of feature theory, underspecification. We allowed segments to be either fully specified for all attributes, for example a HIGH, FRONT, ROUND vowel in a word root; or partially underspecified, for example, the NON-HIGH, NON-ROUND vowel of the plural suffix that only received its valuation for FRONT or NON-FRONT by copying it from a vowel to its left.

11.1 Let's play cards

In this section we illustrate the logic the Innateness of Primitives Principle statement by using model languages consisting of sets of playing cards from a normal deck. In our analogy, cards correspond to strings of words of natural languages. From our point of view as observers, a card c will be grammatical, ungrammatical, or neither to a "speaker" of a card grammar G. The reason for the third possibility ('neither') will become clear below. We further assume that learners of these "card languages" are endowed with an innate card language faculty. We will explore the effect of tinkering with "card UG" below. In general, UG will consist of types of symbols and logical operators for symbols. Our assumptions are sketched in (11.1).

11.1	General Principles:

> • Each card is grammatical, ungrammatical, or neither.
> • A grammar is a set of conditions on cards.
> • UG is a set of primitives, including:
>   • types of symbols (features)
>   • logical operators defined over these symbols
> • A card c is "grammatical" with respect to a grammar G iff c satisfies the conditions imposed by G. In such a case we will say, informally, that c is "in G."

We will now explore how the nature of "card UG" limits the set of possible languages available to a learner.

11.1.1 UG1

Assume first that UG makes available to the learner the (privative) feature NUMBERCARD which characterizes cards that bear the numbers two through ten. Further assume that UG makes available the four suits: clubs, diamonds, hearts, spades (♣, ◇, ♡, ♠). These also function as privative features.[37] Finally, assume that UG makes available the logical operator AND, which allows for the conjunction of features in structural descriptions. We call this version of universal grammar UG1.

---

[37] Note that only one of these suit features can characterize any given card. We could equivalently propose an attribute SUIT that can be paired with one of four values, ♣, ◇, ♡, ♠.

| 11.2 | UG1 |

- Features:
    NUMBERCARD
    ♣, ◇, ♡, ♠
- Operators: AND

11.1.1.1 *Possible grammars given UG1*   Now consider some possible grammars, given the definition of UG1. Our first grammar is G_1, which is characterized as follows: G_1 = [NUMBERCARD]. This is to be read as "A sentence/card is in G_1 if and only if it is a numbercard." So, the king of diamonds is ungrammatical in G_1. This is because a king is not a numbercard. On the other hand the six of diamonds and the three of clubs are both grammatical in G_1.

Consider a second possible grammar G_2, characterized as follows: G_2 = [NUMBERCARD AND ◇]. This is to be read as "A sentence/card is in G_2 if and only if it is a diamond numbercard." In this grammar the king of diamonds is still ungrammatical, but so is the three of clubs. The six of diamonds is obviously grammatical.

Now consider G_3, defined as follows: G_3 = [♠]. That is, "A sentence/card is in G_3 if and only if it is a spade." It is obvious what the grammatical sentences of this grammar are, but we now ask: What is the representation of 5♠? K♠? 5♣? The answers are [NUMBERCARD AND ♠], [♠] and *[NUMBERCARD AND ♣],[38] respectively. Only the third is ungrammatical, since it is not a spade.

Finally, consider G_4, which is characterized by no features at all. In other words, it places no restrictions on which cards are grammatical: G_4 = [ ]. That is to say "Every sentence/card is in G_4." But now, is this completely true? The answer is that it is true of all the cards characterizable by UG1, say the fifty-two cards that can be assigned a representation given UG1. However, a tarot card or even a joker would not be grammatical in G_4, given UG1. (Thinking ahead a bit, what would their representation be?)

---

[38] We are assuming that the learner retains access to the UG-given features, even if these features are not used in the acquired language. Rejecting this assumption would not substantively affect the argument, but would unnecessarily complicate the exposition. We are indebted to Afton Lewis for discussions on this point.

11.1.1.2 *Impossible grammars given UG1*   Since any given UG delimits the set of possible grammars, it is also instructive to consider a few impossible grammars, under the assumption of UG1. Consider first (non-)grammar F_1 described as follows: F_1 = [PICTURECARD]. In other words, "A sentence/card is in F_1 if and only if it is a picturecard." Clearly this is an impossible grammar, since UG1 does not provide for a class of all and only picturecards. (Recall that NUMBERCARD is privative by hypothesis.) Similarly, consider F_2 = [NUMBERCARD OR ◇]: "A sentence/card is in F_2 if and only if it is a numbercard or a diamond (or both)." This is an impossible grammar since UG1 does not provide the logical operator OR. Next consider a potential grammar with severely limited expressive capacity: F_3 = [6 AND ♠], that is "A sentence/card is in F_3 if and only if it is the six of spades." This grammar is impossible given UG1 since UG1 does not provide the means to represent a six as different from any other number.

11.1.2 UG2

Now imagine another species endowed with a different universal grammar called UG2, characterized by the following features: [±PICTURE], which is equivalent to having the mutually exclusive privative features [NUMBER-CARD, PICTURECARD], and [±RED], which is equivalent to having the mutually exclusive features [RED, BLACK]. UG2, like UG1, provides the operator AND.

> 11.3   UG2
>
> • Features:
>   [±PICTURE]
>   [±RED]
> • Operators: AND

11.1.2.1 *Some possible grammars given UG2*   A possible grammar given UG2 is G_5 = [+RED AND −PICTURE]: "A sentence/card is in G_5 if and only if it is a red numbercard." What is the representation of 7◇ in this grammar? What about 7♡? And 7♠? The answers are [+RED AND −PICTURE], [+RED AND −PICTURE] and *[−RED AND −PICTURE], respectively. Since the suits are not distinguishable given UG2, the learner parses the two red cards as [+RED]. Since the numbers are indistinguishable given UG2 (as was the case with UG1) the fact that the three cards in question are all sevens is lost to the learner. They are all just [−PICTURE]. Now consider G_6 = [+RED]:"A sentence/card is in G_6 if and only if it is a red card." This grammar will include all the red cards, hearts and diamonds, number and picturecards, though of course these distinctions are not made by creatures endowed with UG2—they are only made by beings like us whose genetic endowment equips them to represent such contrasts.

11.1.2.2 *Some impossible grammars given UG2*   It should be easy now to see that the following two potential grammars are impossible given UG2.

- F_4 = [♠]
  "A sentence/card is in F_4 if and only if it is a spade."
- F_5 = [+PICTURE OR −RED]
  "A sentence/card is in F_5 if and only if it is a picturecard or a black card (or both)."

The first is impossible since UG2 does not distinguish the suits; the second, because UG2 does not provide OR. Note, however, that although F_4 is impossible assuming UG2, its specification is identical to the grammar G_3 which is allowed by UG1. So, again, the nature of UG determines the set of possible grammars.

11.1.3 UG3

We leave it to the reader to confirm that the following characterization of a third UG, UG3, allows for G_7, G_8, and G_9, but excludes F_6, F_7, and F_8.

11.4   Description of UG3
- Features:
  [PICTURECARD]
  [2,3,4,5,6,7,8,9,10]
  [±RED]
- Operators: AND, OR

11.5   Some possible grammars given UG3:
- G_7 = [+RED AND 9]
  "A sentence/card is in G_7 if and only if it is a red nine."
- G_8 = [−RED AND PICTURECARD]
  "A sentence/card is in G_8 if and only if it is a black picturecard."
- G_9 = [PICTURECARD OR +RED]. "A sentence/card is in G_9 if and only if it is a red card or a picturecard (or both)."

| 11.6 | Some impossible grammars given UG3: |

- $F_6 = [\spadesuit]$
  "A sentence/card is in F_6 if and only if it is a spade."
- $F_7 = [\text{NUMBER}]$
  "A sentence/card is in F_7 if and only if it is a numbercard."
- $F_8 = [-\text{RED AND Q}]$
  "A sentence/card is in F_8 if and only if it is a black queen."

It is worth pointing out that, given UG3, it is possible to acquire a grammar that is *extensionally* equivalent to F_7, call it G_{10}: "A sentence/card is grammatical if it is [2 OR 3 OR 4 OR 5 OR 6 OR 7 OR 8 OR 9 OR 10]." Of course, as we discussed in Chapter 4, the I-language perspective allows us to set as our goal the discovery of the "correct" model of a speaker's grammar, one that is, for example, compatible with a theory of UG that underlies all human languages. Thus if a creature endowed with UG3 appeared to have a grammar extensionally equivalent to F_7 and G_{10}, we would know that the correct characterization of this grammar would be the latter and not the former. We have accessible the term "numbercard" but the species endowed with UG3 does not. So, we have demonstrated how the nature of UG limits the set of possible grammars—the set of achievable final states of the language faculty is partially determined by what is present at the initial state.

11.1.4 An impoverished UG4

Now imagine that UG4 provides only a single privative feature: [$\diamond$]. What happens if we expose a learner to 5$\diamond$? The learner parses (constructs a representation for) [$\diamond$]. The "5" is unparsable. It is not *linguistic* information. Now, expose the learner to "6$\heartsuit$." The learner parses nothing! There is no linguistic information in the input. (A linguistic parallel would be the parse of a belch by a human phonological system.) In fact only two grammars can be defined given UG4. $G_{11} = [\diamond]$ allows all and only diamond cards as grammatical utterances. $G_{12} = [\ ]$ defines, actually, a grammar that is extensionally equivalent to G_{11}, that is the two contain the same sentences but these sentences are generated by different grammars. The reason is that, given G_{12}, cards can either be assigned the representation $\diamond$, or they are not parsed at all. So the only cards that will count as linguistic entities are the diamonds. (What happens if we instead use a binary feature [$\pm\diamond$]? Hint:

In addition to languages with no restrictions, like G_{12}, we can define two languages that contain non-overlapping sets of cards.)

11.1.5 A really impoverished UG5

What if UG provides nothing at all—no features and no operators? Then, no matter what we expose the learner to, nothing will be parsed. The starting point for the grammar we ultimately construct cannot be an empty slate since, to quote Jackendoff again, "Without Mental Grammar, there's no language perception—just noise" (1994:164). To reiterate: The set of primitives supplied by UG determines the set of possible grammars that can be described. Without any primitives, no grammar can be described. So the card language faculty of a creature endowed with UG5 will parse any given card in the same way as it will parse a tarot card, the Mona Lisa, or the smell of pepperoni. Any innate system that parses such entities distinctly must be endowed with a mechanism for distinguishing between them. This mechanism, obviously, must be innate.

Before we move on, consider the contrast between a really large 2♠ (like a prop for a magician) and a really small one (like a card from a travel deck), as depicted in Fig. 11.1. Obviously these two cards differ physically—one is big and one is small. They may even have different patterns on their backs and differ in many other ways. But the two cards are *linguistically identical*. They differ in the same way that whispering and shouting a given word differ, that is, they differ only paralinguistically. From the linguistic perspective they are members of the same equivalence class.

Crucially, our claim is not that the contrast in card size will be imperceptible to an acquirer—merely that no size information will be used in the construction of the representations relevant to the "linguistic" module. That is, given a particular card UG, the relevance of specific contrasts that fall within the perceptual capabilities of the learner for card-grammar learning can be made explicit. The set of possible card grammars consists precisely of those that are UG-consistent. The fact that a learner can perceive the difference between large cards and small ones, or between a card on the ceiling and a card on the floor, will not be relevant to the grammatical learning task. For a learner for whom these contrasts are perceptible, any theory that fails to recognize innate primitives *within the card-grammar domain*

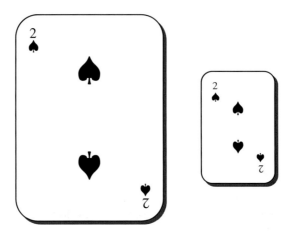

Fig 11.1 A non-"linguistic" card contrast.

will fail to account for the construction of grammars—i.e. the primitives of grammar construction cannot arise from the primitives of perception.

We have been forced to the logical conclusion that there must be something at the initial state of the grammar in order to allow learning to occur. However, one might object: "Maybe the primitives at the initial state are even more basic than what we have posited. For example, if we are sensitive to the difference between straight and curved lines we could discover the distinction between ◇ and ♡." This is perfectly reasonable. It just means that, say, "straight" vs. "curved" are the innate primitives. But YA GOTTA START WITH SOMETHING! That something is Universal Grammar.

It should now be obvious that we are heading towards the conclusion that children must "know" (that is have innate access to) the set of linguistic features used in all of the languages of the world. Of course, they must also have innate access to a set of logical operators or functions—the AND and OR of card grammars or the operators of real human grammars that make phenomena like reduplication and c-command possible.

Obviously, we are not claiming that the set of primitives of phonology corresponds exactly to the set of distinctive features referred to in the literature. There is no question that some of the features have yet to be identified or properly distinguished from others. In some cases a currently assumed feature may represent a conglomeration of the actual primitives of phonological representation. However, by definition, UG, the innate component of the language faculty, consists of the elements of linguistic representation that cannot be derived from anything else.

Consider a proposal that X is necessary for the acquisition of human language and that X is innate. Critics of the proposed innateness of X must formulate their criticism in one of two ways. Either they must provide a learning path that is not dependent on X—i.e. they must challenge the claim that X is necessary for the acquisition of human language, or they must derive X from some other, more basic entities and processes (such as Y), themselves available to the acquirer innately. In the absence of such alternatives, the criticism is invalid. The second alternative is the favorite of so-called constructivist theories of cognitive development. However, note that the appeal to "general learning mechanisms," without specifying in detail what the set of actual primitives involved in any such mechanisms are, is not a responsible critique of the nativist stance.

11.2 Where does this leave us?

It seems to be immensely difficult for many people to come to grips with the idea that in order to learn, the learner must possess the relevant representational primitives *within the learning domain*. We have been forced to conclude that children are born knowing the set of features used in the languages of the world. Is this logical conclusion even remotely plausible? Well, recall our quotations from Zenon Pylyshyn at the end of Chapter 1:

[I]f you believe P, and you believe that P entails Q, then even if Q seems more than a little odd, you have some intellectual obligation to take seriously the possibility that Q may be true, nonetheless.

It is more than a little odd to think that infants have this knowledge. However, researchers who have taken the possibility seriously have found empirical support for this conclusion. For just about every possible contrast in the language of the world that has been tested, experiments indicate that newborn infants are sensitive to the contrast. Well-known and well-replicated results by Janet Werker and her colleagues indicate that language acquisition involves the *loss* of the ability to make distinctions. We are "deafened" by our experience, in some sense, since by around ten months children appear to respond differently to contrasts to which they were sensitive just after birth.[39] This is an exciting topic that has been studied using ingenious techniques showing children's sensitivity to various contrasts, but we will not present the details here.

Werker's results on children's abilities to distinguish adult categories of speech sounds, and thus to represent them as members of different categories, suggest that children's speech output does not provide direct evidence of their underlying representational system. As we will discuss in Chapter 13, the same is true for adults—speech behavior does not provide direct access to the grammar, since many systems, the so-called *performance systems*, intervene between the grammar and the speech output. As in any other domain of behavior,[40] babies' immature cognitive and physiological performance systems make their speech output sound messier than that of adults, thus obscuring their underlying systems even more.

We can distill this presentation of the *IofPP* with what is superficially a paradox: the fact that languages are learned proves that there is an innate basis for language. This is valid, not paradoxical, since in order to learn any aspects of linguistic knowledge, there must necessarily be some body of innate knowledge that allows for the parsing of input into representations from which generalizations can be extracted. Without the innate basis nothing can be parsed, so nothing can be learned.

Before we conclude this discussion of the logical necessity of innate features, we should make it clear that there are many scholars in phonetics, phonology, and psychology who would not accept our conclusions in this chapter. Instead, they believe that by statistical analysis of ambient speech, categories can be constructed without any innate structure. For example, consider the announcement of a recent conference workshop (NELS 38, the 38th meeting of the North East Linguistic Society):

Some of the founding assumptions of Generative Phonology involve abstract units such as distinctive features, timing units, syllables, and constraints. The innateness of these units has been seen as an important part of their nature. Recent work has sought to undermine the claim that innate primitives are necessary for phonological

---

[39] They do not lose the capacity to hear distinctions of sound but only to hear them as linguistic distinctions. However, even this loss appears to be reversible, at least to a certain age, when a new language is learned—something apparently gets the language faculty to "turn on" access to the innately available linguistic contrasts in order to learn a new grammar.

[40] Any domain other than learning, which perhaps should not be considered a behavior—see discussion in Chapter 13. Our position here is controversial—see Hale and Reiss (1998) for detailed arguments.

theory, often drawing more directly upon more concrete factors such as phonetics and language change as sources of explanation.

In our opinion, no empirical evidence by itself can undermine our logical argument for the innateness of primitives. Our conclusions may be false, but this must be shown by a critique of either our premises or our reasoning. This debate relates to a fundamental difference between the rationalist views we represent and a more data-oriented empiricist perspective. We cannot provide a full presentation of all the relevant issues in these debates, but we will revisit some of them in Chapter 13.

11.3 Building blocks in other domains

The notion that all languages are constructed from the same "raw materials," the same innate set of primitive features and operators, what is sometimes called the human language faculty or Universal Grammar, continues to encounter resistance. In this chapter and the previous one, we have provided several arguments to address this resistance. We mentioned the instinct or innate knowledge in birds concerning the visual representation of potential predators. This example suggested the plausibility of innate knowledge in a non-linguistic capacity of a non-human species. It does not prove the existence of UG, but turns the skeptic's doubts around—why should we attribute innate knowledge to a species and a capacity that we tend to think of as less complex than humans and their language, but resist the notion of UG, innate knowledge specific to language? We then presented empirical evidence for the recurrence of the c-command relation across constructions and languages as an illustration of the kind of abstract properties that characterize UG. In this chapter we have presented a logical argument that no learning can occur without an innate set of representational primitives. Before we close, we offer another conceptual argument to counter skepticism about UG.

Start with your own body—run your hands across your face, poke yourself in the eye, floss your teeth until you bleed, fatten your liver with a martini, think about how beautiful life is. Every single part of your body is made up of cells—skin cells, eyeball cells, blood cells, liver cells, brain cells, etc. And it turns out that every single one of these cells contains the exact same genetic material; the diversity of the cells in your body arises from a single set of building blocks (aside from gametes which are missing half of your genetic material). Now let's expand our focus, from your own body to all living things. All genetic material, all DNA, is built out of an alphabet (a feature set) of four, yes, four units called nucleotides. Combinations of these four nucleotides are different enough to provide the code to build a fruitfly, a shark, and you.

Now consider the inanimate world in addition to the biological world: your mother, the sun, the fenders on the passing bus, silk underwear, your cat, the chocolate pudding you ate for breakfast, and every other material object you know about consist of protons, neutrons, and electrons organized in different ways. That is just three, yes, three basic atomic particles that can be combined to make the physical world we experience in all its diversity.

Now let's consider human languages and their diversity: Chinese, French, Greek, Hungarian, to name just a few. They are hugely different from each other. But then again, isn't a shark different from a human? Or chocolate pudding from the sun? And yet, one of the findings of modern science is that sharks, pudding, humans, and the sun are all alike at some level; they are all made of the same basic atomic particles and the differences result from the way in which these atoms are combined. In light of these findings of modern science in other domains, findings that perhaps violate common sense, the possibility that Mohawk, Japanese, English, Greek, and so on, might be modeled by various combinations of some basic elements (locality, c-command, and the like) becomes perhaps more palatable.

11.4 Exercises

Exercise 11.4.1. Defining the initial state: Your task in this exercise is to demonstrate how UG (the initial state of the language faculty) determines the set of grammars that a learner can possibly acquire. You are to create a parallel to the card languages we talked about in the chapter.

Instead of using playing cards your grammars will be based on Canadian coins of the following denominations: 1¢, 5¢, 10¢, 25¢, $1, $2. (Feel free to use some other set of things, for example, another currency or the pizza topping combinations on a menu—mushrooms and pepperoni, pepperoni, anchovies, and extra cheese, etc.)

You should make up some feature systems based on these coins (or pizzas), as well as some operators—please use at least one operator other than AND and OR, and use one privative feature and one binary feature. One possibility for an operator is NOT, a negation operator, but we encourage you to find or invent others—just explain carefully. For this exercise, think of a language as a set of coins (parallel to the sets of cards)—for a given coin, a grammar has to treat it as grammatical or ungrammatical.

Before you begin your answer, read through all the questions. Your earlier choices will affect later ones.

UG$_1$: Define a coin Universal Grammar, UG$_1$, in terms of some operators and symbols (features) that can describe the coins.

   a. Operators:

   b. Features:

- Define two grammars that can be stated in terms of UG$_1$

   c. G$_{1.1}$:

   d. G$_{1.2}$:

- Now define two grammars that cannot be stated in terms of UG$_1$ and explain why each is not possible

   e. F$_{1.1}$:

   f. F$_{1.2}$:

UG$_2$: Define another coin Universal Grammar, UG$_2$, in terms of some operators and symbols (features) that can describe the coins. Before you proceed with defining UG$_2$, read the rest of this question.

   g. Operators:

   h. Features:

- Define two grammars that can be stated in terms of UG$_2$

   i. G$_{2.1}$—a language that generates a set of sentences equivalent to that described by one of the impossible languages, item F$_{1.1}$ or F$_{1.2}$:

   j. G$_{2.2}$—a language that is extensionally equivalent to G$_{1.1}$ or G$_{1.2}$ (generates the same set of sentences), but does so using different symbols or operators:

- Now define two grammars that cannot be stated in terms of UG$_2$ and explain why each is not possible

   k. F$_{2.1}$:

   l. F$_{2.2}$:

Further Readings

In the *Meno* there is a demonstration of innate knowledge that is worth thinking about. Socrates leads an uneducated slave boy through a geometric proof and claims to demonstrate that all he is doing is drawing out knowledge that the boy already had. The paper on the subset principle contains the card language demonstration with more detail on phonological acquisition. Carroll's book is an excellent overview of recent ideas in evolutionary and developmental genetics which shows how diversity can arise out of interactions of a few basic primitives.

- Selection from the Plato's *Meno*—link from course page.
- "The subset principle in phonology: Why the *tabula* can't be *rasa*" by Hale and Reiss (2003).
- *Endless Forms Most Beautiful: The New Science of Evo Devo and the Making of the Animal Kingdom* by Sean Carroll (2005).

PART IV

Implications and Conclusions

12

Social implications

12.1 Prescriptive vs. descriptive grammar

At this point it should be apparent that linguistics is not concerned with so-called *proper* grammar. For a variety of historical and social reasons, certain linguistic forms are associated with a level of prestige that actually has no basis in their linguistic properties—Standard English is not more precise or logical than other dialect forms. We take the position that no language or dialect is more precise or logical than any other, but even applying the same (ultimately misguided) criteria used to argue for the superiority of, say, Standard English, it is trivial to demonstrate that this dialect is often less precise and less logical than less prestigious ones.

In this book we have introduced the terms *grammar* and *rule* as elements of a scientific theory. Scientific grammar is concerned with describing and classifying linguistic data with the ultimate goal of understanding the properties of the human language faculty. This enterprise is sometimes called *descriptive grammar* in contrast to the *prescriptive* grammar that we are taught in school, the main purpose of which is to prescribe "correct" linguistic forms. The notion of correctness has no place in scientific grammar—a particular grammar G generates a form f as an output or it does not. The rules of scientific grammar are thus statements characterizing natural objects—they are either universal rules that are properties of all human languages or particular rules of individual I-languages. Of course, we may sometimes posit the existence of a rule but later revise our view, just as conjectures in any scientific domain are subject to revision.

Focusing on the taxonomic and descriptive work that accompanies attempts at explanation, we can compare the distinction between scientific grammar and prescriptive grammar to that between an anthropological sketch of a society and an etiquette manual. An anthropologist may describe the wedding rites of some community, but will not say that the bride should have worn white and the forks should have been placed on the left of the plate at the reception. While the distinction between scientific grammar and prescriptive grammar should be obvious to *you* at this point, given how much you now know about linguistics, we still find that even, or rather, especially, educated people have a hard time overcoming linguistic prejudices and believing that there is no basis for viewing some linguistic systems as better or worse than others, either in general or for specific tasks. In the following paragraphs we provide further arguments against linguistic prejudice. If you discuss linguistics with "educated" people you may find it convenient to have some of these arguments on hand.

12.2 Negation

How do you react if you hear someone say something like (12.1a.b.)?

 a. Non-Standard Dialect: He didn't eat no cake.
  • Standard: He didn't eat any cake.
b. Non-Standard Dialect: He didn't give nothing to nobody.
  • Standard: He didn't give anything to anybody.

People educated in Standard English, people who use forms more like the glosses given below the non-Standard forms in (12.1), will often react to such utterances as reflecting not only a lack of education but also a lack of precision in thought, since the speaker appears to be unaware of the simple logical principle that "two negatives make a positive." According to everyday conceptions, the negative word *no* in (12.1a.) "cancels out" the negation of the negated verb *didn't*. For sentence (12.1b.) everyday conceptions are not as clear—do *nothing* and *nobody* both cancel out the negation on the verb, or do we have three negatives, which computes to a negative—two cancel out and one remains? In fact, as expected, everyday thoughts about such things do not form part of a coherent theory, and, like most commonsense notions about language, they are just wrong.

While there is no hesitation to condemn the use of multiple nega-tion in modern speakers whose social and educational background differs from one's own, few people are ready to propose that Geoffrey Chaucer, the fourteenth-century poet, philosopher, and diplomat, was lazy, stupid, or incapable of clear thinking because he wrote lines like (12.2) in the *Canterbury Tales*:

12.2   *he nevere yet no villeyneye ne sayde*
    in al his lyf unto no manner wight

A quasi-etymological, word-for-word translation would be "He never did not say no evil to no kind of person." However, an accurate translation from the Middle English would be "He didn't ever say any evil, in all his life, to any kind of person." The form and pattern of negative words, including the negative polarity items we discussed in Chapters 6 and 10, differ in Chaucer's English from our Modern Standard dialect. However, both grammars follow principles of meaning and form that depend upon structural notions like c-command and entailment relations expressible in terms of set theory that we introduced in earlier chapters. These represen-tational and computational primitives are the building blocks of all human languages.

Since speakers who produce utterances like those in (12.1) are humans, the output of their grammars, too, reflects c-command and set theoretic relations. Simply put, our (the authors') mental grammars output NPIs pro-nounced *any* in the same context that the mental grammars of Chaucer and a speaker who produces the dialect forms in (12.1) output NPIs pronounced *no*. All three dialects are equally "logical" and equally capable of expressing precise thoughts.

We now see that there is some contribution to be made to society from linguistic analysis. The crucial step we hope you can make is to go from formal analysis of linguistic differences to an appreciation of the complexity of all languages and the incoherence of claims of superiority, inferiority, or greater or lesser richness for any particular system. In an educational context, the social and economic benefit of teaching standard languages is best achieved via cold but respectful scientific analysis and explanation. Imagine the effect on teacher and student alike of learning that saying *I didn't see nobody* is not an indicator of stupidity but rather shows that one's mental grammar parallels that of Chaucer or an Italian speaker! We ourselves have done such demonstrations to high school students and teachers, and even to high school equivalency students in a maximum security prison. Just as the facts of genetics demonstrate the groundlessness of racial prejudice, linguistic science should serve society by undermining the widespread linguistic misconceptions that affect all social and educational institutions.

12.3 Change is constant

We have records from ancient times of writers complaining about the sloppy speech of the masses and the decay of the language. We even have evidence from graffiti written by less-educated Romans that illustrate the forms criticized by the grammarians.

In addition to the rants of the prescriptive grammarians, we also have writings that criticize their pedantry, such as this passage by St. Augustine (4th–5th century) about solecisms (constructions that do not correspond to prescriptive grammar) and barbarisms (non-standard pronunciations).

What is called a solecism is simply what results when words are not combined according to the rules by which our predecessors, who spoke with some authority, combined them. Whether you say *inter homines* or *inter hominibus* [to mean *among men*] does not matter to a student intent upon things. Likewise, what is a barbarism but a word articulated with letters or sounds that are not the same as those with which it was normally articulated by those who spoke Latin before us? Whether one says *ignoscere* with a long or short third syllable is of little concern to someone beseeching God to forgive his sins. [*De Doctrina Christiana* 2.13.9 (Augustine 1995)]

Augustine sensibly recognizes that language change occurs but that new systems are as good as old ones for the purposes to which we put language.

The linguistic descendants of the average Roman's Latin are the Romance languages French, Spanish, Italian, Romanian, Sardinian, and so on. These languages, of course, are the result of the "decay" bemoaned by the ancients, but this fact does not stop the French Academy and the Office de la Langue Française in Quebec from bemoaning the currently ongoing decay of the language of Molière. Word borrowings from other languages and changes in syntax, morphology, and phonology occur constantly in the course of language transmission from generation to generation—nobody has the same exact I-language as anyone else, so nobody can have the same exact I-language as their parents.

Ironically, the prescriptive grammarians are so confused that they sometimes complain about innovative forms and sometimes archaic forms. Quebec French has retained vowel distinctions from Old French that are lost in Standard French, such as a distinction in the vowels of the words *la* as in *la fille* "the girl" and *là* as in *cette fille-là* "that girl there." Schoolchildren in Quebec are taught that the two words are homophones, pronounced the same, by teachers who only pronounce them the same when teaching that they are homophones, when doing grammar, and never when speaking normally. It is no wonder that the students are confused.

Our daughter, who attends French school in Quebec has even been taught that the order of pronouns in Quebec French differs from that of Standard French because it reflects the fact that the settlers in Quebec were hardworking, unsophisticated rustics who were so busy trapping fur-bearing animals and cultivating the earth that they had no time to cultivate themselves. One teacher at our daughter's elite private school explained that Standard French *dis-le-moi* "tell it to me" is rendered in Quebec French as *dis-moi-le* because the latter is shorter, faster, and easier to say than the former, and thus more suitable for the hardworking, uncultured Québecois. This view seems to reflect a different notion of shortness than what we are familiar with, since the two forms contain the same three units. These personal anecdotes of ours report generally held opinions that even make it into the pages of our local newspapers in opinion pieces signed by university professors.

For a particularly clear case of how silly it is to worry about the fact of language change consider the formation of the future tense in the history of French. Classical Latin had what is called a synthetic future, the future form of a verb was a single word: *amō* "I love" has the future form *amābō* "I will love." Late Latin expressed the future periphrastically by the use of an auxiliary verb identical in form to the verb "to have": *amāre habeō*, literally "to love I have" expressed the future tense. The modern Romance languages, like Latin, have a synthetic form, for example French *j'aimerai*. Modern French also has developed a periphrastic form using the verb "to go": *je vais aimer* "I am going to love." Since we are making a binary distinction between synthetic and periphrastic forms it follows that any two future tense forms from the "same language"[41] will both be synthetic futures, both be periphrastic futures, or they will differ along this dimension.[42] As we see from the history of French, the change can go in both directions. So, the "decay" from Classical Latin resulted in the periphrastic future of Late Latin; but the "decay" from Late Latin to what is (arbitrarily) called, say, French, led to a new synthetic future. If change can both eliminate and introduce synthetic tense forms, then it is clearly silly to view it as "decay" or "degeneration." Yet this is typically how language change is viewed in almost every culture where opinions are expressed on the matter.

Since language is partially learned and since children are not telepathic, they have no direct access to what is in the minds of people around them. Transmission of grammar is imperfect and so-called language change is inevitable. An approach to historical linguistics that takes seriously the I-language perspective can be found in Mark Hale's (2007) *Historical Linguistics: Theory and Method*.

Not only is it the case that change in the rules and meanings vary from speaker to speaker and generation to generation but those who worry about such things cannot possibly be aware of the nature of most of the actual rules and structures of human languages that concern them. The work of modern linguistics over the past fifty years has uncovered patterns that are just now being recognized—explanations are still being sought. It is unlikely that the members of the French Academy or William Safire, who writes on language for *The New York Times*, have an understanding of binding theory that comes anywhere near the sophistication of yours. Excellent discussion of the fact that many of the rules of prescriptive grammar do not even work for the forms they are meant to apply to can be found in "The Language Mavens," Chapter 9 of Steven Pinker's entertaining bestseller *The Language Instinct*.

An old joke about prescriptive grammar illustrates its naiveté with respect to actual linguistic structure: A farmer is touring Harvard Yard and stops

---

[41] Remember, we are using this term in an informal, non-I-language sense in which Classical Latin, Late Latin, Modern Standard French, and Quebec French are the "same language."

[42] Of course, a language can have more than one form that is used to denote future, like Modern French, and it can also have no form—many languages have only a past and a non-past, and specifically future time is denoted by using adverbial expressions like "tomorrow" or "next year."

a passing student to ask "Where's the library at?" The pedantic student replies "At Harvard, we never end a sentence with a preposition," to which the farmer responds "Where's the library at, $*!&@%#©^‡¿" (fill in your favorite epithet). Although we, the authors, do not use this particular construction, we do say things like *Where the heck did that come from?*, ending with a preposition. So, the Harvard student is condemning a structure that is widespread in the speech of people at least as educated as we are (Ph.D. linguists). More interestingly, it is clear that the Harvard student does not understand that linguistic generalizations are structure-dependent, and not formulatable in terms of just linear order—recall the discussion of *Mary's* from Chapter 6. The farmer solves the problem of having a sentence-final preposition, but probably not in a way that would satisfy the student who probably is aware at some level that the farmer's revised utterance does not satisfy the principle he is trying to articulate.

Despite the fact that this so-called preposition stranding is frowned upon in written Standard English, it is widespread in the speech of just about all speakers, regardless of the prestige of their dialect. It turns out that this dangerous phenomenon of preposition stranding is not only threatening English but insidiously endangering the health of French as well. We live in Montreal, Quebec where many people are concerned not only for the survival of French but also with protecting the language from the malignant effects of English. Quebec French allows sentences like the following: *Ça c'est la fille que je parlais avec*, literally "That is the girl that I was speaking with," with the preposition *avec* "stranded" at the end of the sentence. Such forms, which are not accepted by French prescriptive grammars, are often cited as anglicisms, English-influenced forms that should be avoided to maintain the purity of the language. However, it appears to be the case that preposition stranding in Quebec French is very different from the pattern in English. There appears to be a lot of dialect variation but, at least among our students, only certain prepositions can be stranded. The monosyllabic prepositions *à* "to" and *de* "of," for example, appear to be "unstrandable": The string *Ça c'est la fille que je parlais à*, literally "That is the girl that I was speaking to" appears to be ill formed, despite its apparent structural identity with the sentence containing the preposition *avec*. Our goal here is not to analyze these facts but merely to point out that, as usual, they are more complex than they appear at first glance, and that the rules of prescriptive grammarians reflect tremendous ignorance about the nature of language.

As we have pointed out, in addition to the incoherence of their pre-scriptions and their ignorance, prescriptive grammarians fail to recognize that they are fighting a losing battle. Change is a constant and there has never been a linguistic golden age from which today's youth is straying even further than their parents. If archaic forms are somehow taken to be better than innovative forms, then prescriptivists should be telling us to use the (b.) form instead of the (a.) form in the following pairs:

12.3   Are archaic forms more acceptable?

	Modern Standard forms	Unacceptable archaic forms
i. a.	You are losers.	b. *Ye are losers.
ii. a.	You (sg.) are a loser.	b. *Thou art a loser.
iii. a.	The table stands on its legs.	b. *The table stands on his legs.
iv. a.	Both of my brothers are losers.	b. *Both of my brethren are losers.

In (12.3i.), the form *you* is derived from what used to be the form used for objects. The nominative, subject form was *ye*, as in the song *Come all ye faithful*. . . . In the second person plural, Modern English does not make the distinction made, for example, between *we* and *us* in the first person. No prescriptivists tell us to use *ye* anymore.

In (12.3ii.) we see just how "sloppy" Standard English is—not only has it lost a case distinction but the pronoun system does not distin-guish between singular and plural anymore. Older varieties of the lan-guage used *thou* for the singular nominative form, as in *Wherefore art thou Romeo?* "Why are you Romeo?", but no prescriptivists bemoan this "loss of precision".

In (12.3iii.) we see not the loss of an older distinction but an innovative form. The form *its* as a possessive of *it* is only a few hundred years old. Earlier, the form *his* served as possessive of both *he* and *it*. No prescriptivists bemoan this neologism, probably because it has been around for too long by now.

Finally, in (12.3iv.) we see the form *brethren*, which earlier was the normal plural form for *brother* but is now restricted to members of a religious order. Prescriptivists would be outraged by anyone who said *My foots hurt*, yet such a form would have the same status as the now acceptable *brothers* once had. There is no rhyme or reason to prescriptivist proclama-tions.

What do we do with people who say *Me and John went to the store*? A prescriptivist may point out that such people (including your humble authors) never would say *Me went to the store*. So, the prescriptivist would argue, these speakers are not internally consistent—sometimes they use *I* for the nominative singular form and sometimes they use *me*, whereas prescriptive grammar demands consistent use of the nominative *I* whenever there is a first person subject.

The correct response to this view is that *I* ≠ *I*—given our recognition that everyone has his or her own mental grammar, that languages are individual and internal, it is a mistake to equate the *I* and *me* of dialects that generate *I went to the store*, *John and I went to the store*, and *You saw me* with the *I* and *me* of dialects that generate *I went to the store*, *Me and John went to the store* and *You saw me*. The *I* and *me* of the non-Standard dialect cannot simply be analyzed as a case difference, nominative vs. accusative. After going through the discussion of ergativity in Chapter 9, we hope you appreciate that case systems can be fairly complex.

This discussion brings us back to the discussions in Chapters 1 and 4 where we established that English does not exist as a coherent, scientifically definable entity. Different speakers of so-called English have different pronoun systems, as we have just seen. There are lots of other ways in which they can differ. For example, many speakers of Canadian English say things like the sentences in (12.4a.), which are ungrammatical to us, the authors—our grammar does not generate them.

12.4   Some Canadianisms
        a. Canadian
           • *You're allowed playing ball here.*
           • *I'm done my homework.*
        b. Standard
           • *You're allowed to play ball here.*
           • *I'm done with my homework* or *I've done my homework.*

We have labeled the forms that correspond to our forms as "Standard," but it is probably the case that prescriptive grammars typically do not discuss the argument structure of the verb *allow*—in our dialect it takes an infinitival complement like *to play*, whereas in the relevant Canadian dialects it takes an -*ing* form like *playing*. As far as we know, the structural difference reflected in the sentences with *done* is also not discussed in prescriptive grammars.

Once again, we have been talking as if there is a *word* corresponding to Canadian *allow* and our *allow*. But we have already seen that the two differ in the syntactic configurations in which they occur. They also differ slightly in pronunciation. The question then arises of what the word *allow* could be. The answer, from the I-language perspective, is that each of us has different verbs in our mental dictionaries, and that these verbs may be more or less alike in their phonology, their syntax, and their meaning, but each is a mental representation in an individual mental grammar.[43]

Viewed from this perspective of systems of symbolic representations in individual minds, it becomes hard to justify any kind of linguistic prejudice. How could one abstract computational system built upon the resources of the innate human language faculty be better than another?

12.4 Exercises

Exercise 12.4.1.   Reflexives in two dialects: Consider the following forms of the reflexive pronoun from both Standard English and a non-Standard dialect.

Standard		*Non-Standard*	
myself	ourselves	myself	ourselves
yourself	yourselves	yourself	yourselves
herself	themselves	herself	theirselves
himself		hisself	

Assume that these forms are all composed of two parts, a personal pronoun and *-self* / *-selves*. Is there any basis for claiming that the set of Standard forms is more logical than the set of dialect forms? Less logical?

Exercise 12.4.2.   Second person pronouns: In Brooklyn some people say things like *I'll see yous later* (we have adopted Standard orthography.) One of the features of this dialect seen in this sentence is the form of the plural second person pronoun *yous* which is distinct from the singular *you*. Many people argue that speakers of Brooklyn English are clearly more careful and less lazy than speakers of Standard English who do not distinguish a second person singular from a second person plural pronoun. How could you convince such snobs that Standard English speakers are not necessarily

---

[43] Sometimes the grammar refers to the computational system, without the lexicon, and sometimes it refers to both. Here we speak of the lexicon as part of the grammar, but the issue is of no import for our point.

illogical and sloppy people who cannot express basic distinctions of number like that expressed by the Brooklynites? (Can the SE speakers tell if they are talking to more than one person?) Can you suggest a way to help the poor Standard English speakers learn the (superficially, at least) more logical Brooklyn system? (Can you somehow show the SE speakers data from their own dialects that suggests a singular-plural distinction in second person?) You can also relate your answer to other linguistic prejudices you know about.

Exercise 12.4.3. Two dialects of polarity items: Consider the following sentences of Standard English and a non-Standard dialect. Assume that the paired sentences have the same meaning.

		STANDARD	DIALECT
a.	Free choice	He'll eat anything	He'll eat anything
b.	Positive polarity	He ate something nasty	He ate something nasty
c.	Negative object 1	He won't eat anything	He won't eat nothing
d.	Negative object 2	He will eat nothing	He won't eat nothing
e.	Negative subject	Nothing happened	Ain't nothing happened

The two dialects appear to agree in Free choice contexts like (a.) where they both use *anything*. They also agree in Positive polarity contexts where they use *something*. What can you say about the last three sentences? How would you characterize the forms used in each dialect? It may help to know that the form *nothing* in the Standard is sometimes called a negative quantifier. We'll assume that *Nothing happened* is ungrammatical in the non-Standard dialect in question.

How does this dialect difference support the perspective of I-language? Can you incorporate into your response the fact that, like the other forms, *nothing* varies widely in its pronunciation among dialects, with a range including such diverse forms as the following [nəθn̩, nəθŋ̍, nəfn̩, nəʔn̩]?

Further Readings

Labov's article is frightening in showing just how wrong-headed thinking about language can be among many highly educated professionals. Rickford's webpage lists several sources related to the Ebonics controversy in the United States. Hyman's paper surveys traditions of prescriptive grammar in the Greek, Roman, Christian, Muslim and Sanskrit traditions and ties the discussion to religious issues. Pinker's chapter, like the whole book, is a fun read.

- "Academic ignorance and black intelligence" by William Labov (1972).
- Various articles by John Rickford on the Ebonics Controversy. Available at http://www.stanford.edu/ rickford/ebonics/.
- "Bad Grammar in Context" by Malcolm Hyman (2002).
- "The Language Mavens," Chapter 9 of *The Language Instinct* by Steven Pinker (1994).

13

Some philosophy

In this chapter we will discuss various topics in philosophy, some of which traditionally fall into the domain of philosophy of language, such as the nature of reference and meaning, but also others that go beyond the connections between linguistics and philosophy. Broader issues include the mind-body problem and the contrast of rationalism and empiricism. We are not philosophers, yet we will try to convince you that the cognitive biolinguistic I-language perspective we have presented can provide insight into a wide range of philosophical questions that have stumped more traditional philosophy. Our survey will be brief and dogmatic, and our conclusions may seem outrageous, but we encourage you both to take them seriously and to seek out contrasting points of view.

13.1 Rationalism and empiricism

Many philosophers and cognitive scientists are concerned with the question of the sources of knowledge—where does knowledge come from? Broadly speaking, a distinction is often made between *rationalism* and *empiricism*. Rationalism is the view that knowledge is acquired through reason, for

Fig 13.1 Where does knowledge come from?

example, by logical inference. Empiricism is the view that knowledge arises from our sensory experience, what we see, hear, smell, touch, and taste. The two views are not mutually exclusive, but they are typically discussed as contrasting approaches to the question of the source of knowledge.

The distinction between rationalism and empiricism is relevant to two separate issues in linguistics and cognitive science. On the one hand, there is the question of scientific knowledge—where do theories and hypotheses and intuitions come from? This concern is shared with any philosopher of science interested in the activity of scientists. A focus on rationalism would favor the view in which scientists come up with ideas, make inferences and deductions, and only then appeal to observation to confirm or refute predictions. A focus on empiricism would favor a view in which generalizations, theories, and laws arise out of a large body of observation.

On the other hand, the rationalism–empiricism debate in cognitive science is also related to the sources of the kind of knowledge that is the object of study. For example, does the acquisition of knowledge of a specific language by children involve imposing innately determined categories on observed experience, a view in line with a rationalist perspective, or does it arise from observing linguistic output in one's environment and then extracting regularities from this data, a view favored by an empiricist perspective?

The rationalism–empiricism debate at both of these levels is a tremendous topic with a long history, and we cannot even attempt a thorough discussion. In terms of scientific discovery, it is probably the case that the average person is primarily an empiricist, and this corresponds to the popular view that the primary activity of a scientist is to do experiments and make observations from which generalizations will emerge. It is pretty clear that this everyday view cannot be correct, since there are an infinite number of hypotheses compatible with any body of data. It is also the case that there are an infinite number of observations that can be made, an infinite number of experiments to perform. If scientists were not guided by ideas, they would just perform experiments (if that would even be the appropriate term for such activity) at random, with no sense of what they were looking for.

In the domain of human knowledge, especially in linguistics, the rationalism–empiricism debate often revolves around what is called the argument from the poverty of the stimulus. The argument is basically that children end up knowing much more about language than, say, an unbiased pattern recognizer could learn from the same input. Paralleling the discussion above, there are an infinite number of grammars compatible with any corpus that a child will be exposed to, and, yet, children generalize beyond the forms they have encountered. Perhaps they have heard sentences in which *wh*-words are pronounced in a derived position that is up to thirteen words away from the base position, and, yet, they do not end up with rules that limit the linear distance between base and derived positions to thirteen words. Consider this case:

13.1 What did the tall guy with bright green dreadlocks and a friendly pregnant German shepherd really want the fat bald guy in a bright pink tutu to hear ~~what~~?

Twenty-seven words intervene between the derived position copy of *what* at the beginning of the sentence and the base position copy at the end. Perhaps you have never heard an example of *wh*-movement with exactly twenty-seven words between base and derived position, yet you recognize this example as grammatical. And, unless you hang out in some very interesting places, you probably never heard this exact set of words put together in any sentence. Yet, somehow, you recognize the sentence in (13.1) as a member of an equivalence class that includes (13.2a.b.), but not (13.2c.).

13.2   More *wh*-movement
  a. What did the bad dog eat ~~what~~?
  b. Who did the tall guy with bright green dreadlocks and a friendly pregnant German shepherd really want the fat bald guy in a bright pink tutu
   to hear ~~who~~?
  c. *The boy did the tall guy with bright green dreadlocks and a friendly
   pregnant German shepherd really want the fat bald guy in a bright pink
   tutu to hear ~~the boy~~?

The string in (13.2c.) is of course superficially more similar to (13.2b.) and (13.1) than (13.2a.) is. However, this kind of similarity is not relevant to the generalizations that human language learners make. Children's grammars always end up with structure-dependent rules that do generalize beyond what they hear, but they only generalize in some ways and not others—only some analogies to what they have heard work. Children do not generalize about numbers of intervening words, and they do generalize in ways that make reference to subcategories of NPs. Those that belong to the equivalence class of *wh*-items are treated differently from others.

Much ink continues to be spilt on this issue of what can be learned from the observed data, and it has even been claimed that linguists who adopt the argument from poverty of the stimulus are guilty of poverty of imagination about how learning proceeds. However, as Howard Lasnik has pointed out, and as you will appreciate if you did the segmentation exercise in Chapter 2, the poverty of the stimulus exists right at the word level. There are no words in the input signal, words are constructions of the mind. Without an innate category WORD there would be no reason for kids to segment the acoustic signal they receive. In fact, there must already be an innate system to separate speech signal input from other input, just as other species recognize the communication sounds of their conspecifics against a background of other noises.

In an underappreciated paper written in 1976, Robert Hammarberg discussed empiricism in linguistics, specifically with regard to the phonetic and phonological analysis of speech segments. Hammarberg contrasts the then current standard view in phonetics, the field that studies the acoustic and physiological aspects of speech sounds, with the emerging approaches under development by Chomsky and his collaborators.

Chomskian linguistics is explicitly anti-empiricist, and all indications are that current philosophy of science is moving toward a rejection of the empiricist programme (Fodor, (1968), pp. xiv *ff*). A key feature of the new programme is exactly a reevaluation of the concept of observation. Observations are now held to be judgments, and these judgments are made in terms of the criteria provided by the paradigm. Thus the taxonomy of a discipline is to be regarded as imposed from above, rather than emerging from below, i.e., rather than emerging in the form of brute facts before the unprejudiced eyes or ears of the researcher. The relevance of this to the study of phonetics and phonology should be obvious: the concept of the segment, which is indispensable to phonetics and phonology, is a creature of the paradigm, not of the raw data. [Hammarberg 1976:354]

Hammarberg here is mainly concerned with empiricism and rationalism in the domain of scientific inquiry, but it follows that he is also a rationalist when it comes to understanding the sources of linguistic knowledge in speakers' minds, since the learner, like the analyst, cannot discover segments in the signal. Hammarberg is very clearly a mentalist:

[I]t should be perfectly obvious by now that segments do not exist outside the human mind. [354]

But it is also clear that this mentalist position is not at all at odds with taking notions like "segment" as objects of serious scientific inquiry. He addresses the position of phoneticians who treat the segment as merely a convenient fiction for description and categorization, but he responds that

there would be little value in such an approach. Science aims for a theory of the real, and to base one's descriptions and generalizations on a fictional taxonomy could only lead to one's theories being fictional as well. [355]

This point, that theories should be assumed to model real aspects of the world, has also been made by Chomsky in various places (for example, in "Language as a natural object," 2000a:111) where he mentions that there have been periods in the history of chemistry when the formulas and models were assumed to be merely calculating devices. This contrast in attitude concerning theories is sometimes referred to as the difference between "realist" and "instrumentalist" positions.

Unfortunately, Hammarberg appears to have been overly optimistic about the downfall of empiricism.[44] Radical empiricism refuses to die in linguistics and cognitive science, and it even appears to be on the rise recently, a development perhaps tied to the accessibility of data collection and analysis equipment—if such powerful tools are available and one can get large grants to buy them, it is mighty tempting to use them, even if they distract us from what is actually interesting and important. People working in areas of statistical or probabilistic linguistics would scoff at arguments for features and innate categories, such as those we presented in Chapter 11. They would argue that children can extract equivalence classes based on statistical analysis of the input they receive without any innate categories.

Note that dogs, who have very good hearing, do not end up with the phonological categories that a child ends up with upon exposure to the same input, so the categories cannot literally be present in the signal. Even if some kind of statistical analysis is part of acquisition, there has to be innate knowledge (or whatever you want to call it) of what categories to do the statistics *over*. Statistics about loudness and distance from the speaker and the ambient air temperature appear to be ignored in acquiring linguistic representations. In fact, statistics about context and many acoustic details are clearly completely irrelevant to the construction of linguistic representations at some point: a word you learn in a single noon encounter with a skinny, distant screaming woman on the tundra can be whispered at dawn in the ear of a soft-spoken plump man on a tropical island. Any theory of language acquisition that even approaches strict empiricism has a hard time accounting for such facts. And since empiricists claim to like facts, this gets them into trouble.

Lila Gleitman and Elissa Newport (1995) discuss rationalist- and empiricist-oriented approaches to language acquisition in terms of a contrast that we can summarize as follows.

- **Empiricist focus:** Children's speech at a particular age directly reflects the amount of input they have heard and the forms that they have heard—basically they just imitate what they hear, and the more they hear, the better they imitate.
- **Rationalist focus:** Children's speech at a particular age tends to be correlated with other developmental milestones, including non-linguistic

---

[44] Hammarberg himself, who was trained as a phonetician, was scorned by the field for his anti-empiricism and never managed to get an academic position [p.c.].

aspects of cognitive and physical development; they also produce forms that they have never heard and no adult ever would use.

The empiricist focuses on the stimuli the child receives, what is outside, granting minimal responsibility to any domain-specific cognitive apparatus, any innate language faculty, for example. In contrast, the rationalist focuses on what comes from within the learner, and downplays the role of massive amounts of data in attaining a grammar. Gleitman and Newport make a very simple argument in favor of the rationalist position. A child raised in a fully bilingual environment can be assumed to get about half as much input in each language as a child raised in a monolingual environment. If language acquisition was primarily data-driven, then we would expect large delays in the development of bilingual children as measured by various milestones in linguistic performance. It turns out, however, that no such massive delays are observed. Children in bilingual environments tend to be at about the same level of production and comprehension in both languages as children in monolingual environments, despite receiving about half as much data on average.

In our reference to the sense of time in rats (and humans) in Chapter 6 we mentioned that pure duration cannot be observed—events and processes have a duration, but the category itself is an abstraction imposed by the rodent or human mind. We can build a computer that measures duration of sound signals and light signals and treats the results the same, regardless of the input channel of the signal, but we have to make sure that we program the computer to do this—we have to use a single clock or merge the results of a sound clock and a light clock. Duration pure and simple is not in the signal. We already know that the same is true for the sound segments and words we hear, as well as the syntactic structure that is imposed on speech by our minds. A strict empiricist approach to language acquisition fails because without the necessary pre-existing mental apparatus that humans have, but that snakes, fish, and dogs do not have, there are no categories over which to generalize.

13.2 Competence and performance

We have been assuming to this point that it is fairly obvious what a language acquirer has to do and what a linguist has to account for—generalizations and patterns have to be imposed on the data in the form of equivalence classes and computations involving these classes. Throughout this book, however, we have ignored a crucial fact: It is far from clear what the data is over which the generalizations and patterns must apply.

The subject matter of linguistics cannot actually be what people say, if "what people say" is understood to refer to the sounds they make when speaking. Many people speak more than one language and it would be a hopeless task to follow a person around and model in a consistent way (develop a grammar of) their speech output if they sometimes said *dog*, sometimes *chien* (French for "dog") and sometimes *perro* (the Spanish word). Even when we decide that a given utterance provides evidence for a particular grammar, we have to recognize that the output of a person and the output of a grammar are two very different things. By definition, the grammar outputs representations, abstract mental entities that cannot be seen or heard directly. These representations can be fed to other systems, ultimately leading to the sounds of speech emanating from a person's mouth, but many other factors contribute to such sounds:

- did the grammar in fact generate a complete sentence or was it interrupted in its computations?
- did the processors receive into memory buffers an intact representation or were multiple grammar outputs mingled?
- did the processes of attention allocation dedicate enough resources to passing this representation on to other systems?
- was the nervous system functioning "normally" or was it compromised by alcohol or fatigue or drugs?
- were the biomechanical features of the vocal tract and respiratory tract that enter into speaking functioning properly?
- was the oral tract clear of peanut butter and pretzels when articulating speech?

...and so on.

In the linguistics literature the constant knowledge that constitutes an I-language is sometimes referred to as a speaker's *competence*. This term is contrasted with what is called *performance*. Linguistic performance is not a well-defined notion—basically all aspects of speech production and comprehension, and perhaps even the making of grammaticality judgments, that do not reflect the grammar are called *performance*.

In the literature, discussions of performance typically are concerned only with so-called *performance errors*, situations in which the performance systems appear to obscure the grammatical output. For example, when a person pronounces a tongue twister like *She sells sea shells by the seashore* and switches some of the *s* and *sh* sounds, we assume that the representation of the words in memory has not changed, but rather the switch is due to something going wrong in one of the performance systems intervening between grammatical output and the speech signal.

The subject matter of linguistics thus is not speech. It is the knowledge system underlying speech. We must use speech as one source of data, because the knowledge is not directly observable, and the indirect data is all we have. Other forms of indirect data are the judgments people provide when asked if a string is grammatical and the reaction time experiments mentioned in Chapter 7, where structural complexity correlates with the time it takes to judge that a string corresponds to a well-formed sentence.

This situation is not unique to linguistics. In fact, any time a scientist uses meter readings to draw inferences about the nature of the world, the same method is at work—observations must be interpreted in light of some theoretical framework in order to draw inferences about phenomena that are not directly observable. For example, nobody has ever observed an electron with the naked eye, and yet scientists build theories about electrons. In drawing inferences about the underlying linguistic system, we have to be careful to distinguish the underlying knowledge, or competence, from the effects of the various performance systems that lead to observable output.

Thus, we need to constantly be aware of a distinction between the object of study in linguistics and the sources of evidence available to us. All speech output that we observe has to be evaluated to determine how well it reflects the output of the grammar and to what extent various performance factors have influenced the observed speech output. We obviously do not want our theory of Universal Grammar to be modeling aspects of speech output that reflect the effects of performance systems, whether these effects are sporadic and irregular, or systematic.[45]

The distinction between competence and performance and the fact that mental grammars, I-languages, are properties of individual minds are behind the following famous quotation from Chomsky's *Aspects of the Theory of Syntax* (1965:3):

Linguistic theory is concerned primarily with an ideal speaker listener, in a completely homogeneous speech community, who knows its language perfectly and is unaffected

---

[45] See Hale and Reiss (2008) for discussion of what UG should be modeling.

by such grammatically irrelevant conditions as **memory limitations, shifts of attention and interest, and errors (random or characteristic)** in applying his knowledge of
language in actual performance. This seems to me to have been the position of the
founders of modern general linguistics, and no cogent reason for modifying it has
been offered. To study actual linguistic performance, we must consider the interaction
of a variety of factors, of which the underlying competence of the speaker-hearer is
only one. In this respect, study of language is no different from empirical investigation
of other complex phenomena. [emphasis added]

Chomsky is basically pointing out the distinction between our everyday
use of terms like *speaking English* and the kinds of categories we must
consider when undertaking a scientific analysis. Yet, this passage has evoked
incredibly virulent reactions both from within and from outside the linguistics community. You will have no trouble finding examples if you search
the phrase "homogeneous speech community" on the internet. The general
complaint can be paraphrased like this:

Chomsky proposes to study language by modeling an ideal speaker-hearer in a completely homogenous speech community, but there are no languages like this—there
is always intra- and interspeaker variation correlated with temporary or more per-
manent social circumstances, and no speech community is completely homogenous.
Therefore, Chomsky's idealizations are so radical as to be uninteresting and useless
for an understanding of how language really works.

At the time Chomsky wrote the passage in *Aspects of the Theory of Syntax*
he had not introduced the term I-language, and perhaps his expression of
the goals of linguistics, as he conceived them, could have been clearer. We
are not concerned with such issues, but instead with providing you with
an understanding of where the objections represented above are misguided,
even if our terminology is anachronistic.

There are two issues to clarify, neither of which is particularly difficult.
First of all, interpret the term *language* when Chomsky uses it to mean *I-
language*. This is clearly not the same as the everyday word that we use
when we talk about the English language and its variants around the globe.
So, it is simply the case that Chomsky is speaking of a completely different
entity from that referred to in expressions like "the language of Jamaica is
English."

The second issue is that Chomsky would be the first to agree that generative linguistics is basically useless for providing insight into how speech
communities work (whatever that means), or for explaining all aspects of
language behavior. These topics, if they are coherent at all, are clearly far

too complex for scientific inquiry. Science makes progress only when narrow issues are examined, not vague, all-encompassing questions like "How does the world work?"

Chomsky's idealizations allow us to study I-language, and to view the complexity of observed linguistic behavior as arising from the performance factors we have mentioned, including physiological and cognitive factors, as well as the interaction of individuals with grammars that differ to varying degrees, the presence of multiple grammars underlying the speech behavior of a single individual, the arbitrary boundaries on speech communities, and so on. A model of I-language will surely be simpler than a model of the use and interaction of multiple I-languages. And, surely, nobody can deny that the individual members of a speech community each have some kind of cognitive system, so it seems unreasonable for those interested in speech communities to complain about an effort to understand these simpler systems that are components of speech communities.

Now that we have clarified the competence–performance distinction, it should be apparent that Universal Grammar must be a theory of the universal aspects of linguistic competence, since performance factors are not part of grammar by definition.

There are some linguists and other scholars who suggest that the modeling of Universal Grammar must wait until we have more data, until more languages have been observed. We pointed out in Chapter 5 that the demonstration of the insufficiency of Finite State Grammar for a model of the human language faculty is a result that is not subject to revision on the basis of more data: Finite State Grammars cannot model English-type grammars, so they cannot be powerful enough for Universal Grammar.

The preceding discussion of the competence–performance distinction provides yet more grist for the anti-empiricist mill of generative linguistics. There is no reason to wait to observe more languages before building a theory of Universal Grammar, because we have not yet observed a single language! Remember, we are interested in I-languages, mental grammars, and these are not available to direct inspection any more than quarks are—their existence and their nature must be inferred.

Chomsky and others have long advocated the necessity of focusing on competence theories:

In my opinion, many psychologists have a curious definition of their discipline. A definition that is destructive, suicidal. A dead end. They want to confine themselves solely to the study of performance—behavior—yet, as I've said, it makes no sense to construct a discipline that studies the manner in which a system is acquired or utilized, but refuses to consider the nature of this system. [Chomsky 1977:49]

[I]f we confine ourselves to the scientific and intellectual goals of understanding psychological phenomena [as opposed to predicting observed behavior] one could certainly make a good case for the claim that there is a need to direct our attention away from superficial "data fitting" models toward deeper structural theories. [Pylyshyn 1973:48]

One reason for this position is that, despite empiricist claims to the contrary, even performance or behavior is difficult to define. Empiricists also face the difficult problem of defining what the data points are if they want to extract generalizations from them.

In *Species of Mind*, their 1997 book on cognitive ethology, the cognitive science of (non-human) animals, Colin Allen and Marc Bekoff discuss the difficulty of defining behavior. Does behavior imply movement? Aren't freezing or playing dead behaviors? Is secreting a hormone or a noxious odor a behavior? Does movement imply behavior? Allen and Bekoff point out that "One would not, for instance, expect an ethological explanation for the motion of an armadillo dragged fifty meters along a highway by a speeding pickup truck" (p. 42), but what about blinking, breathing, and having a pulse? There is movement involved, but is there behavior? Perhaps behavior is just as abstract a notion as grammar, or even more so, despite the empiricist's insistence that our theories must be grounded in observable data.

Grammars are not directly observable and observable language behavior is clearly the result of many interacting systems—motor planning, attention, learning systems, physical properties of the vocal tract, and so on. This means that it is difficult to build theories, since we are never sure when patterns we see reflect somewhat directly underlying competence. It is difficult, but *c'est la vie.*

It has been suggested that Chomsky invoked the competence–performance distinction to explain away some difficult facts, but we think this represents a misunderstanding of a crucial point that is typically only implicit. Like our discussion of rationalism vs. empiricism, the competence–performance distinction is not only relevant to the linguist's theorizing but it is also relevant to a characterization of the acquiring child. The "data" that children get, the speech behavior they are exposed to, contains numerous mis-starts, mis-pronunciations, switches between grammar, doors closed in the middle of sentences from the next room, and so on. If children attempted to build a grammar based directly on the spoken sounds they heard, the result would definitely not be a possible human language. Children somehow come to the language-learning situation with a learning system that knows that the data will be messy, and that much of what is heard will have to be discarded. Exactly how they sort and discard remains largely a mystery, but a mystery that the theory of Universal Grammar attempts to help solve.

13.3 Reference

One aspect of language that seems to involve learning in a relatively straightforward way is the arbitrary connection between phonological representations and meanings. The everyday notion of meaning is typically related to the idea of "picking out things in the world." We will see that things are not so simple—once again, it is not very clear what the "data" actually is.

Most sane people believe that languages contain words and phrases that refer to things in the world—the phrase *the sun* means "the sun" because it refers to the sun; the phrase *George W. Bush* means "George W. Bush" because it refers to George W. Bush; and so on. Sometimes the situation is a bit more complex—for example, *dogs* apparently refers to the set of all dogs in the world and *a dog* needs to be interpreted as referring to one member of the set of dogs in the world. A phrase like *the dog* seems to have several ways of referring: it can refer to a particular dog that is relevant to a particular discourse—*I have a dog and a cat, but I like the dog more*—or it can function as a generic term referring to the whole set—*The dog is a faithful beast*—or it can refer to a particular dog which is present when the sentence is uttered—*Does the dog bite?*—perhaps said while pointing to a particular dog.

Despite the apparent obviousness of the view that linguistic expressions refer to the world, we will argue that, in fact, such a position is untenable. As in just about every other domain that has been investigated scientifically, the beliefs of most sane people just do not stand up under scrutiny.

The commonsense view can be paraphrased as positing a relation, called *reference*, between words or phrases, which, according to the I-language approach we have developed, are in the heads or minds of individuals, and things in the world outside of individual minds. There are at least two ways to undermine the commonsense, apparently obvious view of language and reference.

First, for a good many words and phrases, everyone is in agreement that no corresponding entities exist "out in the world." We talk about *unicorns*, *universal peace*, *the ether*, and *the United Federation of Planets*, without believing that any of these entities actually exist in the world outside our heads. These examples do not show that no words or phrases refer to things in the world, but only that some fail to refer in this simple-minded way. However, these examples do show that this reference relation is not a necessary component of what a word is or does, since many words do not have this component.

Other examples consistent with the idea that phrases need not refer to the world are conditional statements like *If John arrives early, we'll take him to dinner* or *If I could afford it, I'd have you iced*. These sentences clearly have a meaning, and yet they are built upon descriptions of situations that do not yet or may never exist.

A more radical attack on the simple view of reference comes from the idea that the words or phrases that we use reflect the way in which our minds divide up the world, but the latter does not correspond in any direct manner with the properties of the physical world as characterized by the physical sciences. The claim is not to be confused with some kind of idealist philosophy that denies the existence of the physical world. Physicists can specify regions of space-time with great accuracy, and also characterize the regions with respect to their mass or average molecular kinetic energy or the wavelength of light that they reflect. However, these characterizations cannot be directly correlated with the words and phrases of everyday language and the objects of everyday thought.

There are many examples that can be used to demonstrate that our concepts of things do not correspond to physically definable entities in the world and that the terms of our language correspond to our concepts rather than physically definable entities. Obvious examples are the illusory triangle, rectangle, and blob from Chapter 2. There is ink on the page, but your mind interprets the input to your eyes as a triangle, rectangle, or blob. It is not really useful to ask if there is really a triangle on the page, although it is interesting to explore under what conditions we see a triangle. And, to flog a dead horse, the phonemes, words, c-command relations, and so on, are also constructions of your interpreting, constructing mind. Hammarberg said it, too: "[I]t should be perfectly obvious by now that segments do not exist outside the human mind".

Here is one of those odd conclusions that Pylyshyn warned us about: everything we experience is like the triangle. Your home, your beloved, your nose, your dreams and aspirations, your high school diploma and high school degree, the /t/-s in *cat, cats, atomic, atom, want a*—everything. Your mind carves up the world in certain ways, or rather, constructs a certain kind of world, because it is built to process information in certain ways.

Actually, each component of your mind has, or rather, is a set of world-construction rules. Your visual system creates visual objects and scenes, the components of the visual world; your auditory system creates auditory scenes consisting of auditory streams that in turn consist of auditory events, the components of the auditory world;[46] your language faculty creates sentences, structures that consist of phrases, which in turn consist of morphemes, which in turn consist of symbols that we correlate to variables (as in our reduplication examples) or the speech segments that we described as sets of features (as in our Turkish vowel harmony example); and so on for all our other faculties. Some scholars have even posited components, or modules, of mind that construct the categories in domains such as moral reasoning (Mikhail (2007), and Jackendoff's contribution to Macnamara, Jackendoff, Bloom, and Wynn (1999)). In domains like moral reasoning it is easy to accept that the categories are mental constructs. In vision and language, we have spent a lot of energy trying to convince you that the entities involved are mental constructs, too. Words we perceive, for example, do not correspond to "pieces" of sound separated by silence.

The hard step to take is to accept that our everyday understanding of space and objects is also the product of construction, that the objects that we think of as populating the physical world do not correspond in a straightforward manner to the objects that physics recognizes. In other words, the "physical world" of human experience and the "physical world" of the science of physics are two very different worlds, or, rather, two different structures imposed on the one and only world. We are not heading towards an idealist philosophy and we will even adduce the authority of a physicist later in the chapter on a closely related point, so bear with us.

Maybe you will take us more seriously if we introduce an example from antiquity—the philosophical puzzle of the Ship of Theseus. If we replace a

---

[46] These are technical terms, used in work such as Bregman (1990).

plank from this ship, is it the same ship—does the ship continue to exist? Our intuition is that it does. What if we replace two planks? Or ten? Note that the ship can even be conceived as persisting if we replace every single plank, every single physical part, over time. How can this be if the ship is a physical object? Things get even worse when we consider that the removed planks can be collected and set up in exactly their original configuration and yet the ship thus constructed does not correspond to the original ship, or at least not obviously so.

To update the issue, consider that we typically think of our cars as physical objects, yet if we put on winter tires, replace the windshield, the gas tank, and even the engine, re-upholster the interior, putty, paint and add fins to the body, the law does not require us to get a new license plate. The legal identity of the car seems to transcend its physical composition in a way that is not well understood. In fact, the identity of the car as the same entity appears to depend on our own internal construction of a concept that persists through time. There are no necessary or sufficient physical (in the sense of physics) correlates to the triangles we perceive—they can be black or blue or red or defined by regions of small x's on a background of o's. Similarly, there are no necessary or sufficient correlates to the concept CAR or even to the concept of a particular car—BILL'S CAR—no set of molecules, no space-time continuum can define a car. This lack of necessary and sufficient conditions is characteristic of equivalence classes as discussed by Pylyshyn (1984), and we suggest that both CAR and BILL'S CAR are not labels of objects recognized by the science of physics but rather of objects of human experience of the world, equivalence classes of our faculty of object cognition.

Each of us constructs CAR concepts that relate to aspects in the physical world much like the relation between our triangle percept and ink on the page in Chapter 2. We humans impose "car-ness" on aspects of experience. We tend to appear to agree about what cars are out in the world because we have very similar apparatus for imposing structure on our experience of the world and very similar input systems with which we transduce incoming stimuli, convert them to mental representations. Note that we also can construct CAR concepts without any external stimulus—in visual imagery or other kinds of thought. These concepts, these cars, have no physical correlates whatsoever, despite the fact that we may conceive of them as objects in our world of human physical experience.

Similar considerations apply to living beings, and the argument is perhaps easier to accept in this domain, given notions like self and soul that are part of our everyday concepts. Chomsky mentions the stories of the Frog Prince of the fairy tale and Sylvester the Donkey of the children's story—when the former undergoes the transformation from man to frog and the latter from donkey to rock, children, like adults, have no trouble conceiving of the frog or rock as the same entity as the man or donkey, respectively. The rock has no hair and no ears, the dogs detect no donkey smell on it, and it does not talk or bray. Yet it remains Sylvester the Donkey because our concepts and words refer to a continuity that transcends physical continuity.

Perhaps a good way to think about it is that the names and concepts have been associated with an index. The physical properties associated with the index may change, but the identity remains merely by virtue of being associated with an index.

Chomsky discusses many examples of words whose apparent referent is not simply some physical object. We refer to doors and windows as things that can be installed and painted, but we also refer to the possibility of passing through a door or window, focusing on the space bounded by the frame. The frame and the space have very different properties, but we do not think of the words as being ambiguous. For example, we do not think of a room as having four windows in one sense (frames) and four in the other sense (spaces)—the word refers to a complex concept that cannot be reduced to a consistent physical characterization.

Similar considerations hold for the word *house*. We can make an arbitrary decision that our house ends two meters below the center of the doorknob of the front entrance, but such a decision is exactly that—arbitrary and with no basis in how we conceive of what a house is. Our house can burn down and be rebuilt slightly to the south—its physical properties are completely different and yet we can conceive of it as the same house. Similarly, a city can be destroyed and rebuilt in a different location. An institution such as a university is at the same time a collection of buildings, associations among individuals, legal and social conventions, and so on. So, clearly, words referring to such an institution cannot be referring just to things in the physical world.

The observation that the identity even of simple objects transcends their physical characterization was made in the 1930s by the linguist and anthropologist Edward Sapir in the paper mentioned in Chapter 1. Sapir points out that a given physical object can be described from the point of view of physics as having a certain length, mass, color, and chemical composition, but that a physical description can never tell us if the object is a club or a pole. Two poles may differ greatly in their physical attributes, and a given pole may be identical to a given club from this perspective. What makes us call one a club and the other a pole depends on how we use them or intend to use them, and perhaps our beliefs about the intent of the person who made each object. If we see you take a certain object, plant it in a hole lined up with other similar objects and string barbed wire between these objects, we will refer to them as "poles." If, instead, we see you use the same object to bang someone on the head, we call it a club.

We began this chapter by presenting two ways in which the rationalism vs. empiricism debate relates to language. The first one concerns the source of our theories: do we start with observations and then make generalizations and provide hypotheses, or do we make inferences and deductions, and only then appeal to observation? The position we have argued for is a rationalist one. The second way in which the rationalist vs. empiricist debate applies to language concerns the source of our knowledge of language as speakers. Here, too, we have sided with rationalists, who admit innate knowledge as a possibility, as opposed to empiricists, who advocate that knowledge is primarily derived from experience. Our discussion about reference suggests yet further problems for the empiricist perspective, since the very objects that are part of our experience and observations are actually mental constructs. Acquiring knowledge of language partly consists of constructing "sound-meaning" correspondences for words.[47] And yet, the meanings of words do not directly map to the physical world of science but rather to the world of human experience, the world as perceived by us humans, including both those aspects we consider to be physical, material objects, and other aspects to which we do not attribute these properties. So, there is no sense in which word meaning, as a component of knowledge of language, can be conceived of as being derived from experience and observation, unless what we mean is that it is derived from our own perception of experience and from the way in which we carve or categorize our observations. But, of course, that amounts to actually taking a mentalist, rationalist stand.

13.4 Essentialism

One of the immediate consequences of accepting that language is not about the "real" world is that an essentialist position becomes untenable. Let us explain.

---

[47] Of course, we mean phonological representations, not actual sound.

Our teenaged daughter speaks both English and French, but her first language was Romanian. Once, while crossing the street a few years ago, she jokingly said to Charles: "I hope that car does not step on me." She then explained that this was a literal translation of how you say in Romanian "I hope that car does not hit me." We explained, much to her astonishment, that upon learning this fact about Romanian, some philosophers might actually engage in a discussion of whether cars really step on you.

You probably think we are being unfair to the community of philosophers, but you should consider the kinds of questions that philosophers have been asking for millennia. The Platonic dialogues portray Socrates engaged in discussion of such questions as *What is beauty/justice/virtue?* More recently, retired Princeton philosophy professor Harry Frankfurt engaged in what might be best characterized as meta-bullshit when he explored the question *What is bullshit?* in a book published in 2005 by Princeton University Press entitled *On Bullshit*. These questions are actually no different in kind from questions like *Can a machine think?*, *Can animals do evil?*, or *Can a car step on you?* All these questions presuppose that there is a matter of truth at stake, and the truth depends crucially on what the words in question really mean. If we figure out the real meaning of *thinking*, or *stepping on*, or *beauty*, or *justice*, or *bullshit*, then we will be able to answer the questions correctly. This idea is directly related to the idea that understanding the world involves understanding the essence, or real nature, of the things that words refer to. However, as pointed out in the preceding chapter, we each use words in certain ways, and we have developed similar ways of using words with similar sounds if we acquire our languages under similar circumstances. But there is no truth to the matter, no question of the real, that is, *correct*, meaning of a word.

We have (perhaps unfairly) caricatured philosophers as overly prone to essentialist discourse, and we must point out that, in fact, the most prominent critic of the view that science should attempt to define the *essence* of named entities was the twentieth-century philosopher Karl Popper. He contrasted such methodological essentialism with methodological *nominalism*. The essentialist tries to answer questions like *What is movement?* or *What is an atom?* The nominalist in contrast asks questions like *How do the planets move?* or *Under what conditions will an atom radiate light?*

And to those philosophers who tell [the nominalist] that before having answered the "what is" question he cannot hope to give exact answers to any of the "how" questions, he will reply, if at all, by pointing out that he much prefers that modest degree of exactness which he can achieve by his methods to the pretentious muddle which they have achieved by theirs.

...methodological nominalism is nowadays fairly generally accepted in the natural sciences. The problems of the social sciences, on the other hand, are still for the most part treated by essentialist methods. This is in my opinion, one of the main reasons for their backwardness. But many who have noticed this situation judge it differently. They believe that the difference in method is necessary, and that it reflects an "essential" difference between the "natures" of these two fields of research. [Popper 1945:33. Popper's footnote deleted]

Popper goes on to discuss why the social sciences (and humanities) accept essentialism, and it is interesting, but beyond the scope of this book to compare Popper's discussion with that of methodological dualism in Chapter 3 of this book.

In order to impress upon you how seriously Popper took the issue of essentialism among his fellow philosophers, we provide the following quotation from volume 2 of the same work cited above:

The problem of definitions and of the "meaning of terms" is the most important source of Aristotle's regrettably still prevailing intellectual influence, of all that verbal and empty scholasticism that haunts not only the Middle Ages, but our own contemporary philosophy; for even a philosophy as recent as that of L. Wittgenstein suffers, as we shall see, from this influence. The development of thought since Aristotle could, I think, be summed up by saying that every discipline, as long as it used the Aristotelian method of definition, has remained arrested in a state of empty verbiage and barren scholasticism, and that the degree to which the various sciences have been able to make any progress depended on the degree to which they have been able to get rid of this essentialist method. (This is why so much of our "social science" still belongs to the Middle Ages.) The discussion of this method will have to be a little abstract, owing to the fact that the problem has been so thoroughly muddled by Plato and Aristotle, whose influence has given rise to such deep-rooted prejudices that the prospect of dispelling them does not seem very bright. In spite of all that, it is perhaps not without interest to analyse the source of so much confusion and verbiage. [Popper 1945, Vol. II]

Popper's refusal to mince words made it very difficult for him to find a publisher for what ended up becoming one of the century's most influential philosophical works. The book was rejected by American publishers because of its criticism of Plato and Aristotle and finally published in London in 1945. We have neither the space nor the competence to defend Popper here, but we will just point out that the problem of essentialist thinking appears to lie behind many of the enduring "puzzles" of philosophy of language and mind. We now turn to one such "puzzle."

The great mathematician Alan Turing asked the question *Can a machine think?* in a famous paper in 1951, but sensibly enough immediately provided the following response to his own question:

The original question "Can machines think?" I believe to be too meaningless to deserve discussion. Nevertheless I believe that at the end of the century the use of words and general educated opinion will have altered so much that one will be able to speak of machines thinking without expecting to be contradicted.

Turing explains that whatever we *call* what machines are doing has no bearing on what they are actually doing. It may or may not be useful to apply the label *thinking* to what digital computers do, but Turing predicted that the label would be used by educated people at some point.

The amount of ink that has been spilt on Turing's question, all the while ignoring his dismissal a few paragraphs later, is mind-boggling. Contributors include philosophers, computer scientists, artifical intelligence researchers, psychologists, theologians, and more. A quick web search turns up this example from the kurzweilai.net website in an article "Can a machine think?" by Clinton Kelly from 2001:

Why do we think computers may have the "right stuff?" The reasons are among some of the most significant philosophical concepts of the late 20th century.

In one variant or another, the question "can a machine think" has occupied the attention of philosophers and others for centuries, stimulated from time-to-time by the emergence of ingenious mechanisms which suggested at least the possibility of an affirmative answer. In our own times, we have seen the creation of machines that are autonomous—robots, for example, that can perform tasks without constant human supervision. Does this mean that the device thinks? Thinking about what it means for a machine to think means thinking, as well, about ourselves. Indeed, what does it mean to think? Does thinking define humanity? Do animals think?

Chomsky has pointed out that the meaninglessness of these questions follows from the I-language perspective in which we *use* words to refer and to mean things, but do not attribute reference and meanings to the words themselves:

[I]t is not a question of fact, but a matter of decision as to whether to adopt a certain metaphorical usage, as when we say (in English) that airplanes fly, but comets do not—and as for space shuttles, choices differ. Similarly, submarines set sail, but do not swim. There can be no sensible debate about such topics; or about machine intelligence, with the many familiar variants. [Chomsky 2000a:114]

Whatever we call what computers do or what gorillas do, it may or may not be useful to compare them to what we think humans do when we say they are *thinking*. As we have seen in our discussions of the verb *see* in Chapter 2 and in our discussions of the word *language*, everyday terms used to describe human behavior and cognition tend to cover a wide range of different phenomena when we begin to subject them to scientific inquiry. The question of whether machines "really" think is no more useful than the question of whether cars "really" step on people.

You can probably see how the discussion of reference and essentialism ties in with the Platonic, P-language conception of language introduced in Chapter 4. If the words of languages exist outside of human minds, as ideal forms, then they have true meanings—the ones they actually have. It follows, then, that one can judge usages that do not conform to these true meanings as "wrong" or "false." This chain of reasoning helps to explain why there exists a strong prescriptivist strain among philosophers. (We won't try to substantiate this characterization—all you need to do to convince yourself is try explaining the positions on I-language and prescriptive grammar we have presented to a philosophically "sophisticated" friend. They will assume that you are being crazy, stupid, or both.)

13.5 Mind and body

In this section we will briefly discuss one of the most enduring topics of philosophical discussion, the so-called "mind-body" problem. This issue is sometimes referred to as the "ontological problem" since ontology is the study of what exists, and the issues we are concerned with are whether "mind" and "body" both exist and whether or not the distinction between them is a principled one. A related question, of course, is why the two can apparently interact if they are completely distinct—we know that a vodka martini with three olives or a good workout (physical things) can make us feel happy (a mental thing), for example.

We use the term "mind" in the context of the ontological problem, to refer to what throughout history has been called *mind, thought, spirit*, and *soul*, and various roughly equivalent terms in other languages. Even restricting ourselves to *thought*, we find that discussion is further confused by a failure to distinguish cognition of the kind we have been discussing, visual, auditory, and linguistic computation for example, from conscious (self-)awareness and conscious thought.

This is not the place to review the history of the ontological problem, but we can briefly mention some of the major themes and positions that have been proposed and defended. The view that mind stuff and body stuff are both real but fundamentally distinct is referred to as *dualism*. The most famous advocate of dualism is the great seventeenth-century French mathematician and philosopher René Descartes, from whose name derives a view of the ontological problem known as *Cartesian dualism*. Descartes is famous for his skepticism—he began his investigations into the ontological problem by doubting everything. You are probably familiar with his famous statement *I think, therefore I am*, which was the first conclusion he accepted: the fact that he thinks shows that he must exist. So, Descartes accepted first the existence of thought and thus mind. It took some further argumentation for him to accept that his body was real.

Idealism, whose most famous representative was Bishop Berkeley writing in the eighteenth century, is the position that only mental stuff exists. The universe is just thought, and things exist just by virtue of being thought about or perceived. Since everything is always in the mind of God, things that we think of as physical objects do not go in and out of existence according to *our* thoughts about them—God has a lot more attentional resources than we do (probably infinitely more) and so He can keep everything in mind, thus ensuring the permanence of the so-called physical world.

In our everyday lives, most of us are probably dualists. Whether we believe in the soul in accordance with some religious tradition or because we experience our minds as independent of our bodies in so many ways, we tend to talk and act like dualists of one sort or another. These everyday beliefs show many incoherent and inconsistent properties upon examination. For example, Descartes defined the physical as that which has location and extension in space, and most people would readily agree that the soul or the spirit or the mind lacks this property. However, at the same time, we tend to think of the mind/soul/spirit as somehow inhabiting or being inside the body and departing upon death of the body. How can something both not have location and extension *and* be located inside our head or hearts?

When thinking about these issues as scientists or philosophers, many modern thinkers reject dualism for a form of *materialism*—the idea that only physical stuff exists. Thus the body is real, but the mind is not real in the same way. There are many varieties of materialism and an excellent survey is provided in Paul Churchland's 1984 *Matter and Consciousness*. Two popular versions of materialism are *reductive materialism* and *eliminative materialism*. Reductive materialism takes the position that the phenomena of mental life, thoughts and consciousness, will be reducible to categories of the natural sciences. For example, thinking about *cockroaches in the jungle* is ultimately reducible to, or describable as, a certain electrochemical state of the brain. Eliminative materialists go even further. They do not want to reduce the mentalistic talk to physical neurological terms, but rather eliminate the mentalistic talk altogether.

In the history of science there have been many proposals for entities that are no longer thought to exist. The whole universe was assumed, until the early twentieth century, to be full of "the ether" that served as a medium of electromagnetic radiation. Sound and water waves require a medium, so the same was assumed for light and other waves emitted from distant stars. We now know that electromagnetic radiation does not require a medium, and thus the ether has been eliminated from physics. Eliminative materialists, including Churchland, who wrote an excellent review of the philosopher John Searle's views on these matters called "Betty Crocker's theory of consciousness" (Churchland 1988), propose that mentalistic terms like *thought*, *knowledge*, and *belief* should be eliminated from the science of the mind. From a scientific perspective, the eliminativists argue, thought is as unnecessary an element for an understanding of cognition as the ether is for an undertanding of the physical universe.

In our opinion, Chomsky has cut the Gordian knot of the mind/body problem by arguing that the issue is incoherent, not because of the difficulty of identifying what the mental is, but because of the incoherence of the notion "body"—the physical world cannot be defined or identified in any coherent fashion. Eddington, in the quotation repeated below from Chapter 3, had in mind the divergence of everyday experience of space and time from what we know about the scales of particle physics and cosmology. Cognitive science has gone further in showing that even on the middle scale of everyday life, perception of time, space, motion, etc. can be greatly at odds with what physical measurements record.

At one time there was no very profound difference between the two versions. The scientist accepted the familiar story [of the perceiving mind] in its main outline; only he corrected a few facts here and there, and elaborated a few details. But latterly the familiar story and the scientific story have diverged more and more widely—until it has become hard to recognise that they have anything in common. Not content with upsetting fundamentally our ideas of material substance, physics has played strange pranks with our conceptions of space and time. Even causality has undergone transformations. Physical science now deliberately aims at presenting a new version of the story of our experience from the very beginning, rejecting the familiar story as too erratic a foundation.

Chomsky's insight about the vast gulf between everyday experience and scientific understanding is not new, but his application of this idea to the mind/body problem apparently is new, and almost universally ignored or rejected by the philosophical community.

As the familiar story and the scientific story diverge it becomes impossible to understand in any direct sense what the world is like according to the scientific view. As Chomsky puts it, science no longer aims to make the world intelligible but only to construct intelligible theories that appear to give us some insight into phenomena in very narrow domains, far removed from everyday experience.

So what Chomsky (2000:106) proposes is to use the term "mental" informally, "with no metaphysical import" as pre-theoretically defining a domain of inquiry in the same way that terms like "optical," "chemical," or "biological" are used. Nobody wastes their time trying to determine the essence of the optical. But there are certain interfacing explanatory theories that have been constructed that we group together for the purposes of writing textbooks or organizing departments in universities. Because of a fairly informal naming practice we should not assume to have discovered a coherent, distinct aspect of reality. The mind-body "problem" is just another essentialist fallacy under this view.

Instead of asking whether the triangle of Chapter 2 exists, or whether Maranungku foot structure exists, or NPs exist, the cognitive science approach to the study of the mind asks questions like *What are the binding conditions on NPs in English?* Positing NPs and their c-command relations allows us to build an explicit explanatory theory that appears to give insight into some aspect of the world (in this case one that we happen to call linguistic, part of the mental world). Questions about whether NPs really exist, just like similar questions about gravitational fields or electrons, do not provide any insight. According to Chomsky (1997:132) in Johnson and Erneling (1997) such "[o]ntological questions are generally beside the point, hardly more than a form of harrassment."

The fairly arbitrary labeling of domains is made apparent in a passage from *The Computer and the Brain* (2000) by the mathematician John von Neumann describing a nerve impulse propagated along an axon:

One of its characteristics is certainly that it is an electrical disturbance; in fact, it is most frequently described as being just that. This disturbance is usually an electrical potential of something like 50 millivolts and of about a millisecond's duration. Concurrently with this electrical disturbance there also occur chemical changes along the axon. Thus, in the area of the axon over which the pulse-potential is passing, the ionic constitution of the intracellular fluid changes, and so do the electrical-chemical properties (conductivity, permeability) of the wall of the axon, the *membrane*. At the endings of the axon the chemical character of the change is even more obvious; there, specific and characteristic substances make their appearance when the pulse arrives. Finally, there are probably mechanical changes as well. Indeed, it is very likely that the changes of the various ionic permeabilities of the cell membrane (cf. above) can come about only by reorientation of its molecules, i.e. by mechanical changes involving the relative positions of these constituents. [40–41]

So is the neural impulse an electrical, chemical, or mechanical phenomenon? Nothing depends on the answer and so the question is probably not a useful one. The names of these domains roughly delineate topics of study in which some progress has been made developing explanatory theories, and the same is true of linguistics, vision and quantum mechanics. There is no chemical world or mechanical world or optical world or linguistic world. There is just *the world*, and more or less explanatory theories that we can make about aspects of the world. The world itself will not be intelligible to what Eddington calls the "storyteller" of the perceiving mind, but our scientific theories can be intelligible.

Chomsky argues, and much of this book has attempted to support this view, that under a certain perspective of what language is, we can develop explanatory formal models that give us some insight into phenomena under the same kinds of idealizations made in all pure sciences. The decision to treat human language as a natural object is vindicated by the insight achieved. The same can be said for the study of vision and other mental faculties.

So, Chomsky solves the mind-body problem by denying a principled distinction between what is mental and what is physical. Not only is the world of physics remote from our own pre-scientific notions and understanding, but physics changes to include whatever physicists posit. Before Newton there were no gravitational fields in physics. Rather than *reducing* mentalistic notions, including linguistic ones like *word*, *c-command*, or *phoneme* to materialist definitions in terms of neurons and chemicals or quarks and ions, Chomsky proposes that various domains in which intelligible theories have been constructed may perhaps one day be *unified*. Just as the unification of chemistry and physics in the twentieth century required changes in the theories of both fields, the unification of linguistics with neuroscience, if it is ever possible, will require the positing of neural properties that are currently not known. Why would we want to try to reduce linguistics to a neuroscience that we know to be incomplete? In fact, by paying attention to what computational properties human language exhibits (such as recursion and c-command) neuroscientists can design research programs that will lead to the discovery of the necessary computational apparatus.

13.6 A view from neuroscience

In order to convey what a bad job linguists have done at communicating their ideas it will be useful to compare the views we have developed with the discussion of language and cognition presented recently in a popular book by a prominent neuroscientist. Gerald Edelman won a Nobel Prize for his work on antibodies, but he is also director of the Neurosciences Institute and president of the Neurosciences Research Foundation. In his 2004 book *Wider Than the Sky: The Phenomenal Gift of Consciousness*, Edelman takes a very skeptical view of *mental representations* which he defines as

a term used by some cognitive psychologists who have a computational view of the mind. The term is applied to precise symbolic constructs or codes corresponding to objects and, by their computation, putatively explaining behavior. [167]

Not surprisingly, topics like Warlpiri reduplication or conditions on anaphor binding are not handled in Edelman's discussions of language. Instead, Edelman muses on the origins of language in evolution, not only via the development of the vocal tract and the auditory system but also with regard to our upright posture which he assumes is a necessary precursor of language:

In freeing the upper extremities from brachiation (climbing or hanging) or walking, a whole precursor set involving the interpretation of gestures by the self and by others may have been opened up for early hominines. [102]

Edelman continues by suggesting that this evolutionary history may be repeated in child development:

Whether infants who have learned to walk, and have their upper limbs free, develop similar capabilities before the exercise of extensive speech acts is a question that remains. The acquisition of language may be enormously facilitated by the development of conscious imagery related to movements and motor control. Almost certainly, concepts of objects, events, and succession must exist in a child's mind before the exercise of language. According to these ideas, the sequences of actions of the free upper extremities may prepare the basal ganglion–cortical loops for the emergence of syntactical sequences, establishing what might be called a protosyntax.

Clearly, one of the largest steps towards the acquisition of true language is the realization that an arbitrary token—a gesture or a word—stands for a thing or an event. When a sufficiently large lexicon of such tokens is accumulated, higher-order consciousness can greatly expand in range. Association can be made by metaphor, and with ongoing activity, early metaphor can be transformed into more precise categorization of intrapersonal and interpersonal experience. The gift of narrative and an expanded sense of temporal succession then follow. [102–3]

Where do we start? Edelman is certainly hedging with all these *may*s and *might*s, but let's assume that he wants us to take these ideas seriously. Basically, he seems to be suggesting that upright posture freed the hands to use gesture, which in turn led to conscious imagery related to movements, which in turn led to (proto-)syntax. Combined with the "realization" that arbitrary signs or tokens stand for a thing or event and a bit of metaphor; this all leads to the "gift of narrative." If Edelman were not such an important figure, this just-so story would hardly warrant a response. However, an analysis of the factual and conceptual errors reflected in this passage should prove instructive.

We start with some points about children's capacities at birth. Let's first note that a vast body of research suggests that children have "concepts of objects, events, and succession" as soon as they can be tested, basically from birth. Elizabeth Spelke (1994), for example, has some very concrete proposals concerning children's initial concepts about the physical world. If this research is valid, then making such concepts a prerequisite for language is an empty requirement, since the concepts are there from the beginning and so "language" can be as well.

Second, the idea that cognitive development must be preceded by motor and spatial experience and learning is an obsolete notion associated most strongly with the great developmental psychologist Jean Piaget. A concrete example of such ideas would be that children should have to be able to line up sticks in size order (a task involving motor skills and spatial perception) before they could correctly use comparatives, like *Pat is taller than Kim* (a linguistic construction). As Annette Karmiloff-Smith, a student of Piaget's, has shown, children with Williams Syndrome, a severe form of mental retardation, are able to use comparatives in speech, but they are completely incapable of lining up sticks in size order.

Third, some linguistic knowledge, or knowledge that ends up being used by the language faculty, can be shown to be present in newborns. Based on the low frequency signals that make it into the uterus through the mother's belly, newborns can distinguish the rhythmic properties of their mother's language from that of a wide range of other languages. As mentioned in Chapter 11, newborns also appear to be sensitive to any phonetic contrast that can appear in a language of the world, while at the same time they ignore contrasts that are not used linguistically.

It is clear from the passage that Edelman is ignoring the competence–performance distinction presented above. As just mentioned, very young infants have speech perception capacities that are completely out of line with their lousy abilities at articulating sounds. Later, it is clear that their comprehension of complex syntactic constructions far outstrips the complexity of their produced sentences. Like aphasics, or even people with paralyzed vocal apparatus, children's syntactic knowledge cannot be determined by just observing their behavior.

Notice that Edelman is after big game—consciousness. He is not satisfied to investigate the neuroscience of, say, how the brain computes Warlpiri reduplication or subject–verb agreement in English or how you recognize your mother's face from the side, topics about which nothing at all is known at the level of neurons. One would think that normal scientific practice would entail the preliminary investigation of simpler aspects of cognition before proposing a solution for what is perhaps the greatest mystery of the mind, consciousness. Not only is there little evidence that consciousness is actually amenable to scientific study but Edelman bizarrely suggests that it is clear that language itself involves conscious thought—he refers to *conscious imagery* and the *realization* of the arbitrariness of linguistic signs. So, he not only tackles the most difficult problem, the basis of consciousness, but he also assumes that the evolution and acquisition of language necessarily involve consciousness. Recall the analyses of phonology, morphology, syntax, and semantics in Chapters 6–9 which proceeded without any reference to consciousness. We are certain that no reader of this book who was not already trained as a linguist had conscious knowledge of the binding conditions, for example. In fact, even after reading Chapter 8, the workings of your grammar with respect to binding remain as inaccessible to consciousness as his own enzyme secretion remains to a gastrologist.

Edelman continues the passage above to discuss "past recollections and future imaginations," which relate to one of the most wondrous properties of human language. We use language to refer not only to objects we see now but also to things we saw yesterday or last year, events we hope to witness, situations that did not arise and could never arise, and so on. The term *displaced reference* is commonly applied to a subset of these uses of language, those that do not refer specifically to things in the immediate environment. Despite Edelman's willingness to sketch a plausible evolutionary scenario for the development of language, and given his latitude in discussing the nature of language, it is striking that he does not mention that the only well-established case of displaced reference in a communication system is in the waggle dance of honey bees, which, performed in the hive, conveys the distance, direction, and abundance of a food source. Presumably, Edelman does not attribute to bees and humans the same evolutionary path to displaced reference.

Finally, let's comment on Edelman's appeal to metaphor. The discussion is so vague that it is hard to criticize, yet it is reminiscent of a recurrent anti-nativist appeal to *analogy* as the basis of language acquisition. The problem is that the child acquiring language has no way of knowing which metaphors or analogies will work and which will not. Since we have at least some idea of how to formalize the notion of analogy, we will continue the discussion in that vein.

Here is a simple example, borrowed from Ivan Sag and Tom Wasow, of how analogy fails the learner. Fill in your favorite profane verb in the following contexts:

13.3   A failure of analogy
   a. *@#$&*% yourself!*
   b. *Go @#$&*% yourself!*
   c. *@#$&*% you!*

Reasoning by analogy, we ask "Sentence 1 is to sentence 2 as sentence 3 is to x. What is x?" Clearly x should be the following:

13.4   **Go @#$&*% you!*

But (13.4) is clearly ungrammatical, as any native speaker can attest. Analogy fails.

Here is another example. Consider the difference between the sentences that end in an NP and those that do not.

| 13.5 | Another failure of analogy |

    a. John is too tough to eat tofu
    b. John is too tough to eat
    c. John is too tough to talk to Bill
    d. John is too tough to talk to

In (13.5a.) the object of *eat* is *tofu*. Example (13.5b.) is ambiguous: it can mean that John is so tough that he won't engage in eating of anything, or that John is so tough that we can't eat him. We might expect, reasoning *by analogy*, that leaving the NP *Bill* off of (13.5c.) would yield an ambiguous string, but (13.5d.) is not ambiguous. Example (13.5d.) can only mean that John is so tough that we can't talk to him, and not that he is so tough that he won't engage in talking to anyone at all. Simple analogy fails again.

If analogy or metaphor sometimes work and sometimes do not, then we cannot claim that they provide an explanation in just those cases where they work. This would constitute opportunistic appeal to analogy—kind of like the way people invoke astrology. Typically, linguists say that analogy is irrelevant to language learning. Another way to think about it is that Universal Grammar is the theory of just which analogies are entertained by children in the course of language acquisition. The language faculty specifies certain analogies that play a role in learning, but not others.

Let's consider one more, fairly complex example where analogy fails. One might expect that, *by analogy*, a string of words would contribute a consistent meaning to any string it is embedded in. Consider a possible and an impossible reading of the following string, as indicated by the indexation:

| 13.6 | The men$_m$ expected to see them$_{*m/n}$ |

The pronoun *them* cannot be coindexed with *the men* as you now understand from our discussion in Chapter 8. However, *them* can be indexed with any index distinct from that borne by *the men*. Now consider the same string embedded in a larger context.

| 13.7 | I wonder who$_i$ the men$_j$ expected to see them$_{*i/j/k}$ |

Here we see that *them* can indeed be coindexed with *the men* (or with anything else other than *who*). Why should this be? Why does the analogy between (13.6) and (13.7) fail?[48]

You actually already have almost all the tools to answer this question. Like the base- and derived-position copies of NPs that we introduced for *wh*–movement, we will assume that there are base- and derived-position copies of NPs in a sentence like *John expects to go*. The abstract structure will be assumed to have two copies of *John*:

13.8   • *John expects to go*
        • John expects John to go

We can now apply this to the sentences above. Here is the tree for (13.6):

13.9

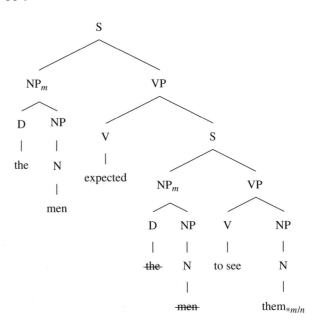

You can see that *them* is locally c-commanded by the base-position copy of *the men*, and thus, they must not be coindexed—pronouns like *him* cannot occur in such an environment.

Now look at the tree for (13.7):

---

[48] If you have trouble getting the two readings consider the following:
 • The men are dressed up for Halloween; they expect to be seen by someone. I wonder who$_i$ the men$_j$ expected to see them$_j$.
 • The women are dressed up for Halloween; the men expect that someone will see the women. I wonder who$_i$ the men$_j$ expected to see them$_k$.

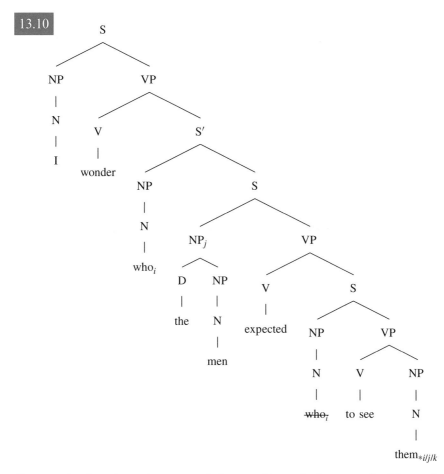

Once again there is an instance of *the men* (the only instance, in this case) which can bind *them*. However, this is not *local binding*, since *the men* is not in the minimal clause that contains *them*.

There is no need to appeal to consciousness in this discussion, and in fact it is pretty clear that the binding conditions are not accessible to consciousness or related to consciousness in any other way, except that humans have both. Furthermore, we have already learned that the sentence structure, and even the words, do not have invariant physical correlates—there is no sense in which "the actions of the free upper extremities" lead to a "proto-syntax," if proto-syntax has anything to do with the actual syntax of c-command and the like.

Edelman appears to scorn an approach to cognition (well, he keeps referring to consciousness, but it looks like he means any cognition complex enough to be specific to human language) based on symbolic equivalence classes and "programs and algorithms" (p. 33) such as we have presented, which he refers to (repeating a common and misleading characterization) as "computer models" of the mind (see his Chapter 4, especially). He rightly insists (p. 33) that

it is important to construct a brain theory that is principled and compatible with evolution and development. By principled, I mean a theory that describes the principles governing the major mechanisms by which the brain deals with information and novelty.

There is nothing to argue with here, but Edelman continues: "One such theory or model is the idea that the brain is like a computer . . . ", a view he rejects in no uncertain terms: "Once more with feeling: the brain is not a computer and the world is not a piece of tape" (p. 39).

But isn't it also right to insist on a brain theory that can handle reduplication, vowel harmony, binding, negative polarity items, and whatever else we need to model human language? If neuroscience has no insight to offer into these issues, then that is a problem for neuroscience, given the robustness of the linguistic accounts. Neuroscience is clearly not ready for unification with linguistic theory, but that is no bad reflection on linguistics, which has enough problems of its own, to be sure, but also has offered intelligible explanations with predictive power for a wide range of observable phenomena.

13.7 Exercises

Exercise 13.7.1.   We began this book claiming that we would relate Turkish vowel harmony to important philosophical questions. Have we succeeded? Can you trace a line of thought from vowel harmony to the mind-body problem, for example?

Exercise 13.7.2.   Chomsky (2000b:12) says that

it is a rare philosopher who would scoff at [the] weird and counterintuitive principles [of physics] as contrary to right thinking and therefore untenable. But this standpoint is commonly regarded as inapplicable to cognitive science, linguistics in particular . . . This seems to be nothing more than a kind of "methodological dualism," far more pernicious than the traditional metaphysical dualism, which was a scientific hypothesis, naturalistic in spirit. Abandoning this dualist stance, we pursue inquiry where it leads.

In a page or so, unpack this quotation, and explain the distinction between the two kinds of dualism that Chomsky is describing.

Exercise 13.7.3.   At some point children are able to play a game in which they name an "opposite" for words you provide to them, even for new pairs. For example, given *hot–cold* and *up–down*, a child will provide *dry* when prompted with *wet*, *small* when prompted with *big*, and so on. Sketch two theories for how children can come to be able to do this, a more empiricist theory and a more rationalist theory. What observations could lead children to develop the concept of "opposite"? What challenges are faced by a rationalist, nativist approach?

Further Readings

- "Initial knowledge: six suggestions" by Elizabeth Spelke (1994).
- "The problem of reality" by Ray Jackendoff (1992).
- "Review of Skinner's *Verbal Behavior*" by Noam Chomsky (1959).
- "The metaphysics of coarticulation" by R. Hammarberg (1976).

14

Open questions and closing remarks

14.1 You and your grammar

Two of our primary concerns in this book can be stated in such a way as to seem contradictory. On the one hand, we wanted you to accept a narrow conception of what language is—we wanted to abstract away from issues like communication and other purposes to which we apply language. On the other hand, we want you to appreciate the complexity of linguistic phenomena, even when we restrict ourselves to looking at the vowel patterns of Turkish or the "contracted" verb *'s* in English. Paradoxically, by narrowing our focus, we are able to make discoveries that have broad implications for our understanding of the rich complexity of the human mind.

People are complex, a sentiment expressed in the rant against superficiality and narrowness in the song containing lines from the movie *Fight Club*:

You are not your bank account.
You are not the clothes you wear.
You are not the contents of your wallet.
You are not your bowel cancer.
You are not your grande latte.
You are not the car you drive.
You are not your $*!&@%#^‡¿ © khakis.

...and you are not your grammar.

You speak and assign interpretations to utterances you hear or imagine, but these tasks are not the result of the deaf, dumb, and blind grammar. Your grammar is just one component of a complex individual with memories of the past and predictions about the future (which may or may not be consistent with those held by others). Using language to communicate, lie, seduce, inform, and pray is something people do, not grammars. But science demands that we be narrow in our investigations, that we try to find evidence concerning individual phenomena that enter into our complex behavior. Studying what somebody will say on a given occasion or whether someone will raise his arm overhead when asked will not lead to interesting results. Studying somebody's binding conditions or the nature of impulse transmission in motor neurons has led to scientifically interesting results.

Abstracting away from the massive complexity of human behavior is very difficult, but is probably a necessary component of a naturalistic approach to the study of the mind. Even among certain linguists we find resistance to the idea that binding or vowel harmony can be studied as isolable systems. Such linguists advocate blurring the line between phonetics and phonology or between syntax and semantics. For example, there is a current trend of assuming that phonetic facts about articulation and acoustics of speech sounds are directly available to the phonological grammar.[49]

Our views concerning isolability of grammatical components follows those of philosophers of science such as Lawrence Sklar (2000:54–5), who has even made the point that without such isolability, science itself would probably be impossible:

> ...without a sufficient degree of isolability of systems we could never arrive at any lawlike regularities for describing the world at all. For unless systems were sufficiently independent of one another in their behavior, the understanding of the evolution of even the smallest part of the universe would mean keeping track of the behavior of all of its constituents. It is hard to see how the means for prediction and explanation could ever be found in such a world... it can be argued that unless such idealization of isolability were sufficiently legitimate in a sufficiently dominant domain of cases, we could not have any science at all.

If we take Sklar seriously, then to the extent we have gained scientific insight into the nature of vowel harmony, binding, negative polarity, and

---

[49] See Hale and Reiss (2008) for discussion of these issues under the rubric of "markedness" theory.

the like, it must be that our "idealizations of isolability were sufficiently legitimate."[50]

As people, not scientists, other approaches to language are more suitable for getting insight into what is important to us emotionally, socially, esthetically. Despite stereotypes to the contrary, it is not the case that taking an appropriately narrow scientific view within a domain, such as language, prevents one from taking a broader view in everyday life. Just as biologists do not lose their capacity to enjoy the beauty of a flower, linguists are able to enjoy all the uses to which language is put, literature, song, rhetoric, and so on. Repeating a quotation we have already used, we see that his scientific approach does not prevent Chomsky (2000:77) from appreciating art, literature, or any other aspect of life.

Plainly, a naturalistic approach does not exclude other ways of trying to comprehend the world. Someone committed to it can consistently believe (I do) that we learn much more of human interest about how people think and feel and act by reading novels or studying history or the activities of ordinary life than from all of naturalistic psychology, and perhaps always will; similarly, the arts may offer appreciation of the heavens to which astrophysics does not aspire.

Your grammar is only one aspect of you that determines what you say and how you interpret sentences. As an illustration of other aspects, apart from grammar, that influence the interpretation and acceptability of what we say, consider the following sentences.

14.1   What influences acceptability?
   a. John told Bill to kiss himself.
   b. John told Bill to kiss him.
   c. Bill kissed himself.
   d. Bill outlived himself.
   e. The pilot called the flight attendant into the cabin because she needed his help.

In interpreting (14.1a.), binding conditions determine that *himself* can only be interpreted as referring to *Bill*. In (14.1b.) binding conditions do not uniquely determine the interpretation of *him*, but they do rule out *Bill* as a possible interpretation. Examples (14.1c.) and (14.1d.) have the same form, but the second seems odd. This has nothing to do with binding, but rather with the nature of mortality. This sentence is odd to us, but it is not the grammar's business to take mortality into account. Many people judge

---

[50] We are indebted to Mark Hale for this quotation. Further discussion of isolability and language can be found in Hale (2007) and Hale and Reiss (2008).

sentence (14.1e.) to be ungrammatical when they first hear it, but if it is pointed out that the sentence makes perfect sense if the pilot is a woman and the flight attendant a man, they immediately change their judgment. The judgment of the string as unacceptable has to do with preconceptions about typical matches between gender and profession, surely something we do not want to build into the grammar. The grammar had better be isolable from such factors, or else studying it is a hopeless enterprise.

Grammars are symbolic computational systems, and as such they cannot care whether the sentences they generate result in utterances that are ambiguous, contain sequences that sound like taboo words, or fail to communicate. Your legs cannot go for a walk, since going for a walk involves intentions, goals, beliefs—things that legs do not have. People have intentions, goals and beliefs, and people go for walks. In the same way, *you*, not your grammar, can decide to disambiguate your utterances. The view we are opposing is part of what is sometimes called a *functionalist* approach to language, an approach that aims to explain aspects of language structure from the perspective of language as a communication system. We have not addressed this issue directly in this book, but have rather assumed what is sometimes called the *formalist* position that attempts to merely understand the computational properties of language. Our examples from syntax, semantics, morphology, and phonology lead us to accept the sentiment expressed by Morris Halle (1975), already quoted in Chapter 3:

Since language is not, in its essence, a means for transmitting [cognitive] information—though no one denies that we constantly use language for this very purpose—then it is hardly surprising to find in languages much ambiguity and redundancy, as well as other properties that are obviously undesirable in a good communication code

Halle prefers to look at language as an abstract code, like a pointless game, rather than as a form of purposeful behavior, and we think that this is a useful perspective—whatever we use it for, a language, a mental grammar, has certain properties. Linguists want to find out what those properties are. Obviously those properties must allow us to use language for the things we use it for, but there is no reason to believe that the accidental and arbitrary properties we observe in language make it particularly bad (or good) at what we use it for. We don't have any choice but to use what we have, so the question of the goodness of language is empty.

There is no obvious way in which *wh*-movement or the generation of allophones are good for communication, for example. In a sentence like

What did Bill eat? a speaker has to generate a tree with *what* as the object of *eat* but pronounce a copy in a different position; a listener hears the copy in sentence-initial position, but has to reconstruct a meaning with *what* as the object of *eat*, basically undoing the speaker's derivation. Why did the speaker apply *wh*-movement (notated by us as a copy) at all? It can't be for reasons of communication, since the listener just undoes the movement for interpretation. If we note that even when we engage in an internal monologue, "thinking in words," we apply *wh*-movement, it becomes apparent that such syntactic processes have no communicative function. In fact, in the context of internal monologue, the whole notion of communication becomes strange—who is communicating with whom?—and its irrelevance to understanding grammar becomes apparent.

Similarly, a speaker generates a word like *Tom* from a stored representation that begins with the phoneme /t/, then applies a phonological derivation that turns /t/ into the allophone [tʰ]. A listener has to strip off the aspiration in order to search his or her own mental lexicon for an item that begins with the phoneme /t/. Why doesn't the speaker just pronounce an unaspirated initial [t]? There is no physiological reason for aspirating— Spanish speakers don't aspirate their initial voiceless stops.

One might even argue, as Chomsky (1971:44) has, that the non-functional aspects of language are most interesting.

Where properties of language can be explained on such "functional" grounds, they provide no revealing insight into the nature of mind. Precisely because the explanations proposed here are "formal explanations," precisely because the proposed principles are not essential or even natural properties of any imaginable language, they provide a revealing mirror of the mind (if correct).

It is hard to imagine how the adding and deleting of aspiration or the construction and interpretation of *wh*-movement in a conversation aids in communication—it does seem like a pointless game, but a game whose rules linguists rejoice in discovering.

14.2 Retracing the links among key *-isms*

By treating language as a code or a symbol-manipulating process, by adopting *computationalism*, we were able to focus on its formal properties— what kinds of rules manipulate the symbols? Once we posited such symbol-manipulation processes, we were able to ask what these processes are, and we were led to conclude that they must be contained in or constitutive of individual minds: we adopted *mentalism*; and since minds are assumed to be an aspect of brains, which are inside of us, this leads in turn to *internalism*. We called the information encoded as one component of our mind "linguistic knowledge." This led to the further question of asking how this knowledge comes to be part of individual minds. Since the categories over which the computations apply are not directly contained in the signal, we adopted the position of *constructivism*, the idea that input is organized by the mind by the imposition of structure on stimuli.

However, not all linguistic knowledge can be constructed on the basis of merely making generalizations about the physical signals we receive as children, so we rejected constructivism in a stronger sense, sometimes associated with the psychologist Jean Piaget. This sense of constructivism is closely related to *empiricism* in that it posits that categories of, say, linguistic knowledge can somehow be discovered or induced by analogy to patterns experienced through the senses and motor activity. We rejected this view of the origins of the fundamental categories, the fundamental equivalence classes, of cognition.

The recurrence of equivalence classes and of highly specific patterns, like c-command, across languages, as well as the logical argument that no learning can occur without an initial representational system led us to posit *nativism*, the idea that a certain amount of linguistic knowledge is determined by the human genome.[51] Nativism refers to knowledge prior to experience, and thus is tied to *rationalism*, in the sense that we can have knowledge in the absence of experience. The innate endowment is what we use to process input, to construct representations. Because we treat language as a property of biological entities, we allow ourselves to study it as a property of the natural world, subject to the normal principles used in the natural sciences. This position of *naturalism* also allows us to justify bringing data from one language (say, Weri) to bear on our analysis of another language (say, Maranungku)—both represent possible states of a natural system, the human language faculty.

---

[51] Some of what we call linguistic knowledge is potentially also determined by the genome of other species—innateness in humans does not rule out innateness in other species any more than the claim that our genes determine production of certain proteins that make us develop into humans implies that we do not share those genes and proteins with other species.

This naturalistic approach also allows us to bring non-linguistic data to bear on our analyses—we should not attribute to the human language faculty any property that is inconsistent with the fact of language being a trait of individual biological organisms. This constraint on our hypothesis space cannot be exploited if we reject internalism for *externalism*, treating languages as sets of sentences "out in the world."

Inquiry into language can be broken down into (at least) the following four questions:

14.2   Questions about language
    a. What constitutes knowledge of language?
    b. How is knowledge of language acquired?
    c. How is knowledge of language put to use?
    d. What are the physical mechanisms that serve as the material basis for this system of knowledge and for the use of this knowledge?

We pointed out in Chapter 1 that question (14.2a.) is logically prior to the others—for example, we need to understand what is being acquired before we study language acquisition. As obvious as this should be, it is probably the case that most scholars working on language acquisition, whether in psychology, linguistics, or education departments, have a much less sophisticated understanding of what language (mental grammar) is than you do after working through this book. Given what you now know about the nature of language, you are better prepared to attack the other questions. For example, as a neuroscientist you would have a better idea of what kinds of properties you should be looking for. Your theory of the nervous system has to be compatible with some linguistic theory that can account for Turkish vowel harmony and Warlpiri reduplication, for example.

The phenomenon of language is particularly useful for understanding the links among the -*isms* we have adopted: computationalism, mentalism, internalism, constructivism, rationalism, nativism, and naturalism. Given the relevance of these themes to a wide variety of disciplines, a better understanding of the nature of language will have broad implications.

14.3 Bearing on philosophical questions

In Chapter 1 we promised that we would relate Turkish vowel harmony to some of the most ancient and challenging philosophical questions, repeated here:

| 14.3 | Big philosophical issues we addressed |

- The Nature–Nurture debate: How much of what we are is innate and how much depends on our experience?
- What is knowledge? How is it acquired?
- What is reality?
- Is there a distinction between mind and body?
- How can our study of these issues bear on social questions and educational practice?

We raised the Nature–Nurture debate in our discussions of Universal Grammar, which also relates to the questions about knowledge. In the domain of language, knowledge has to include a computational system that can use variables in order to account for reduplication, for example. Some linguistic knowledge is acquired, since languages differ, but we argued that some must be built into the system—there is a human language faculty. We illustrated the mind's construction of visual percepts, such as the edges of the illusory triangle, and of linguistic objects such as words and syntactic structures. The words we hear seem to be real to us, so it seems like a good idea to consider more of the world as real than just what belongs to the domain of physics. We need to recognize words as constructs of our mind, but real at the same time, since our minds are real parts of the natural world. We now see that our discussion had bearing on yet another set of *-isms*, those relating to the mind/body problem: dualism, idealism, and a whole slew of variations on materialism.

We have tried to convince you that by accepting language as a valid object of scientific inquiry, we can ask questions that make no sense under other approaches, and that we can even find some answers. In all fields science posits theoretical entities that are far removed from everyday experience in the world—this is as true in particle physics and syntactic theory, and thus we see that the study of the mental and the study of the physical proceed in the same manner. The physical world is just whatever is posited by current physics, but this has no actually intelligible correspondence to how we experience the world. So, the mind-body problem disappears—the two terms are just loose denominations for aspects of *the world* that one can study. As in the other natural sciences, naturalism in linguistics leads to *realism*—we assume that our theories are not about fictions, but about aspects of the world, since they give unforeseen insight, allow us to make predictions, and so on, just like the theories in other domains.

We have pointed out in several places that experts in a variety of fields make claims about language that are either completely unsupported or actually even refuted by available evidence. In the realm of academic discourse such ignorance is fairly innocuous, but there are cases where misunderstanding of the nature of language is harmful. One example is the case of medical doctors and educators who advise parents of deaf children to not expose their child to a signed language, or who advise immigrant parents to not speak their native language to their children. There is no evidence that learning multiple languages in childhood is difficult or leads to confusion or problems in language development.

Despite the fairly widespread (but not universal) acceptance of formal approaches to language as a valid research program within the academic community, there is still tremendous ignorance about and resistance to such perspectives in society at large. Two examples familiar to us are the reactions to the Ebonics controversy in the United States over the last ten years, as well as the constant stream of outright nonsense concerning the nature of local French dialects in the mainstream media and in school curricula in Quebec. These cases demonstrate that linguists, as a community, have failed to effectively communicate their findings to the public. Such communication is crucial since ignorance about the nature of language is not only unacceptable in a scientifically advanced society but also generates discrimination and misguided educational policy. Crucially, some of the most ignorant statements about non-Standard languages often come from members of the ethnic group that is associated with the language. Many African-American leaders fail to understand the fact that the dialects loosely referred to as Ebonics or "Black English" are not impoverished or illogical just because their negative polarity items look like Chaucer's. Similarly in Quebec, even many people with strong separatist political leanings decry the use of words and patterns of Quebec French that differ from International Standard French in some arbitrary way. Imagine children in New York being ridiculed and punished in school for referring to *elevators* (the normal American form) instead of *lifts* (the British term). Yet, this is directly analogous to what goes on in French schools in Quebec.

As an extreme case of the ignorance of "experts" consider the case of an indigenous community in Alaska, reported to have incredibly high rates of Fetal Alcohol Syndrome leading to language disorders. Lily Wong Fillmore, a linguist who studied the community, was able to ascertain that the "problem" turned out to be that the community speaks a language known as "Village English," an English-based Creole whose divergences from Standard English obviously do not reflect any kind of pathology. Under the *biolinguistic* approach, "English" does not exist—the object of study is the set of *internal, individual* I-languages instantiated in human minds/brains. One would hope that better understanding of the nature of language by the academic and public sectors would make misdiagnosis of dialect differences as mental retardation less likely.

We must stress that it is the responsibility of linguists to better educate the public and members of other professions, many of whom are quite interested in learning more about language. Recently, we received an invitation from a doctor friend to speak to medical personnel in the infectious diseases unit of a hospital in New York City. One requested topic for us to address was whether the Creoles spoken by many of the hospital's Caribbean patients are as good as "real" languages like English and Spanish at describing symptoms! Any budding linguist who reads this should be heartened by the opportunities you will have to contribute to society as a scientist—there is so much work for us to do.

A prerequisite for undertaking the dissemination of ideas to fight ignorance and social ills and to improve education is to understand the nature of human language. Answering, at least partially, *What is knowledge of language?* is the logical first step. We hope we have helped you to take this step.

Further Readings

- *New Horizons in the Study of Language and Mind* by Noam Chomsky (2000b).
- Article on Lily Wong Fillmore's work in Alaska: follow the link from the companion website.

References

ALLEN, COLIN and BEKOFF, MARC (1997). *Species of Mind: The Philosophy and Biology of Cognitive Ethology.* Cambridge, MA: MIT Press.

AUGUSTINE SAINT, BISHOP OF HIPPO (1995). *De Doctrina Christiana.* Oxford: Clarendon Press.

BAKER, MARK C. (2001). *The Atoms of Language.* New York: Basic Books.

BOAS, FRANZ, POWELL, JOHN WESLEY, and HOLDER, PRESTON (1966). *Introduction to the Handbook of American Indian languages.* A Bison book, BB301. Lincoln: University of Nebraska Press.

BREGMAN, ALBERT S. (1990). *Auditory Scene Analysis: The Perceptual Organization of Sound.* Cambridge, MA: MIT Press.

BRYSON, BILL (1990). *The Mother Tongue: English & How It Got That Way* (1st edn). New York: W. Morrow.

CANTY, NORA and GOULD, JAMES L. (1995). 'The hawk/goose experiment: sources of variability'. *Animal Behaviour* **50**(4), 1091–1095.

CARROLL, SEAN B. (2005). *Endless Forms Most Beautiful: The New Science of Evo Devo and The Making of the Animal Kingdom.* New York: Norton.

CHOMSKY, NOAM (1957). *Syntactic Structures.* The Hague: Mouton.

CHOMSKY, NOAM (1959). 'Review of *Verbal Behavior* by B. F. Skinner'. *Language* **35**(1), 26–58.

CHOMSKY, NOAM (1965). *Aspects of the Theory of Syntax.* Cambridge, MA: MIT Press.

CHOMSKY, NOAM (1971). 'Deep structure, surface structure and semantic interpretation', in *Semantics, an Interdisciplinary Reader in Linguistics, Philosophy and Psychology* (ed. D. Steinberg and L. Jakobovits). Cambridge, MA: Cambridge University Press, pp. 183–216.

CHOMSKY, NOAM (1986). *Knowledge of Language: Its Nature, Origin, and Use.* New York: Praeger.

CHOMSKY, NOAM (1988). *Language and Problems of Knowledge: The Managua Lectures.* Cambridge, MA: MIT Press.

CHOMSKY, NOAM (2000a). 'Language as a natural object'. See Chomsky (2000b), pp. 106–33.

CHOMSKY, NOAM (2000b). *New Horizons in the Study of Language and Mind.* Cambridge, MA: Cambridge University Press.

CHURCHLAND, PAUL M. (1984). *Matter and Consciousness: A Contemporary Introduction to the Philosophy of Mind.* Cambridge, MA: MIT Press.

CHURCHLAND, PAUL M. (1998). 'Betty Crocker's theory of consciousness', in *On the contrary: Critical Essays, 1987–1997* (ed. P. M. Churchland and P. S. Churchland). Cambridge, MA: MIT Press, pp. 113–22.

DEACON, TERRENCE WILLIAM (1997). *The Symbolic Species: The Co-evolution of Language and the Brain.* New York: W. W. Norton.

EDDINGTON, ARTHUR STANLEY (1934). 'Science and experience,' in *New Pathways in Science.* Messenger lectures. New York: The Macmillan Company, pp. 1–26.

EDELMAN, GERALD M. (2004). *Wider Than the Sky: The Phenomenal Gift of Consciousness.* New Haven: Yale University Press.

FODOR, JERRY A. (1968). *Psychological Explanation: An Introduction to the Philosophy of Psychology.* A Random House study in problems of philosophy. New York: Random House.

FODOR, JERRY A. (2000). 'It's all in the mind'. Review of Chomsky's *New Horizons. Times Literary Supplement.*

FOUCAULT, MICHEL (1966, 1973). *The Order of Things: An Archaeology of the Human Sciences.* New York: Vintage Book.

FRANKFURT, HARRY G. (2005). *On Bullshit.* Princeton, NJ: Princeton University Press.

GLEITMAN, LILA R. and NEWPORT, ELISSA (1995). 'The invention of language by children: Environmental and biological influences on the acquisition of language'. See Osherson and Gleitman (1995), pp. 1–24.

HALE, MARK (2007). *Historical Linguistics: Theory and Method.* Blackwell textbooks in linguistics. Malden, MA: Blackwell.

HALE, MARK and REISS, CHARLES (1998). 'Formal and empirical arguments concerning phonological acquisition'. *Linguistic Inquiry* **29**, 656–83.

HALE, MARK and REISS, CHARLES (2003). 'The subset principle in phonology: Why the *tabula* can't be rasa'. *Journal of Linguistics* **39**, 219–44.

HALE, MARK and REISS, CHARLES (2008). *The Phonological Enterprise.* Oxford: Oxford University Press.

HALLE, MORRIS (1975). 'Confessio grammatici'. *Language* **51**, 525–35.

HAMMARBERG, R. (1976). 'The metaphysics of coarticulation'. *Journal of Phonetics* **4**, 353–63.

HANDEL, STEPHEN (1989). *Listening: An Introduction to the Perception of Auditory Events.* Cambridge, MA: MIT Press.

HOFFMAN, DONALD D. (1998). *Visual Intelligence: How We Create What We See.* New York: W. W. Norton.

HYMAN, MALCOLM (2002). 'Bad grammar in context'. *New England Classical Journal* **29**(2), 94–101. Also at http://archimedes.fas.harvard.edu/mdh/.

IDSARDI, WILLIAM JAMES (1992). *The Computation of Prosody.* Ph.D. thesis. Cambridge, MA: MIT Press.

JACKENDOFF, RAY (1990). *Semantic Structures.* Cambridge, MA: MIT Press.

JACKENDOFF, RAY (1992). 'The problem of reality', in *Languages of the Mind: Essays on Mental Representation*. Cambridge, MA: MIT Press, pp. 157–76.

JACKENDOFF, RAY (1994). *Patterns in the Mind: Language and Human Nature*. New York: Basic Books.

JACKENDOFF, RAY, BLOOM, PAUL, and WYNN, KAREN (1999). *Language, Logic, and Concepts: Essays in Memory of John Macnamara*. Cambridge, MA: MIT Press.

JOHNSON, DAVID MARTEL and ERNELING, CHRISTINA E. (1997). *The Future of the Congnitive Revolution*. New York: Oxford University Press.

LABOV, W. (1972). 'Academic ignorance and black intelligence'. *The Atlantic Monthly*, 59–67.

LASNIK, HOWARD, DEPIANTE, MARCELA A., and STEPANOV, ARTHUR (2000). *Syntactic Structures Revisited: Contemporary Lectures on Classic Transformational Theory*. Current studies in linguistics. Cambridge, MA: MIT Press.

MARANTZ, ALEC, MIYASHITA, Y., and O'NEIL, WAYNE A. (2000). *Image, Language, Brain: Papers from the First Mind Articulation Project Symposium*. Cambridge, MA: MIT Press.

MIKHAIL, JOHN (2007). 'Universal moral grammar: theory, evidence and the future'. *Trends in Cognitive Sciences* **11**(4), 143–52.

NIEDER, A. (2002). 'Seeing more than meets the eye: Processing of illusory contours in animals'. *Journal of Comparative Physiology* **188**, 249–60.

NUTI, MILENA (2005). *Ethnoscience: Examining Common Sense*. Ph.D. thesis. University College London.

OSHERSON, DANIEL N. and GLEITMAN, LILA R. (1995). *An Invitation to Cognitive Science* (2nd edn). Cambridge, MA: MIT Press.

PARTEE, BARBARA HALL, MEULEN, ALICE G. B. TER, and WALL, ROBERT EUGENE (1990). *Mathematical Methods in Linguistics*. Dordrecht: Kluwer Academic.

PAYNE, THOMAS EDWARD (1997). *Describing Morphosyntax: A Guide for Field Linguists*. Cambridge, U.K.: Cambridge University Press.

PINKER, STEVEN (1994). *The Language Instinct* (1st edn). New York: W. Morrow and Co.

POPPER, KARL RAIMUND (1952). *The Open Society and Its Enemies*. London: Routledge & Kegan Paul.

PULLUM, GEOFFREY K. (1991). *The Great Eskimo Vocabulary Hoax, and Other Irreverent Essays on the Study of Language*. Chicago: University of Chicago Press.

PULLUM, GEOFFREY K. and SCHOLZ, BARBARA C. (2001). 'On the distinction between model-theoretic and generative-enumerative syntactic frameworks', in *Logical Aspects of Computational Linguistics* (ed. G. M. Philippe de Groot and C. Retoré). Lecture Notes in Artificial Intelligence. Berlin: Springer Verlag, pp. 17–43.

PYLYSHYN, ZENON W. (1973). 'The role of competence theories in cognitive psychology'. *Journal of Psycholinguistic Research,* **11**, 21–50.

PYLYSHYN, ZENON W. (1984). *Computation and Cognition: Toward a Foundation for Cognitive Science.* Cambridge, MA: MIT Press.

PYLYSHYN, ZENON W. (2003). *Seeing and Visualizing: It's Not What You Think.* Cambridge, MA: MIT Press.

SHOPEN, TIMOTHY (ed.) (1979). *Languages and Their Status.* Cambridge, MA: Winthrop Publishers.

SKLAR, LAWRENCE (2000). *Theory and Truth: Philosophical Critique within Foundational Science.* Oxford: Oxford University Press.

SPELKE, ELIZABETH (1994). 'Initial knowledge: six suggestions'. *Cognition,* **50**, 431–45.

VON HUMBOLDT, WILHELM (1836). *Über die Verschiedenheit des menschlichen Sprachbaues und ihren Einfluss auf die geistige Entwickelung des Menschengeschlechts.* Berlin: Royal Academy of Sciences of Berlin.

VON NEUMANN, JOHN (2000). *The Computer and the Brain* (2nd edn). New Haven, CT: Yale University Press.

WERKER, JANET (1995). 'Exploring developmental changes in cross-language speech perception'. See Osherson and Gleitman (1995), pp. 87–106.

WONG FILLMORE, LILY. http://gse.berkeley.edu/admin/publications/termpaper/spring00/fillmore_alaska.html.

Index